ULTIMATE X-MEN

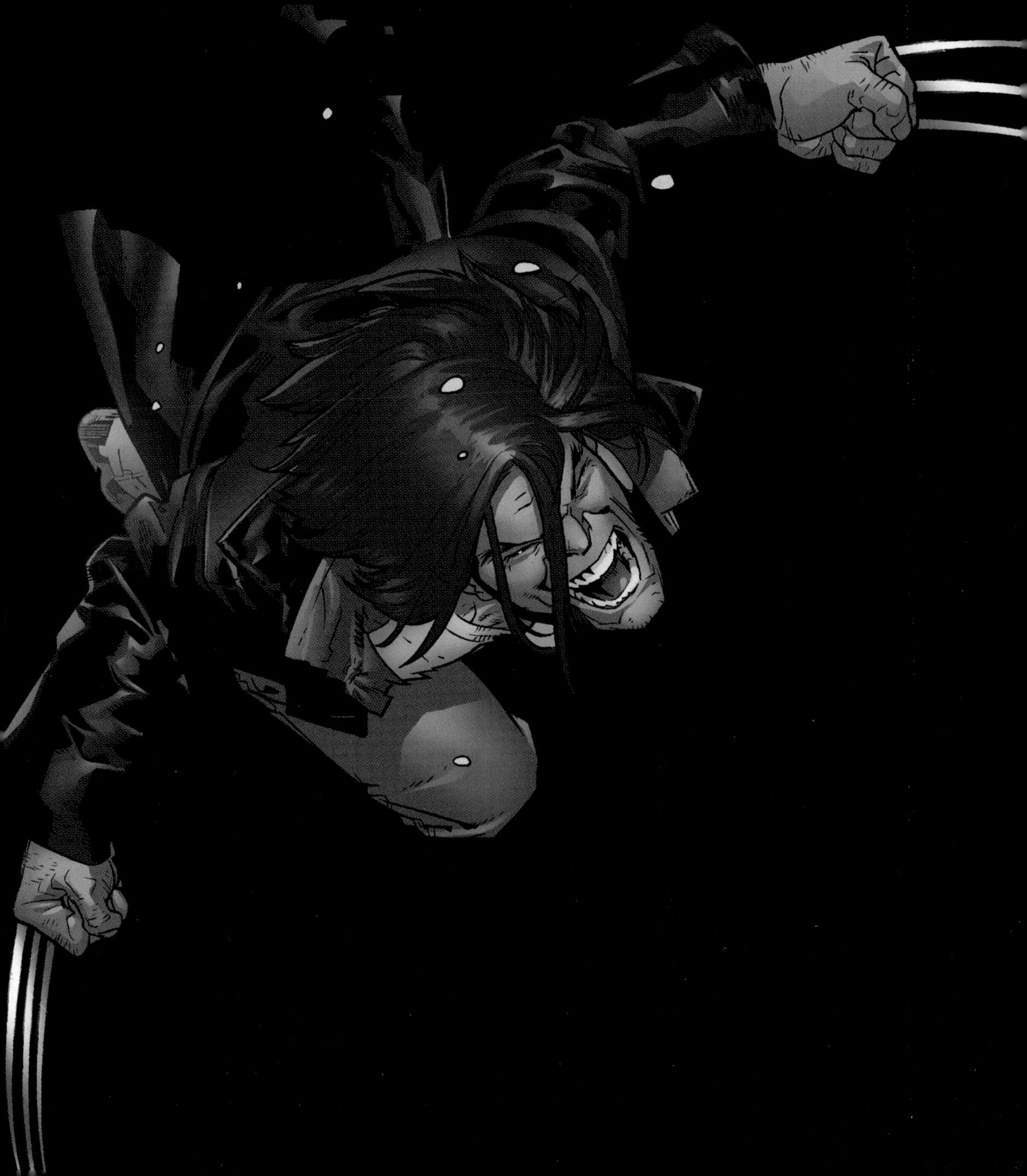

ULTIMATE X-MEN

HARD LESSONS

writer: **BRIAN K. VAUGHAN**

"A Hard Lesson"
art: **STEVE DILLON**
colors: **PAUL MOUNTS**

"Shock and Awe"
pencils: **STUART IMMONEN**
inks: **WADE VON GRAWBADGER**
colors: **JUSTIN PONSOR**

"Ultimate Sacrifice"
pencils: **TOM RANEY**
inks: **SCOTT HANNA**
colors: **GINA GOING-RANEY**

letters: **CHRIS ELIOPOULOS**
covers: **STUART IMMONEN,**
WADE VON GRAWBADGER &
RICHARD ISANOVE
assistant editors: **JOHN BARBER**
& NICOLE WILEY
editor: **RALPH MACCHIO**

collection editor: **JENNIFER GRÜNWALD**
assistant editor: **MICHAEL SHORT**
senior editor, special projects: **JEFF YOUNGQUIST**
director of sales: **DAVID GABRIEL**
production: **JERRON QUALITY COLOR**
creative director: **TOM MARVELLI**

editor in chief: **JOE QUESADA**
publisher: **DAN BUCKLEY**

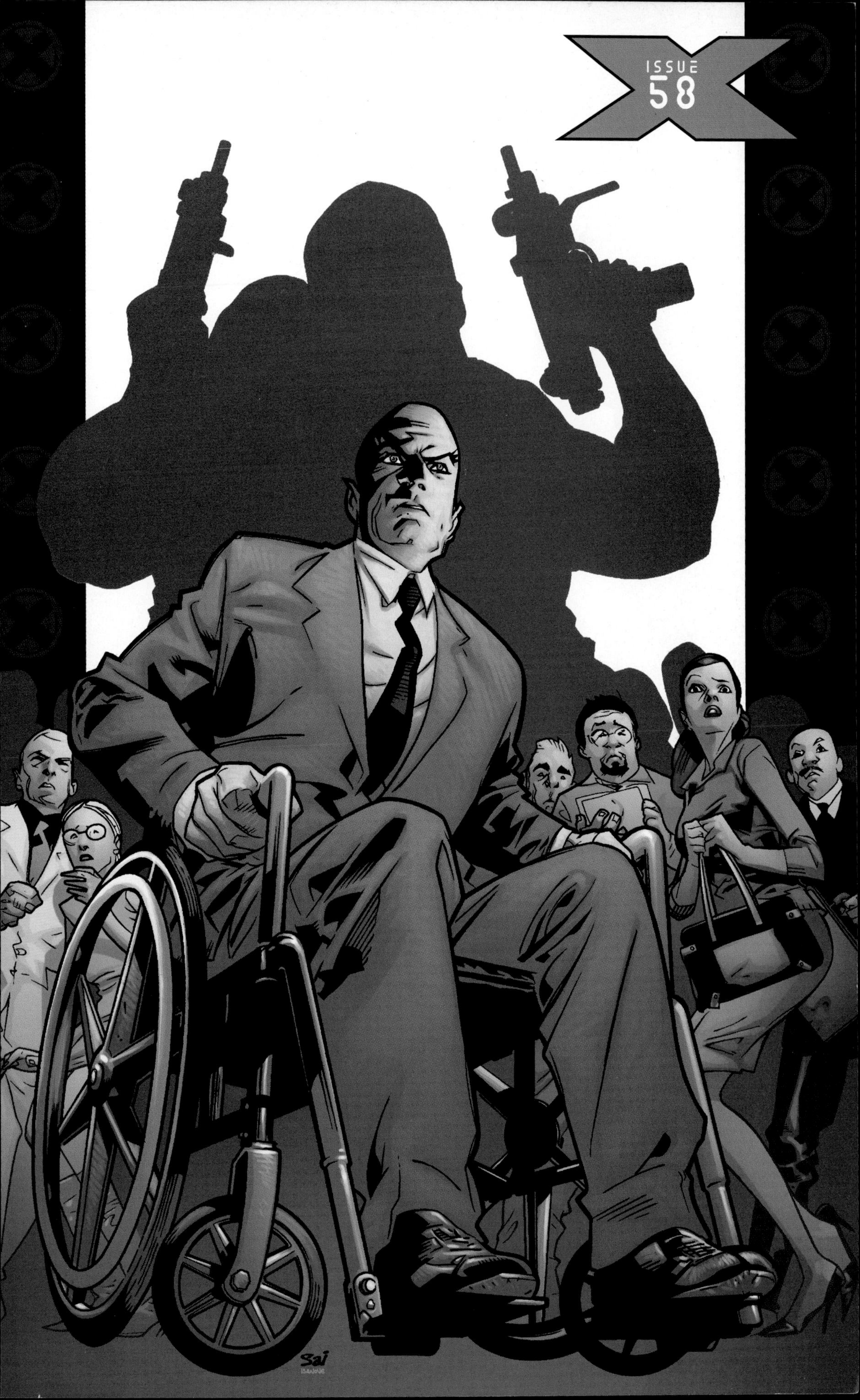
ISSUE
58

PREVIOUSLY IN ULTIMATE X-MEN:

Born with strange and amazing abilities, the X-Men are young mutant heroes, sworn to protect a world that fears and hates them.

Leading these students is Professor Charles Xavier, an avowed pacifist, and the most powerful telepath on the planet.

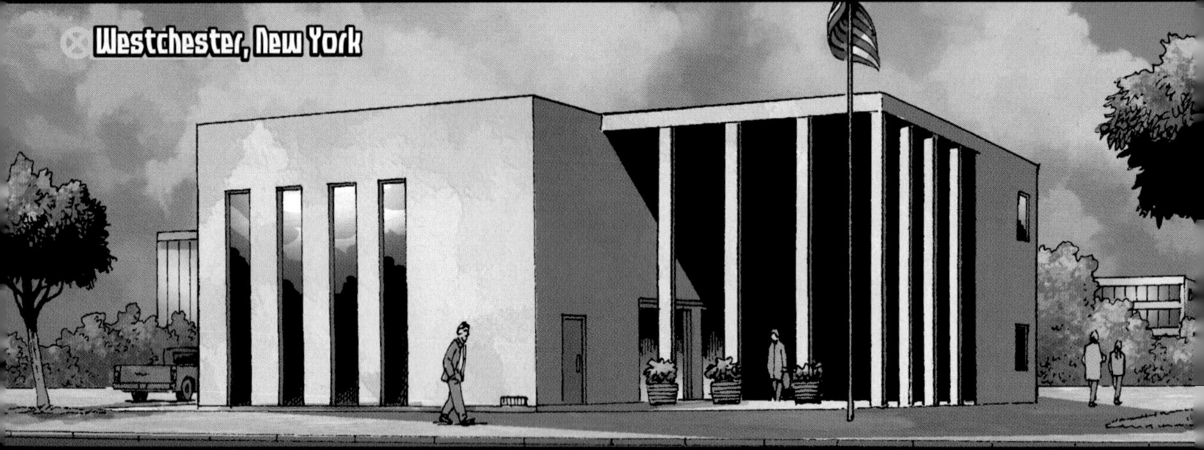
Westchester, New York

A HARD LESSON

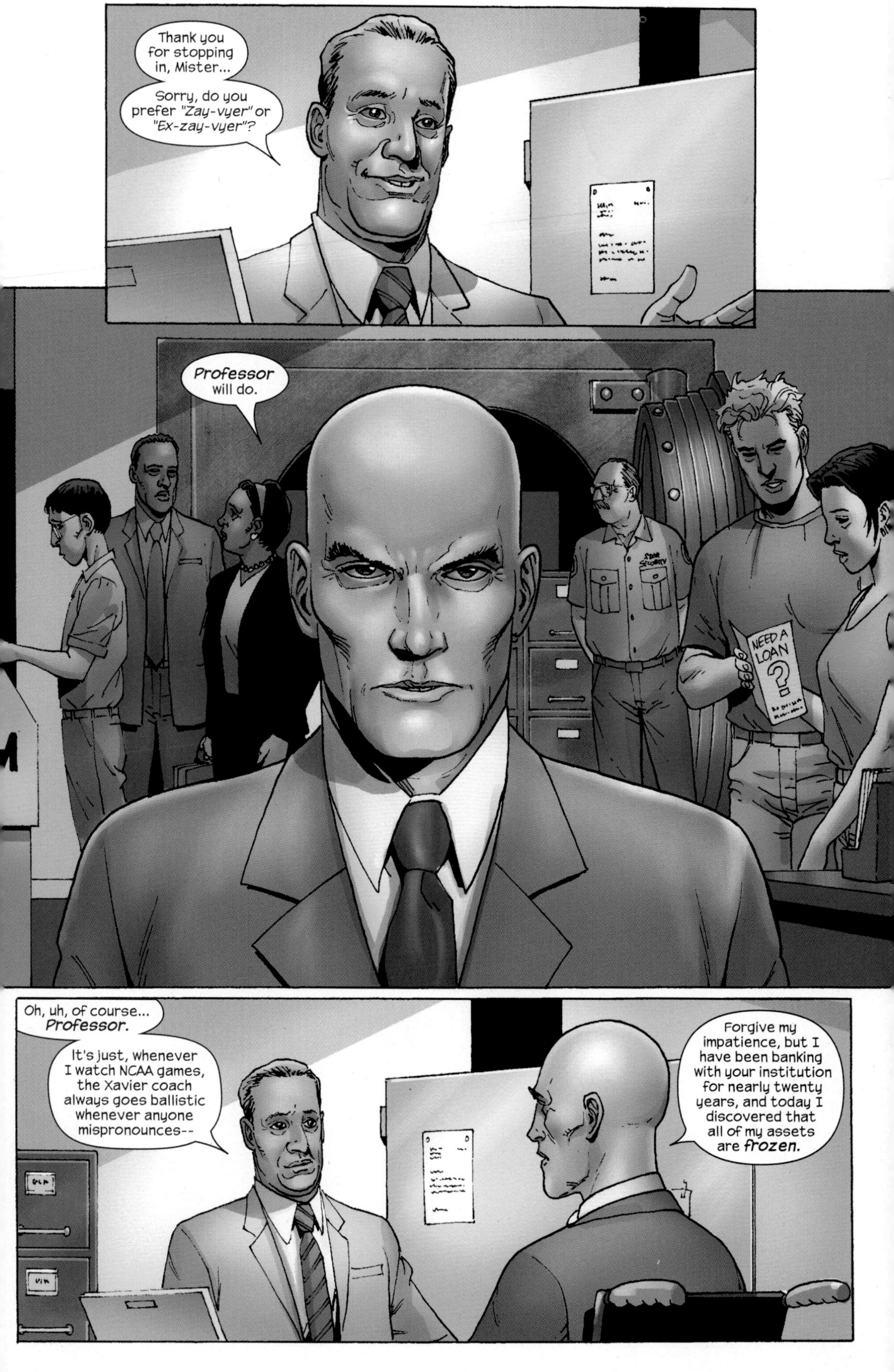
Thank you for stopping in, Mister...
Sorry, do you prefer "Zay-vyer" or "Ex-zay-vyer"?
Professor will do.
NEED A LOAN ?
Oh, uh, of course... Professor.
It's just, whenever I watch NCAA games, the Xavier coach always goes ballistic whenever anyone mispronounces--
Forgive my impatience, but I have been banking with your institution for nearly twenty years, and today I discovered that all of my assets are frozen.

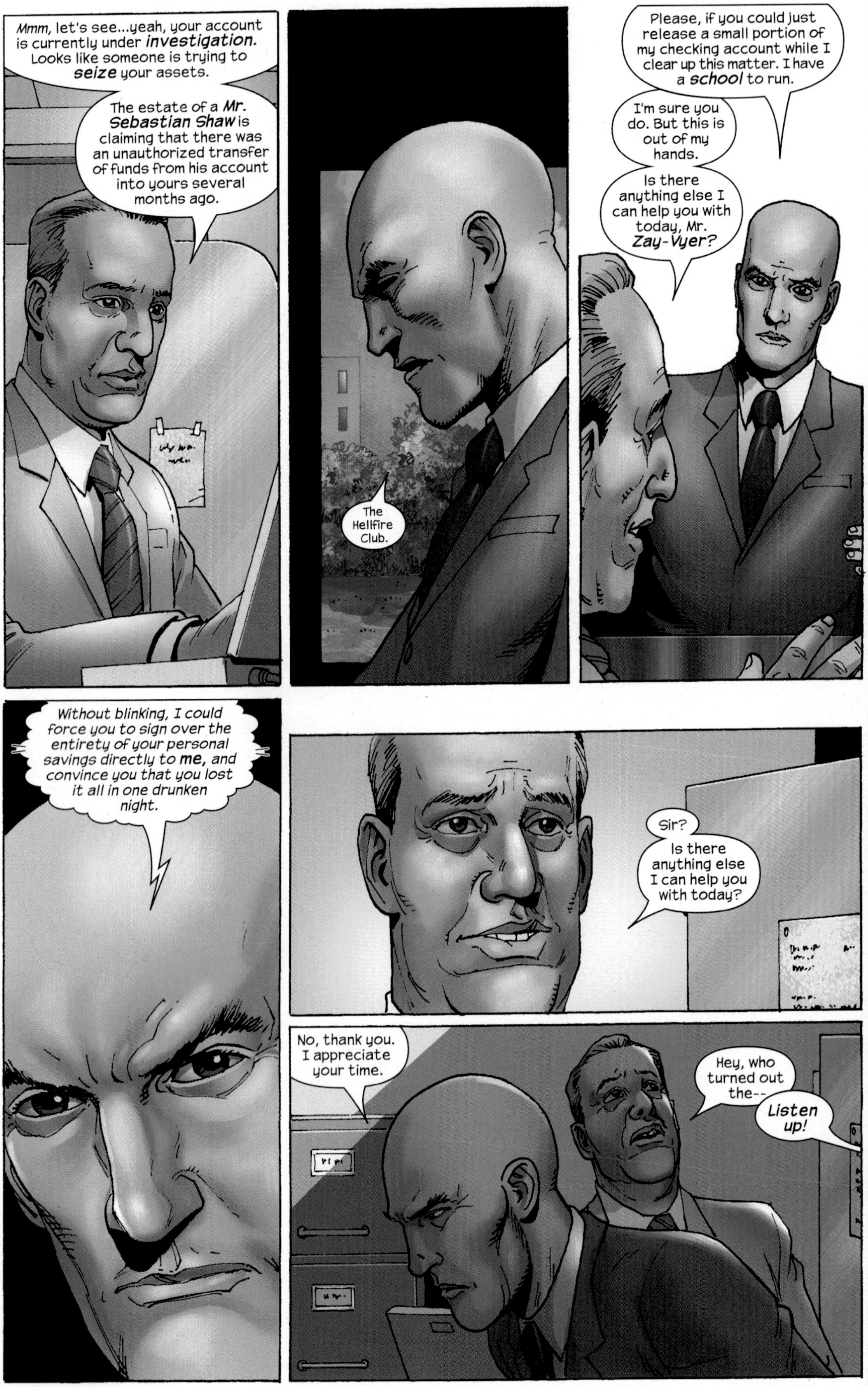
Mmm, let's see...yeah, your account is currently under investigation. Looks like someone is trying to seize your assets.
The estate of a Mr. Sebastian Shaw is claiming that there was an unauthorized transfer of funds from his account into yours several months ago.
The Hellfire Club.
Please, if you could just release a small portion of my checking account while I clear up this matter. I have a school to run.
I'm sure you do. But this is out of my hands.
Is there anything else I can help you with today, Mr. Zay-Vyer?
Without blinking, I could force you to sign over the entirety of your personal savings directly to me, and convince you that you lost it all in one drunken night.
Sir?
Is there anything else I can help you with today?
No, thank you. I appreciate your time.
Hey, who turned out the--
Listen up!

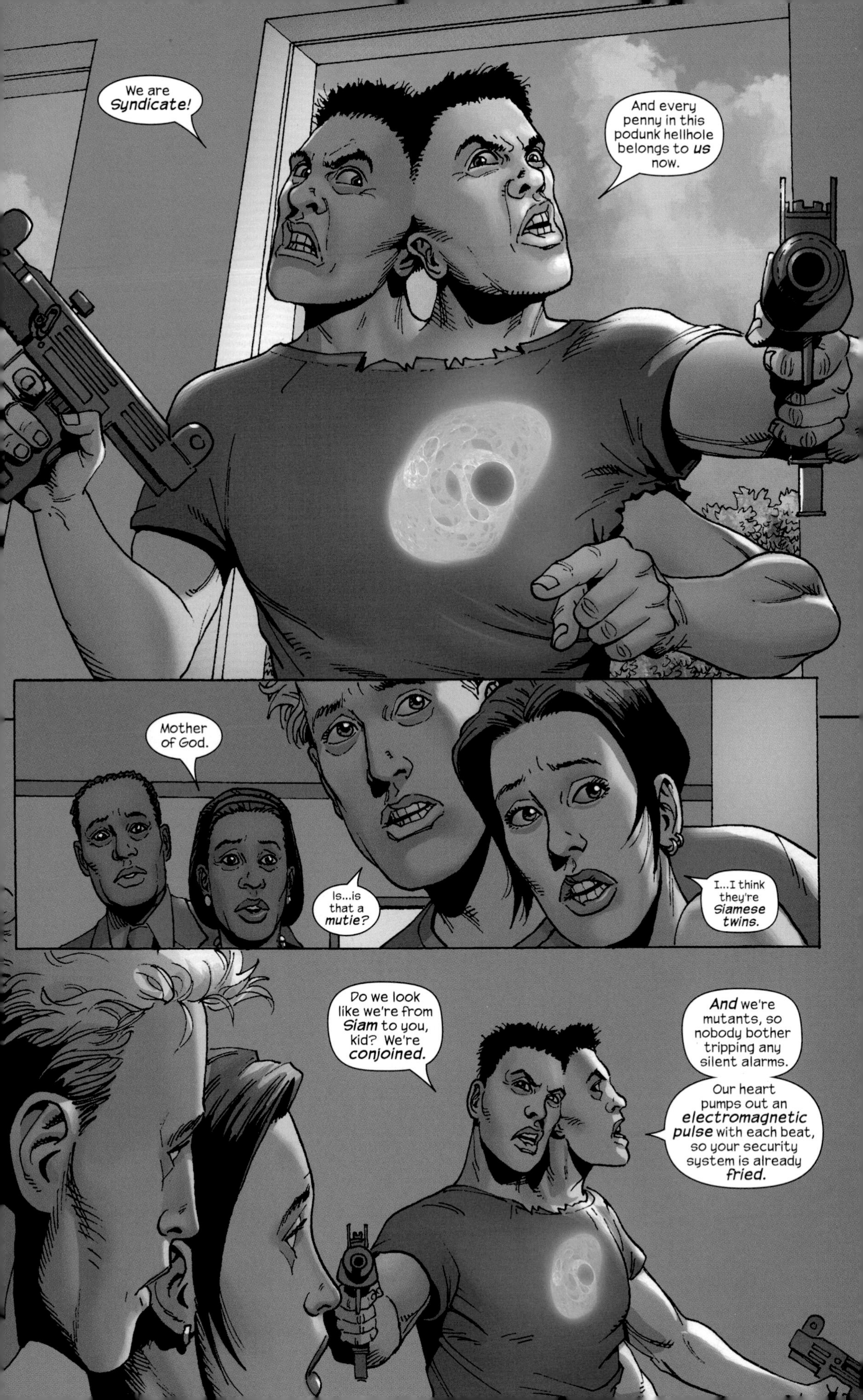

We are Syndicate!
And every penny in this podunk hellhole belongs to us now.
Mother of God.
Is...is that a mutie?
I...I think they're Siamese twins.
Do we look like we're from Siam to you, kid? We're conjoined.
And we're mutants, so nobody bother tripping any silent alarms.
Our heart pumps out an electromagnetic pulse with each beat, so your security system is already fried.

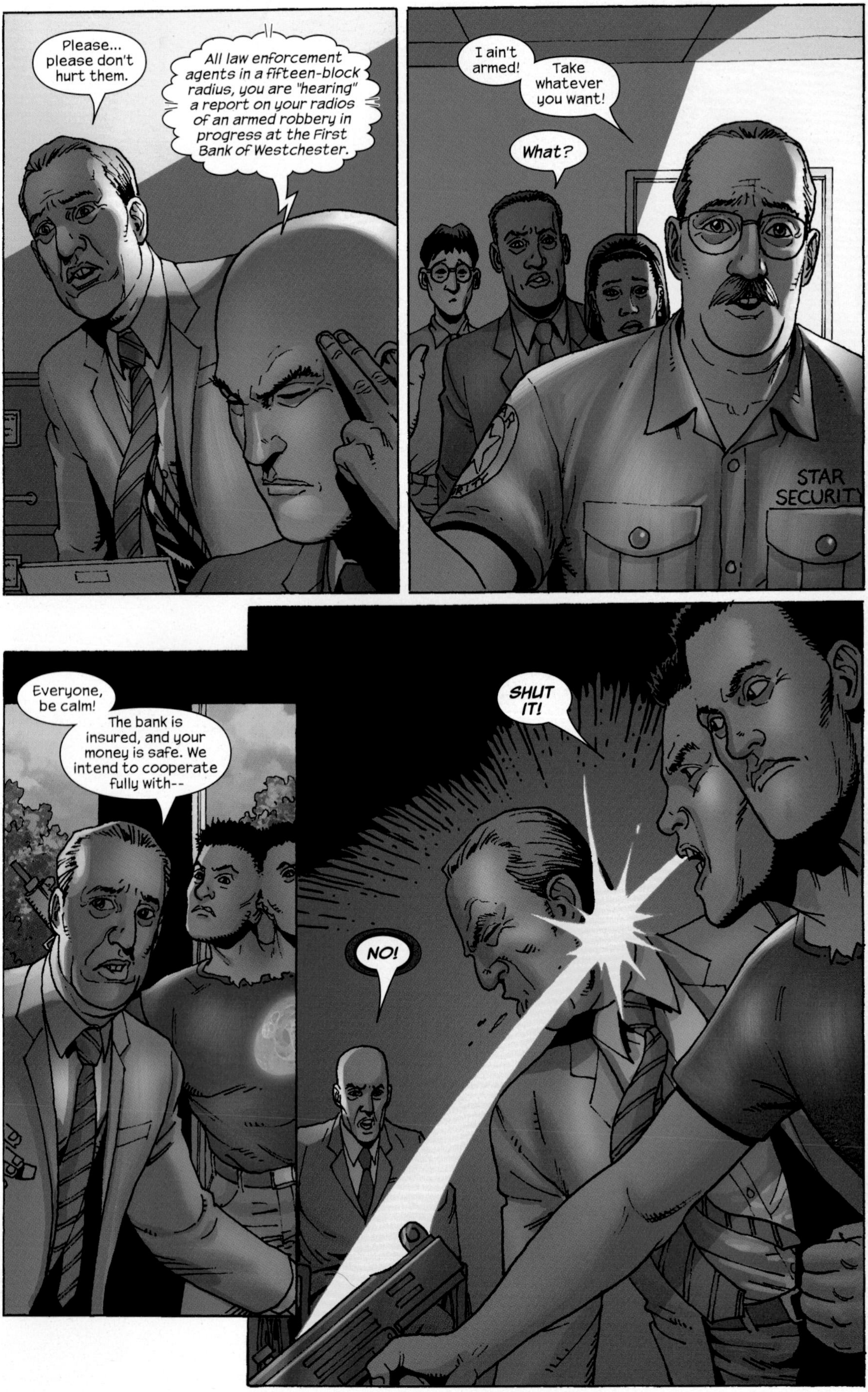
Please... please don't hurt them.
All law enforcement agents in a fifteen-block radius, you are "hearing" a report on your radios of an armed robbery in progress at the First Bank of Westchester.
I ain't armed!
Take whatever you want!
What?
STAR SECURITY
Everyone, be calm!
The bank is insured, and your money is safe. We intend to cooperate fully with--
SHUT IT!
NO!

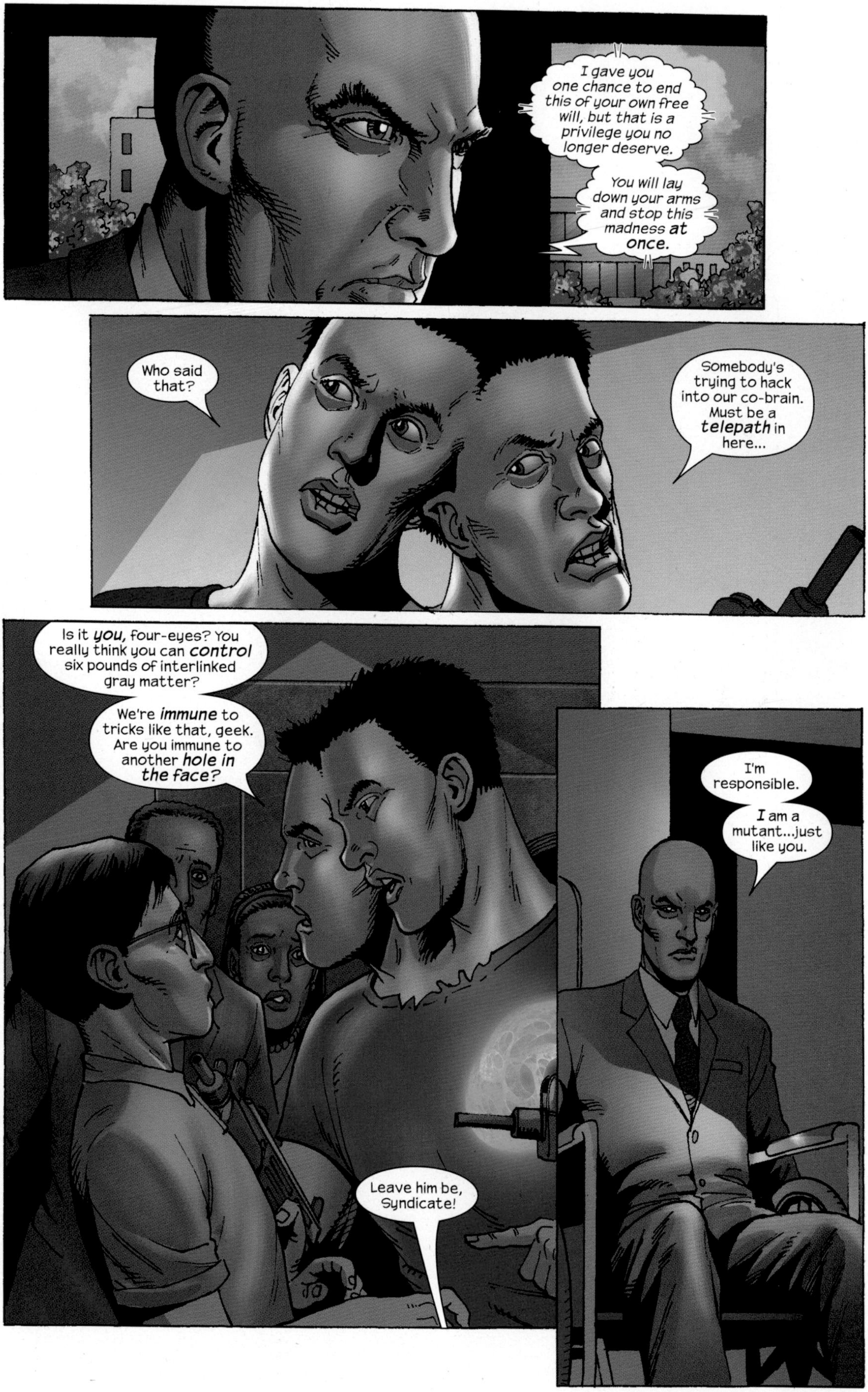
I gave you one chance to end this of your own free will, but that is a privilege you no longer deserve.
You will lay down your arms and stop this madness at once.
Who said that?
Somebody's trying to hack into our co-brain. Must be a telepath in here...
Is it you, four-eyes? You really think you can control six pounds of interlinked gray matter?
We're immune to tricks like that, geek. Are you immune to another hole in the face?
Leave him be, Syndicate!
I'm responsible.
I am a mutant...just like you.

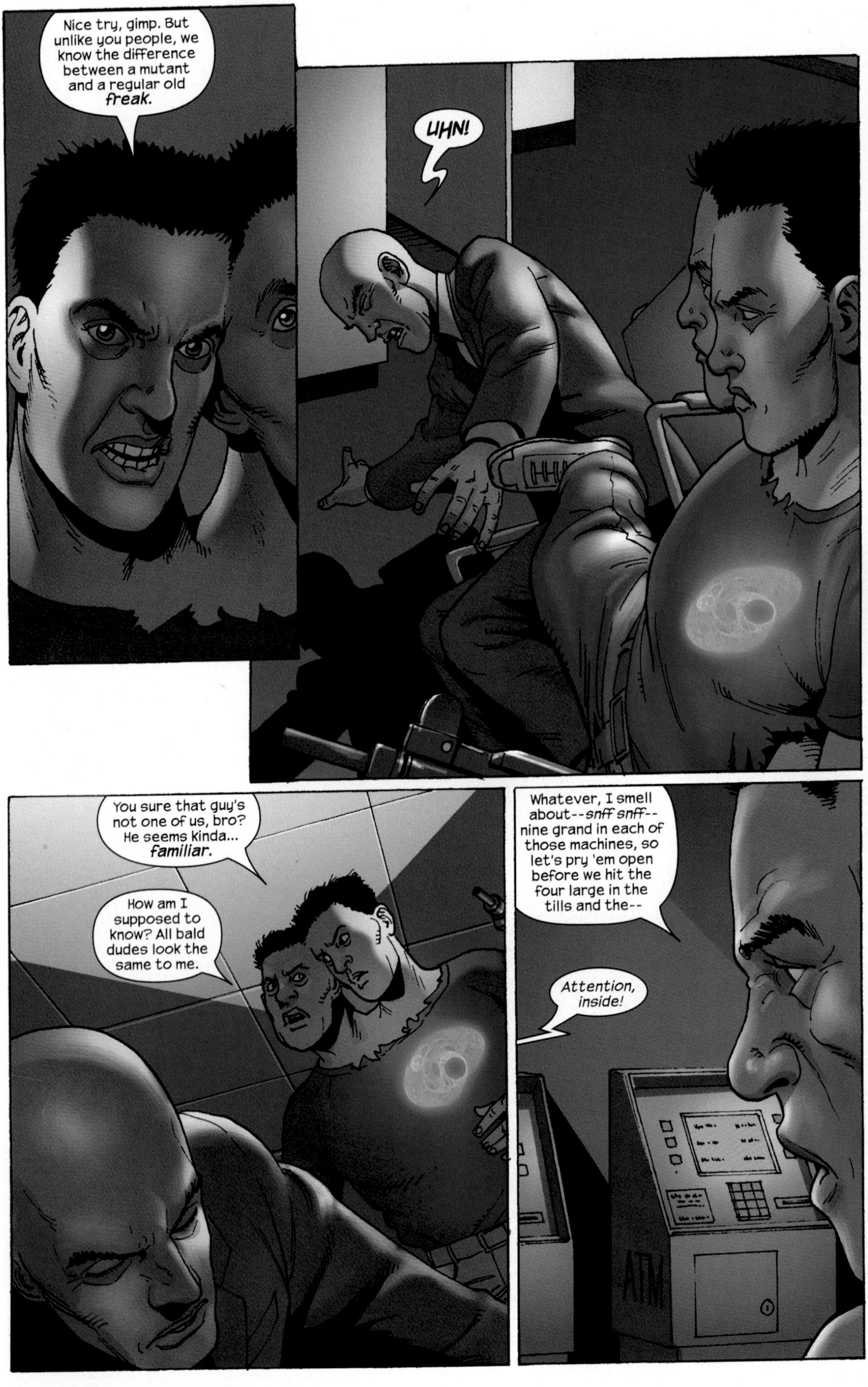

Nice try, gimp. But unlike you people, we know the difference between a mutant and a regular old *freak.*
UHN!
You sure that guy's not one of us, bro? He seems kinda... *familiar.*
How am I supposed to know? All bald dudes look the same to me.
Whatever, I smell about--*snff snff*--nine grand in each of those machines, so let's pry 'em open before we hit the four large in the tills and the--
Attention, inside!
ATM

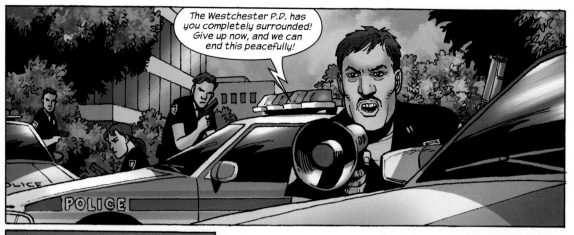

The Westchester P.D. has you completely surrounded! Give up now, and we can end this peacefully!

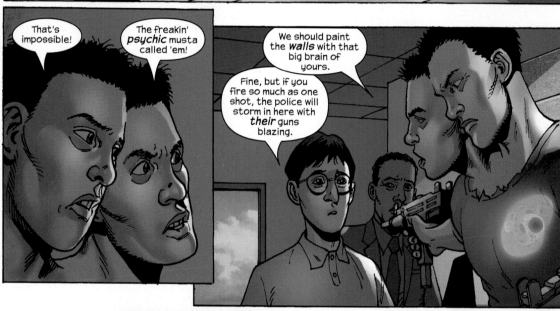

That's impossible!

The freakin' *psychic* musta called 'em!

We should paint the *walls* with that big brain of yours.

Fine, but if you fire so much as one shot, the police will storm in here with *their* guns blazing.

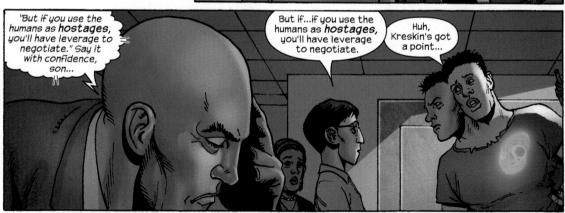

"But if you use the humans as *hostages*, you'll have leverage to negotiate." Say it with confidence, son...

But if...if you use the humans as *hostages*, you'll have leverage to negotiate.

Huh, Kreskin's got a point...

Jean, this is your Professor.

Have you and the other X-Men contained the situation in New Jersey yet?

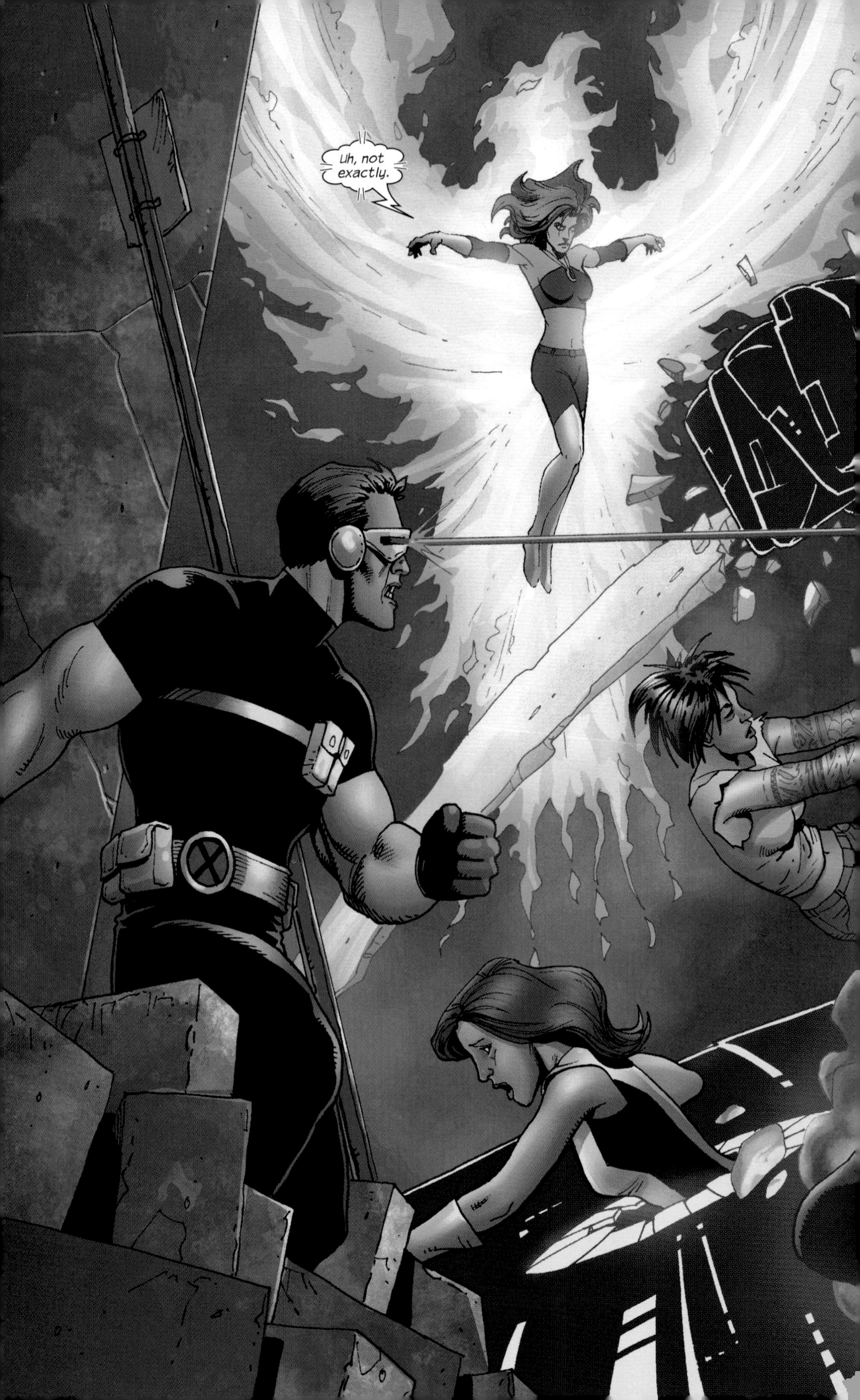
Uh, not exactly.

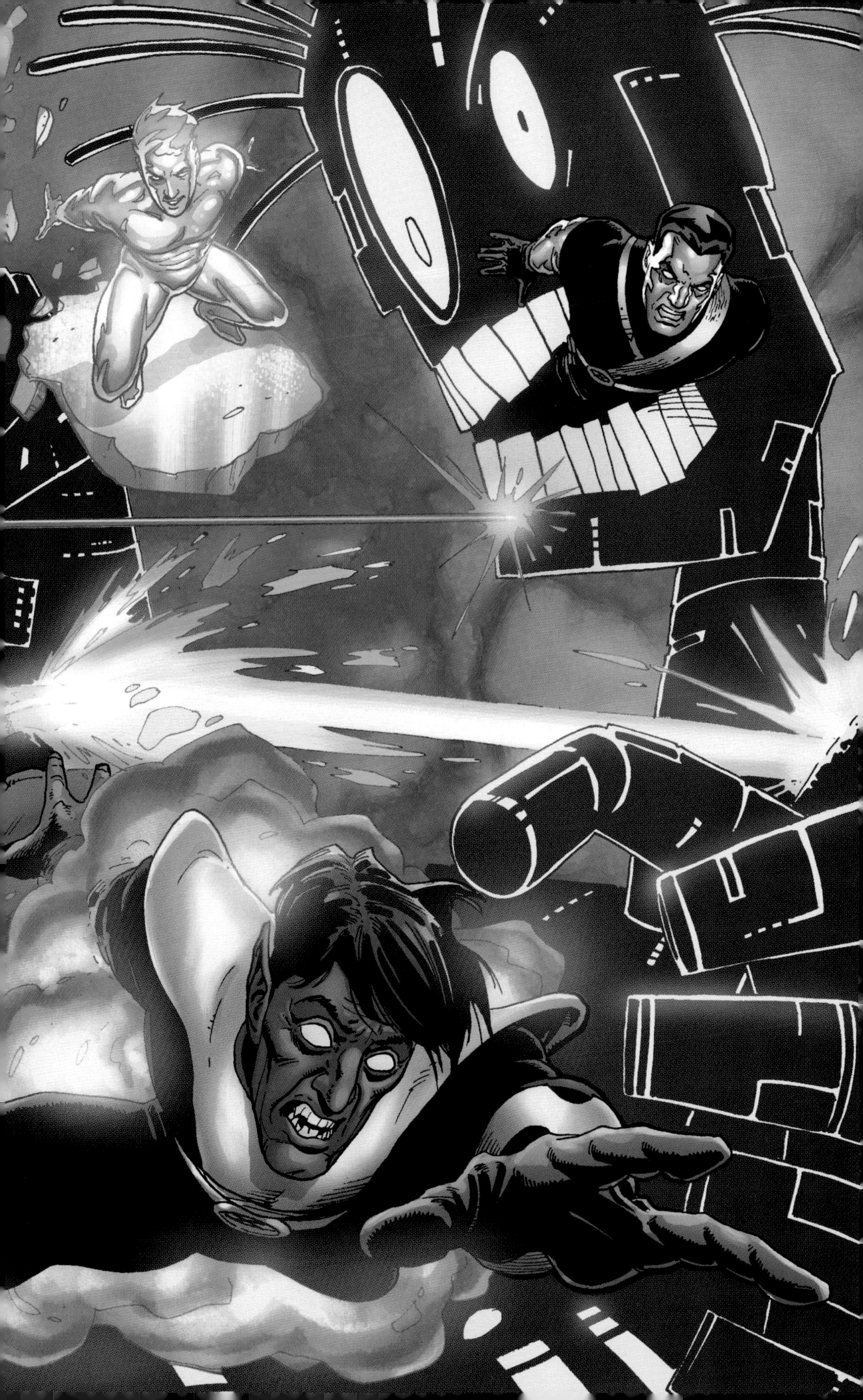

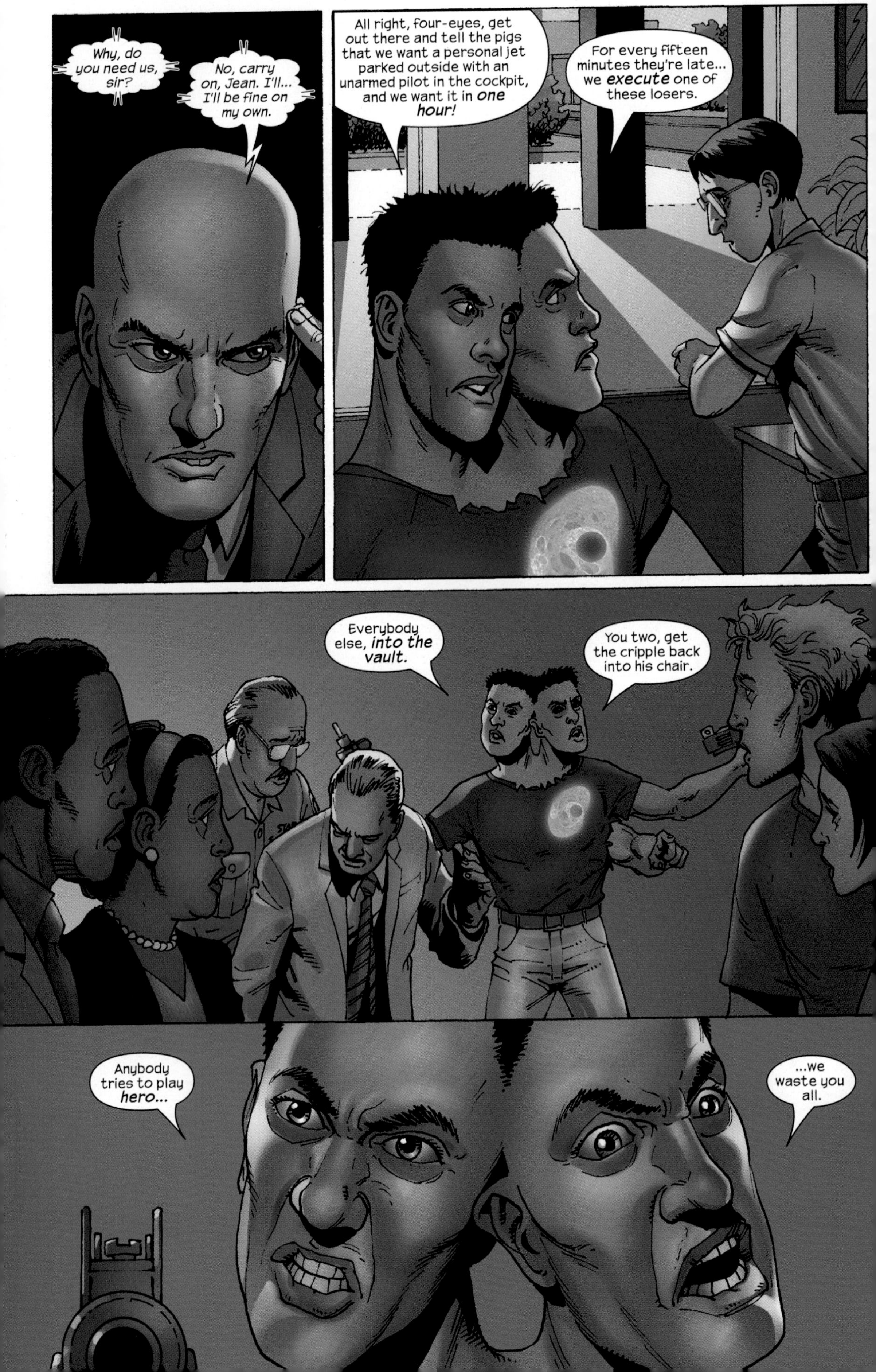
Why, do you need us, sir?
No, carry on, Jean. I'll... I'll be fine on my own.
All right, four-eyes, get out there and tell the pigs that we want a personal jet parked outside with an unarmed pilot in the cockpit, and we want it in *one hour!*
For every fifteen minutes they're late... we *execute* one of these losers.
Everybody else, *into the vault.*
You two, get the cripple back into his chair.
Anybody tries to play *hero...*
...we waste you all.

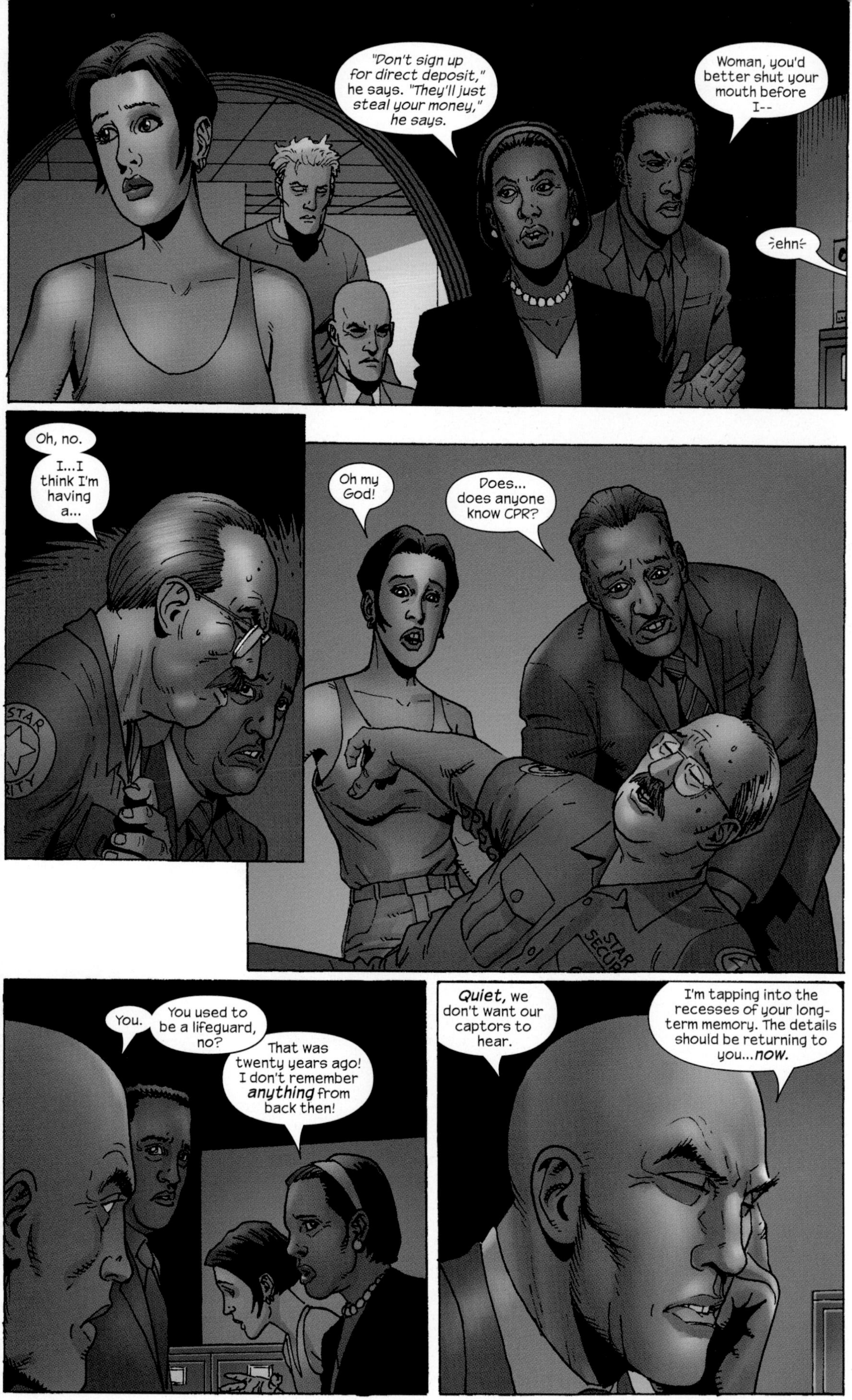
"Don't sign up for direct deposit," he says. "They'll just steal your money," he says.
Woman, you'd better shut your mouth before I--
ehn
Oh, no.
I...I think I'm having a...
Oh my God!
Does... does anyone know CPR?
You.
You used to be a lifeguard, no?
That was twenty years ago! I don't remember *anything* from back then!
Quiet, we don't want our captors to hear.
I'm tapping into the recesses of your long-term memory. The details should be returning to you...***now.***

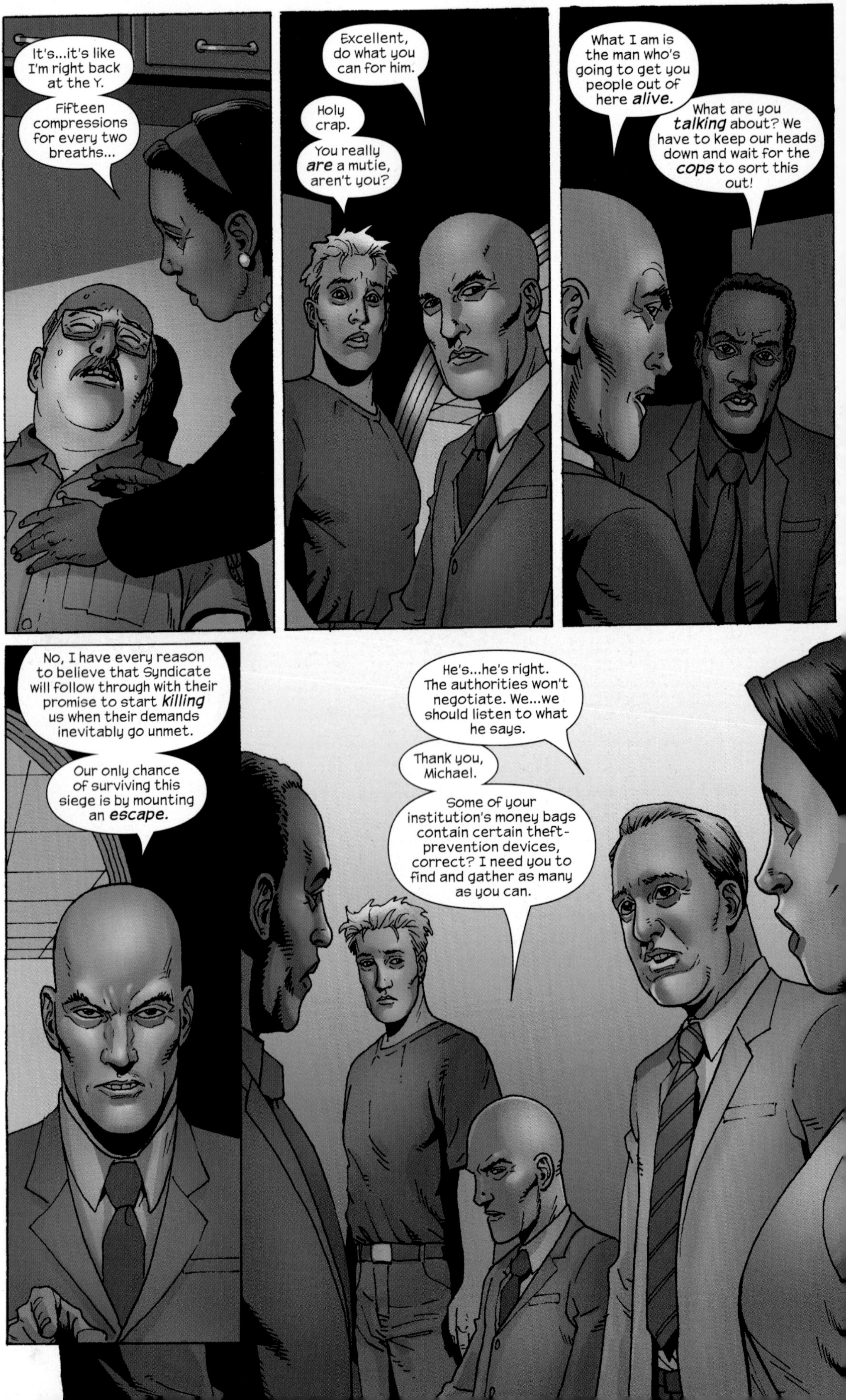
It's...it's like I'm right back at the Y.
Fifteen compressions for every two breaths...
Excellent, do what you can for him.
Holy crap.
You really are a mutie, aren't you?
What I am is the man who's going to get you people out of here alive.
What are you talking about? We have to keep our heads down and wait for the cops to sort this out!
No, I have every reason to believe that Syndicate will follow through with their promise to start killing us when their demands inevitably go unmet.
Our only chance of surviving this siege is by mounting an escape.
He's...he's right. The authorities won't negotiate. We...we should listen to what he says.
Thank you, Michael.
Some of your institution's money bags contain certain theft-prevention devices, correct? I need you to find and gather as many as you can.

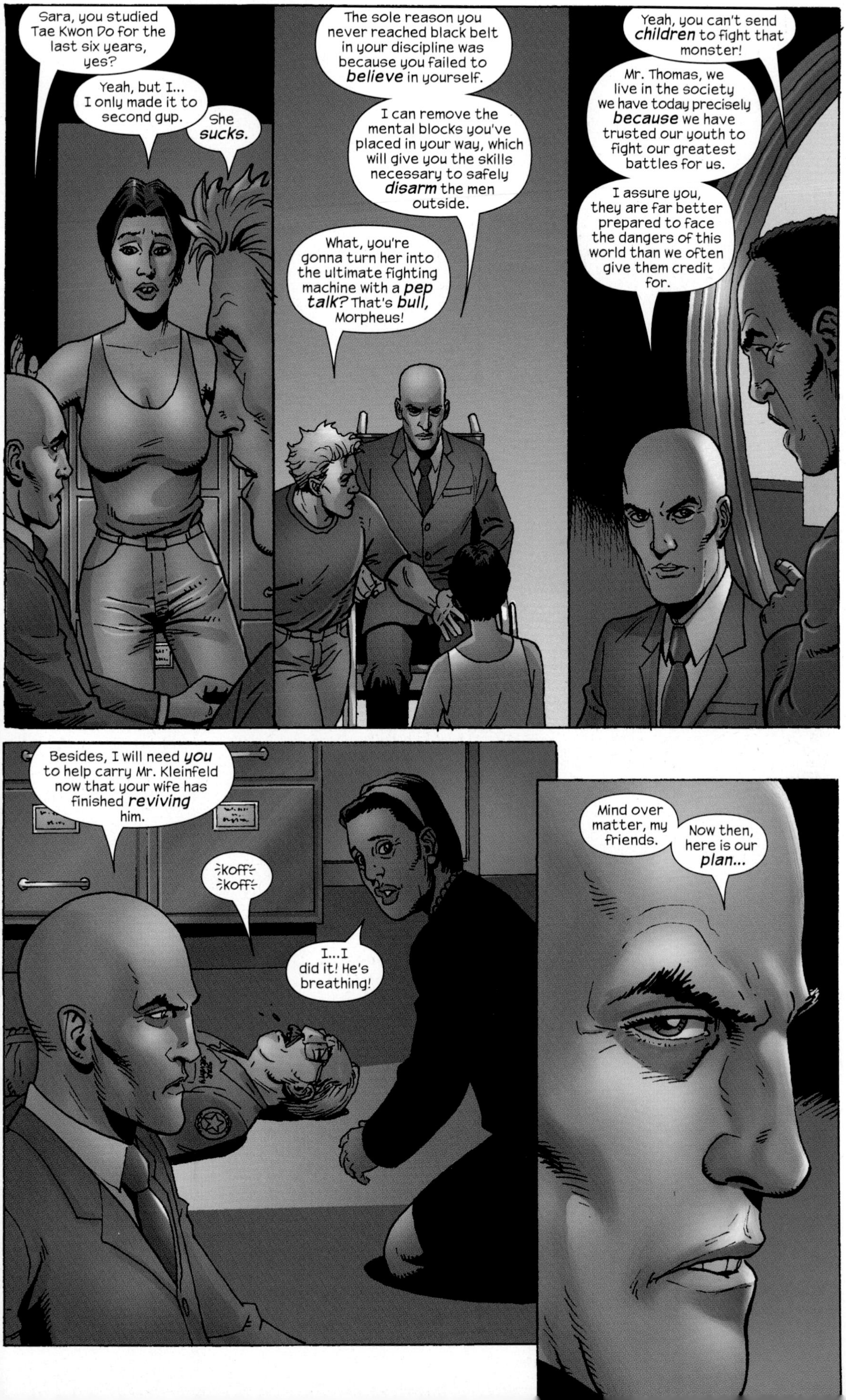
Sara, you studied Tae Kwon Do for the last six years, yes?
Yeah, but I... I only made it to second gup.
She sucks.
The sole reason you never reached black belt in your discipline was because you failed to believe in yourself.
I can remove the mental blocks you've placed in your way, which will give you the skills necessary to safely disarm the men outside.
What, you're gonna turn her into the ultimate fighting machine with a pep talk? That's bull, Morpheus!
Yeah, you can't send children to fight that monster!
Mr. Thomas, we live in the society we have today precisely because we have trusted our youth to fight our greatest battles for us.
I assure you, they are far better prepared to face the dangers of this world than we often give them credit for.
Besides, I will need you to help carry Mr. Kleinfeld now that your wife has finished reviving him.
koff koff
I...I did it! He's breathing!
Mind over matter, my friends.
Now then, here is our plan...

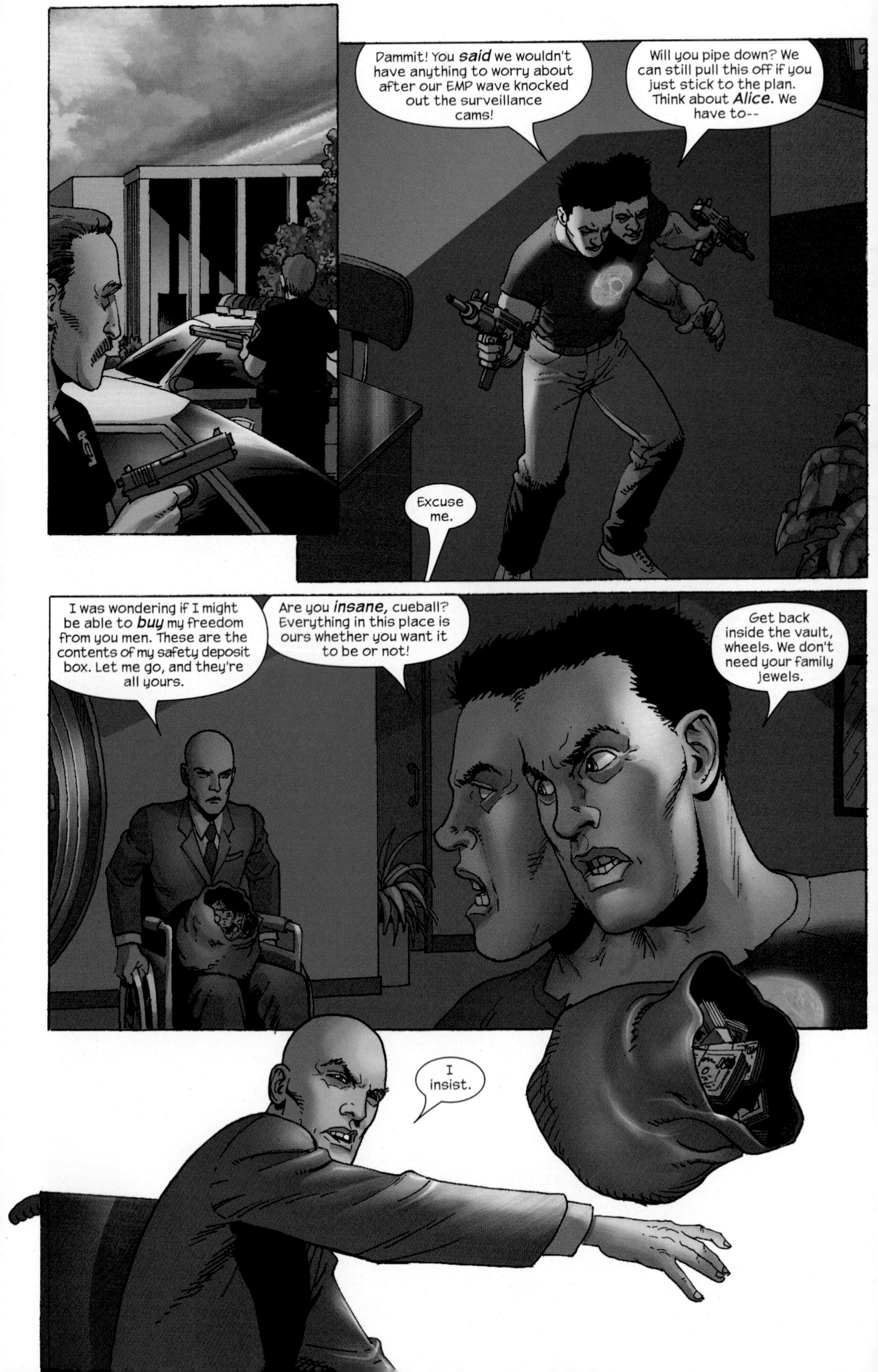

Dammit! You *said* we wouldn't have anything to worry about after our EMP wave knocked out the surveillance cams!
Will you pipe down? We can still pull this off if you just stick to the plan. Think about *Alice.* We have to--
Excuse me.
I was wondering if I might be able to *buy* my freedom from you men. These are the contents of my safety deposit box. Let me go, and they're all yours.
Are you *insane,* cueball? Everything in this place is ours whether you want it to be or not!
Get back inside the vault, wheels. We don't need your family jewels.
I insist.

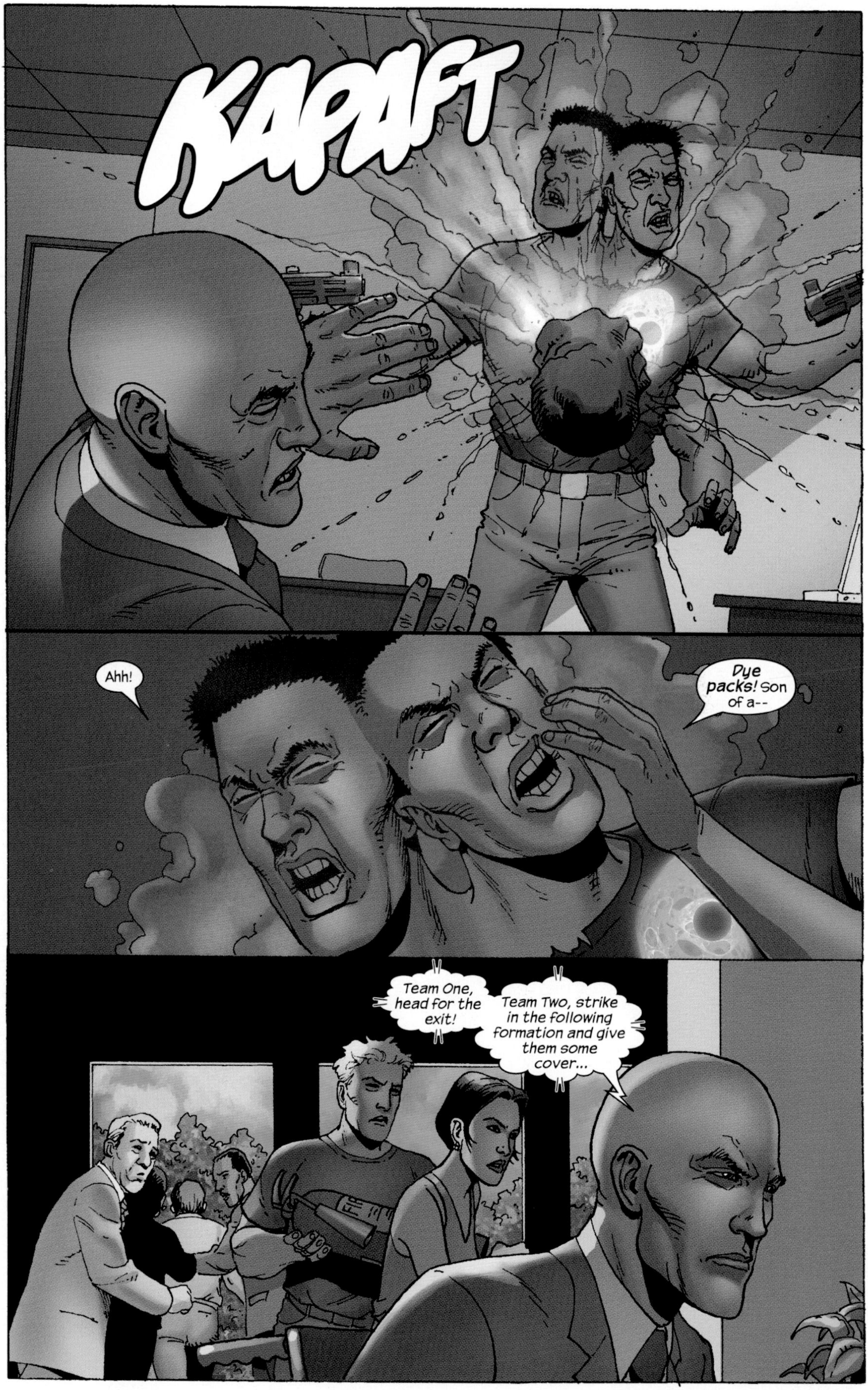
KAPAFT
Ahh!
Dye packs! Son of a--
Team One, head for the exit!
Team Two, strike in the following formation and give them some cover...

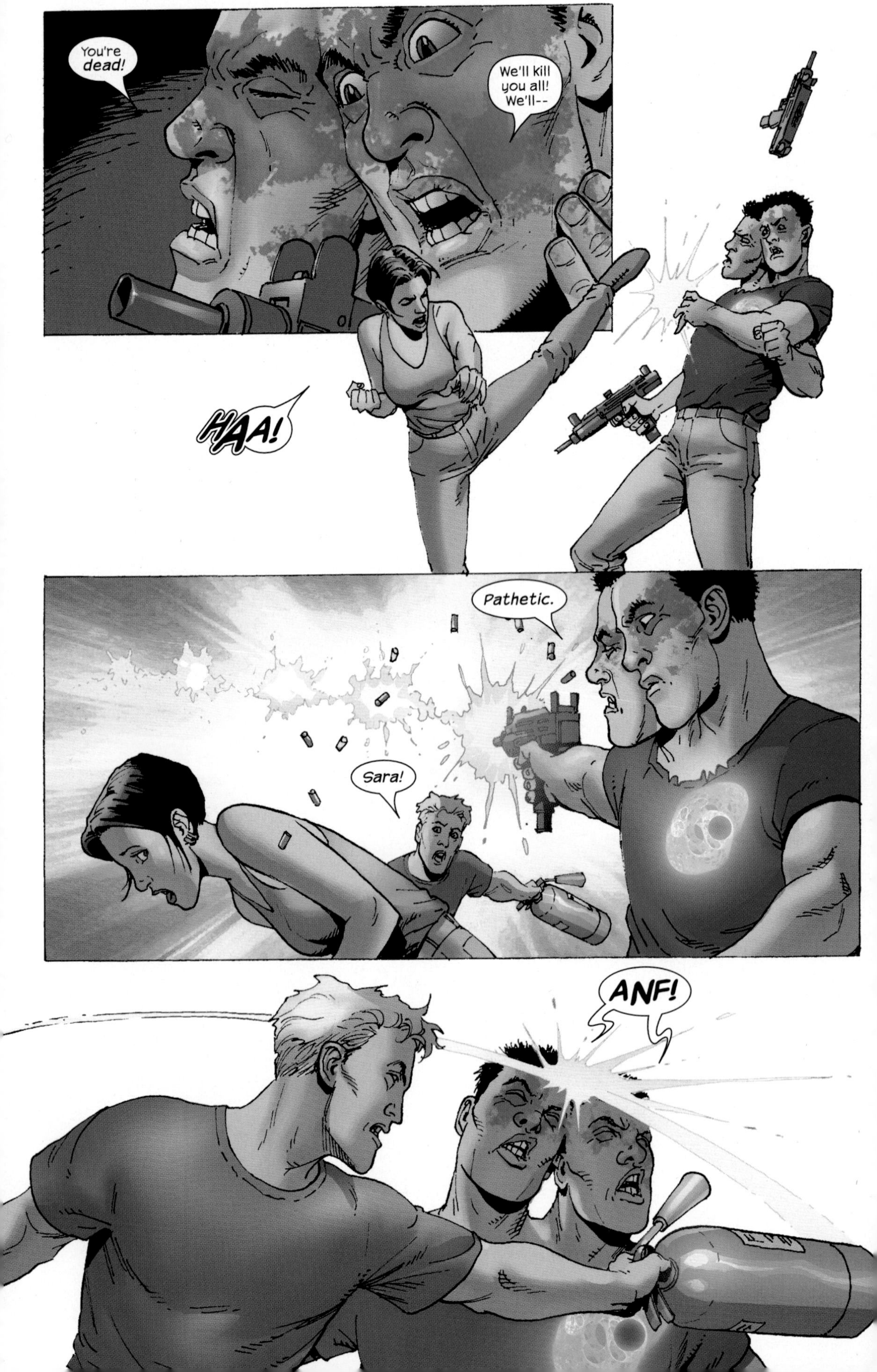
You're dead!
We'll kill you all! We'll--
HAA!
Pathetic.
Sara!
ANF!

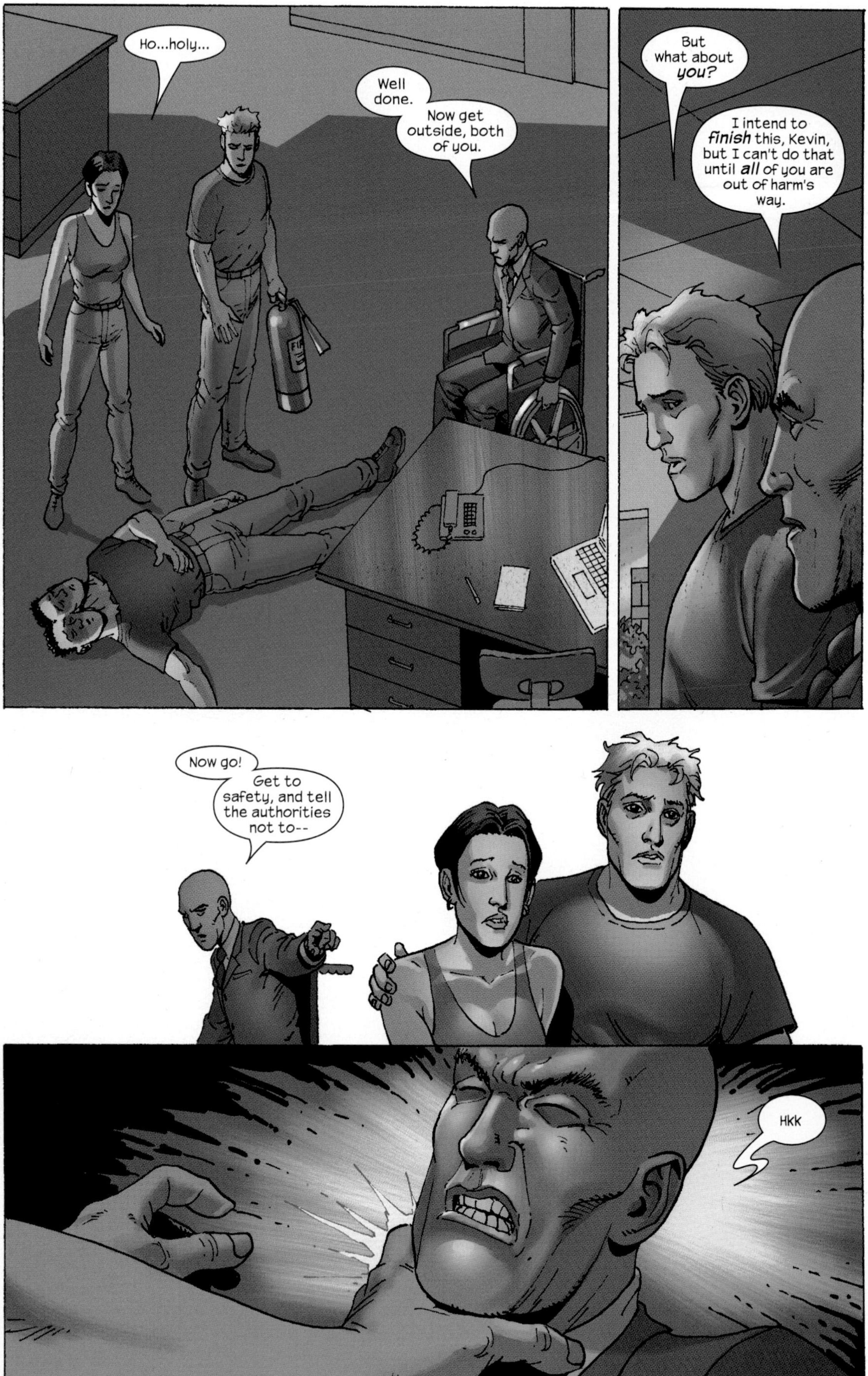
Ho...holy...
Well done.
Now get outside, both of you.
But what about *you?*
I intend to *finish* this, Kevin, but I can't do that until *all* of you are out of harm's way.
Now go!
Get to safety, and tell the authorities not to--
Hkk

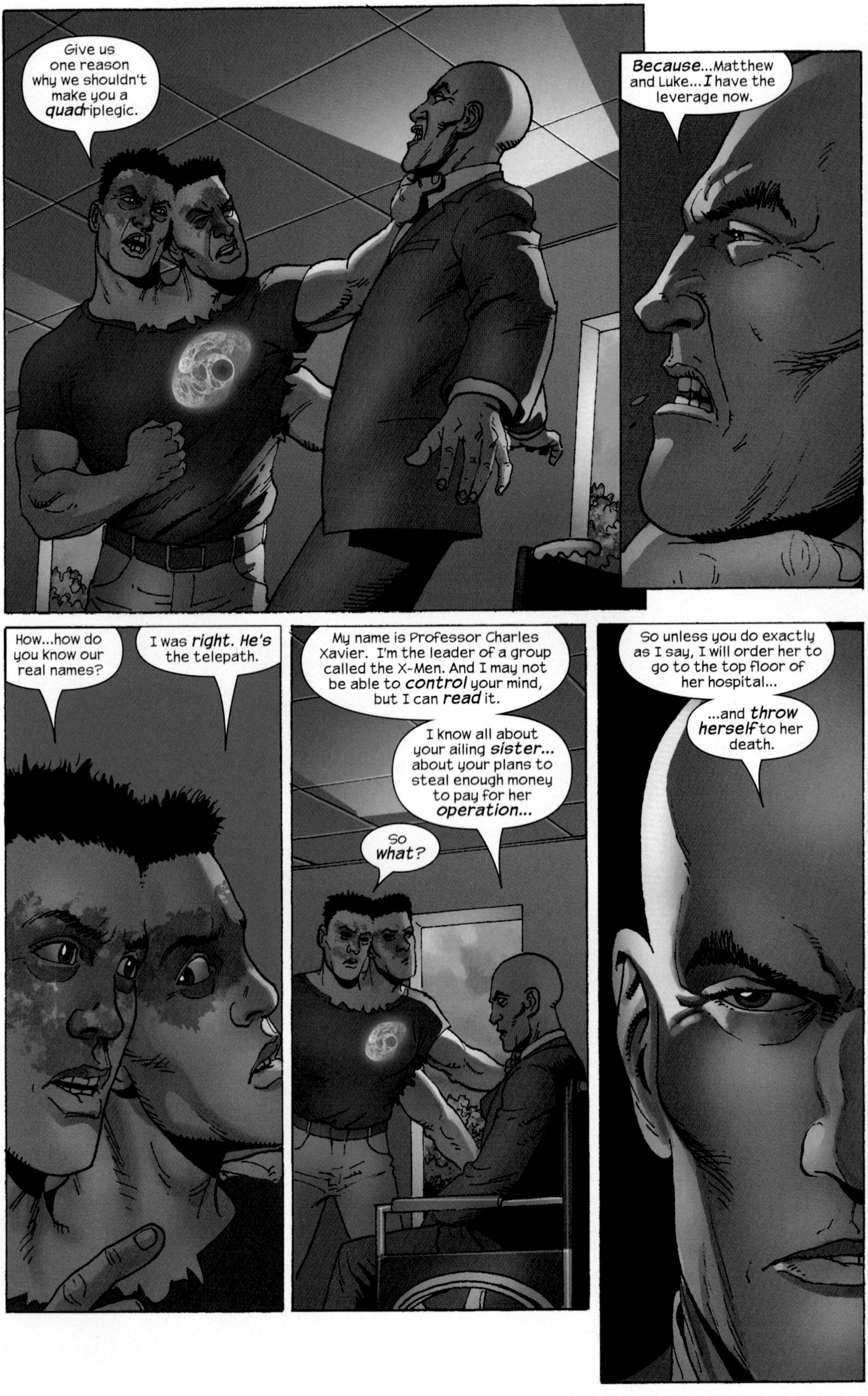

Give us one reason why we shouldn't make you a quadriplegic.
Because...Matthew and Luke...I have the leverage now.
How...how do you know our real names?
I was right. He's the telepath.
My name is Professor Charles Xavier. I'm the leader of a group called the X-Men. And I may not be able to control your mind, but I can read it.
I know all about your ailing sister... about your plans to steal enough money to pay for her operation...
So what?
So unless you do exactly as I say, I will order her to go to the top floor of her hospital...
...and throw herself to her death.

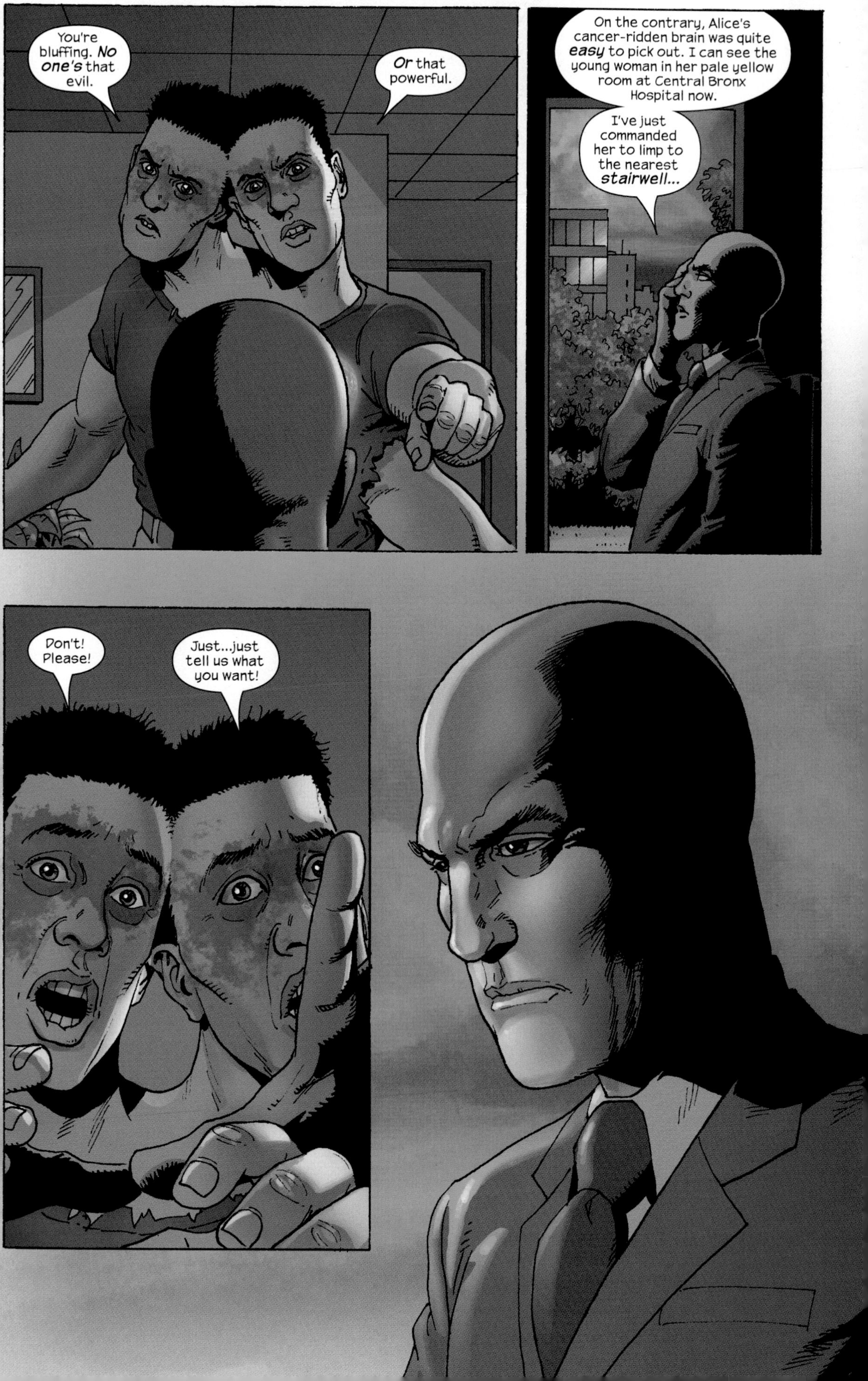

You're bluffing. No one's that evil.
Or that powerful.
On the contrary, Alice's cancer-ridden brain was quite easy to pick out. I can see the young woman in her pale yellow room at Central Bronx Hospital now.
I've just commanded her to limp to the nearest stairwell...
Don't! Please!
Just...just tell us what you want!

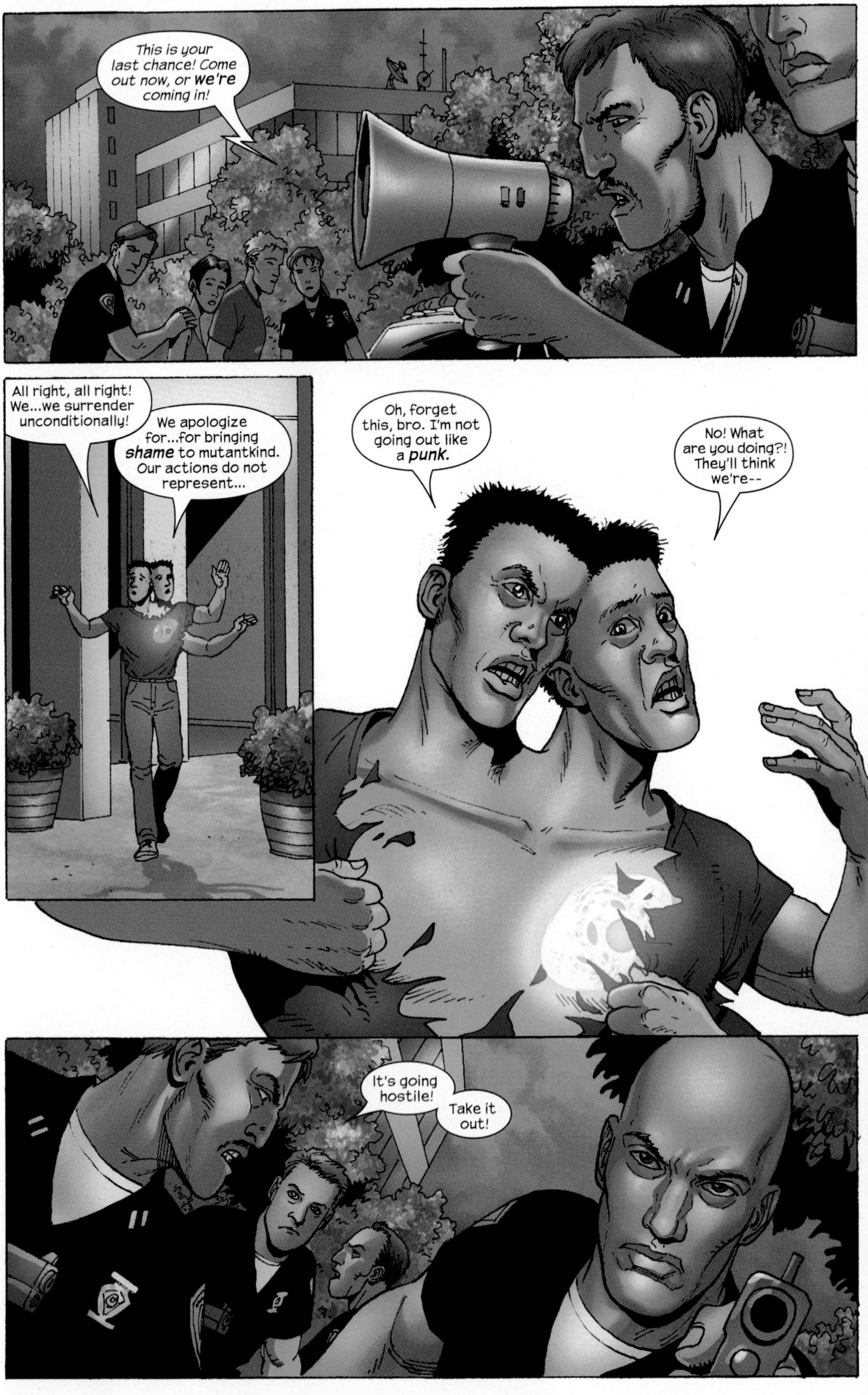
This is your last chance! Come out now, or we're coming in!
All right, all right! We...we surrender unconditionally!
We apologize for...for bringing shame to mutantkind. Our actions do not represent...
Oh, forget this, bro. I'm not going out like a punk.
No! What are you doing?! They'll think we're--
It's going hostile!
Take it out!

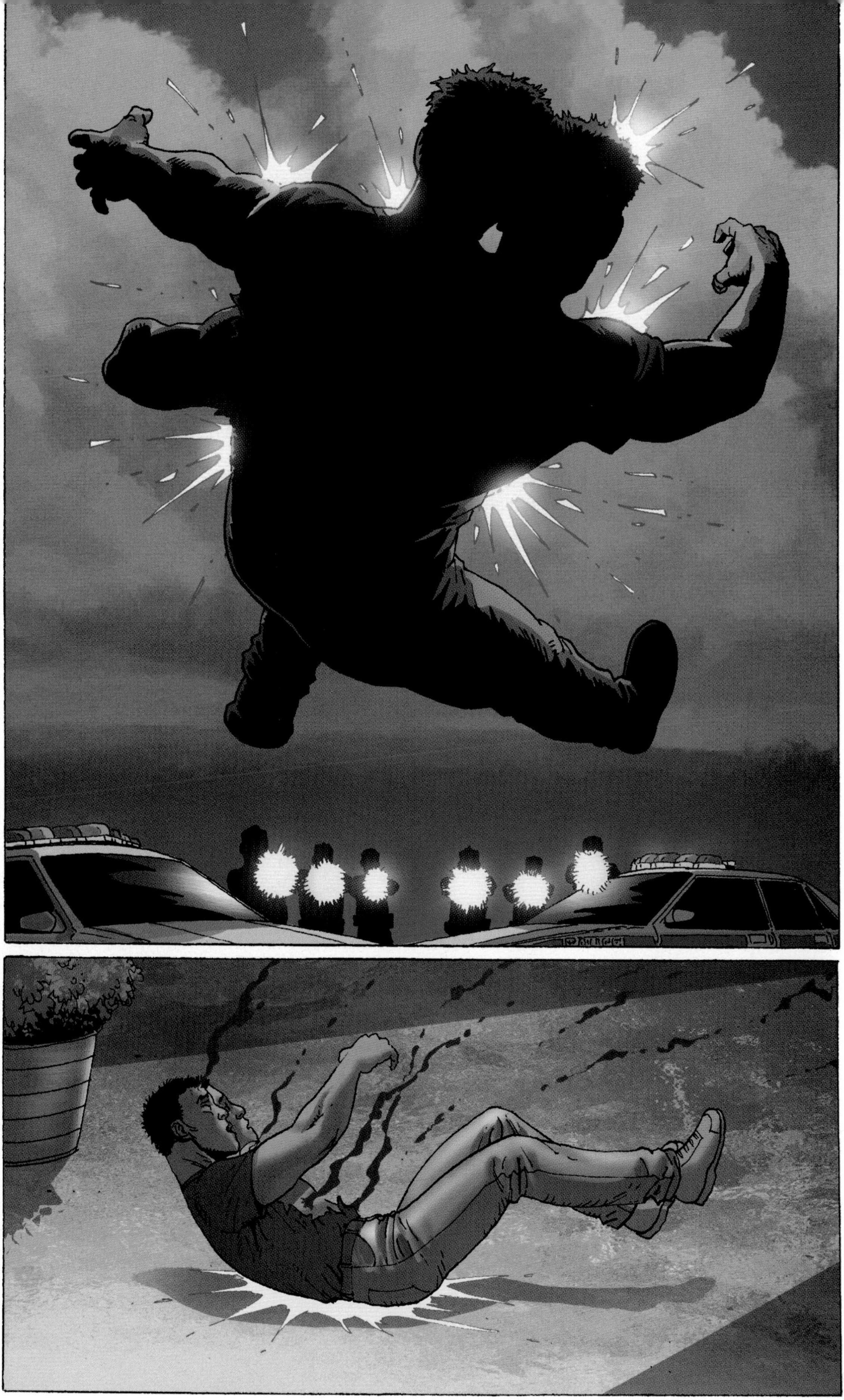

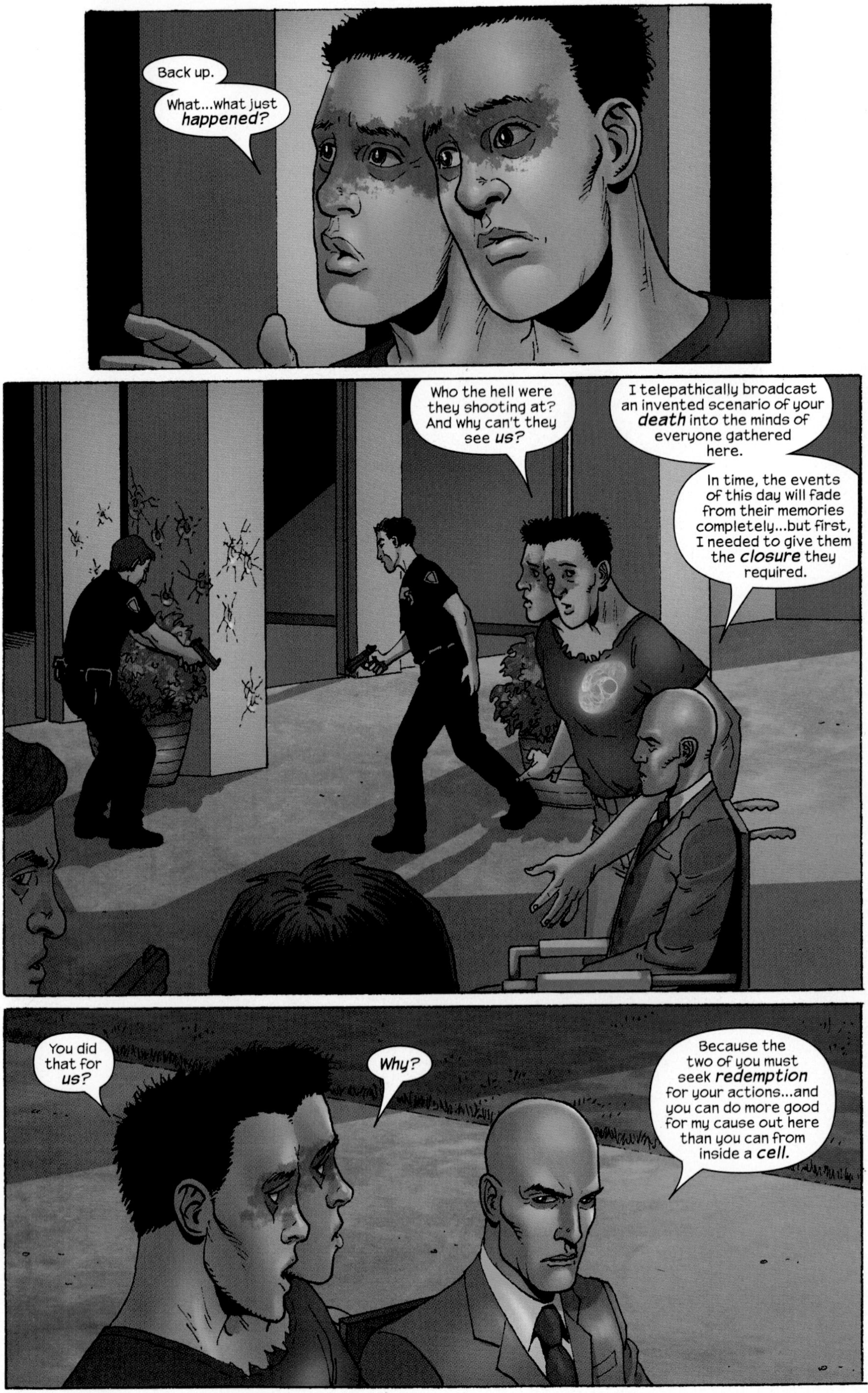
Back up.
What...what just *happened?*
Who the hell were they shooting at? And why can't they see *us?*
I telepathically broadcast an invented scenario of your *death* into the minds of everyone gathered here.
In time, the events of this day will fade from their memories completely...but first, I needed to give them the *closure* they required.
You did that for *us?*
Why?
Because the two of you must seek *redemption* for your actions...and you can do more good for my cause out here than you can from inside a *cell.*

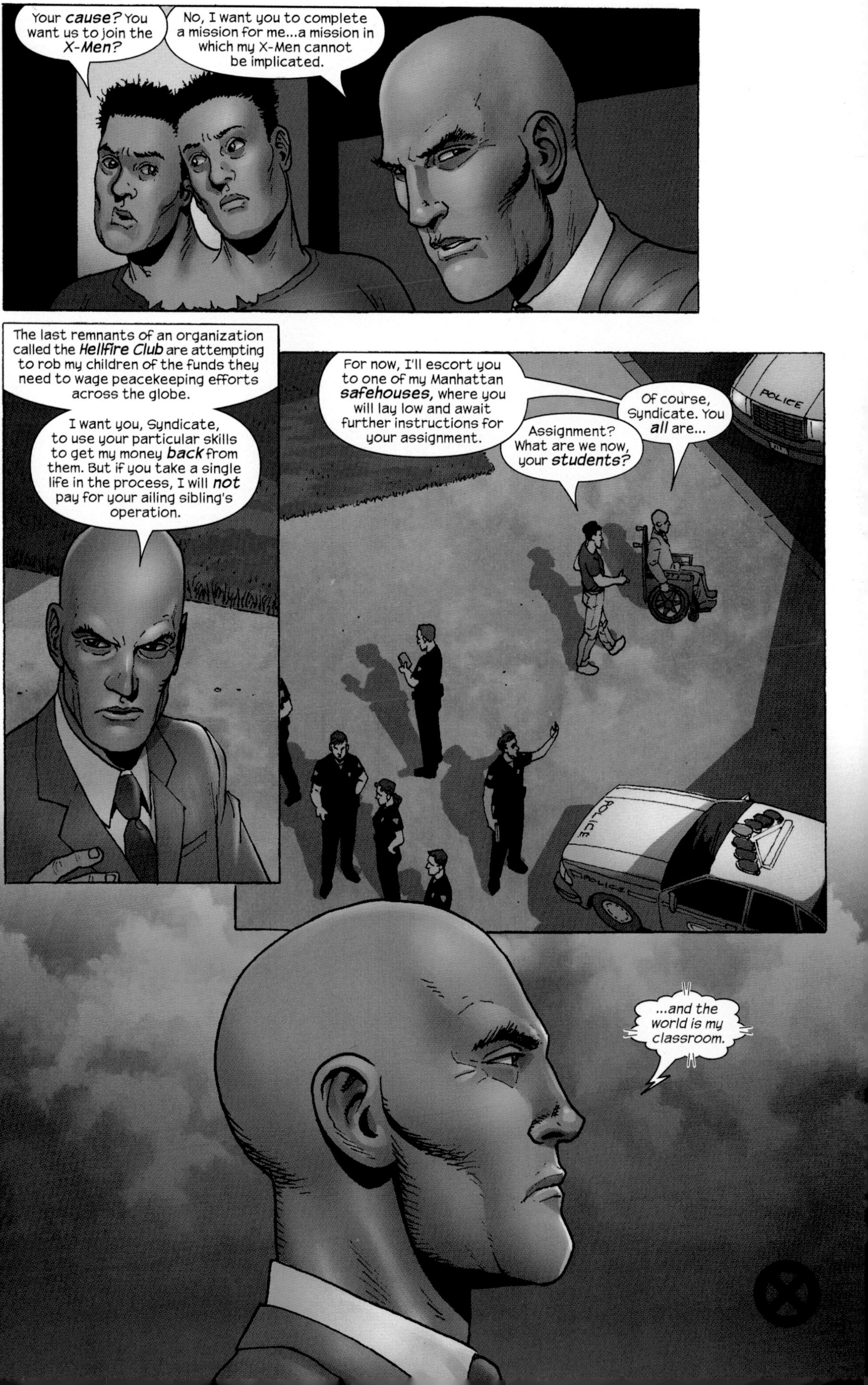

Your cause? You want us to join the X-Men?
No, I want you to complete a mission for me...a mission in which my X-Men cannot be implicated.
The last remnants of an organization called the Hellfire Club are attempting to rob my children of the funds they need to wage peacekeeping efforts across the globe.
I want you, Syndicate, to use your particular skills to get my money back from them. But if you take a single life in the process, I will not pay for your ailing sibling's operation.
For now, I'll escort you to one of my Manhattan safehouses, where you will lay low and await further instructions for your assignment.
Assignment? What are we now, your students?
Of course, Syndicate. You all are...
POLICE
POLICE
...and the world is my classroom.

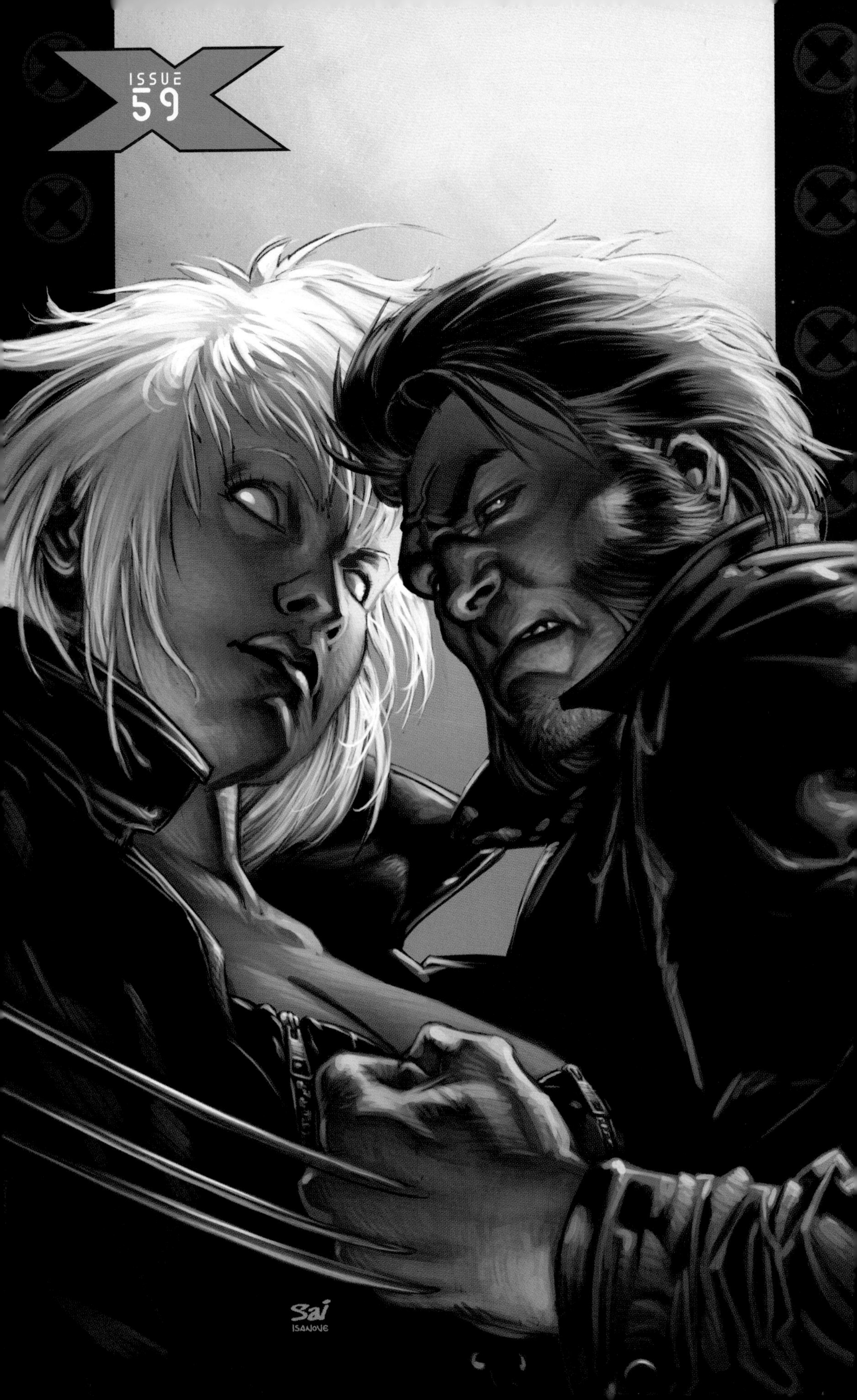
ISSUE
59
SAI
ISANOVE

PREVIOUSLY IN ULTIMATE X-MEN:

Born with strange and amazing abilities, the X-Men are young mutant heroes, sworn to protect a world that fears and hates them. One of these "gifted teens" is Ororo Munroe, also known as Storm, a mutant able to manipulate the weather with only a thought. Having recently lost her boyfriend, the late Hank McCoy, Storm has grown closer with a man named Logan.

Blessed with an incredible healing factor, Logan became the assassin codenamed Wolverine after a covert military organization called Weapon X wiped his memory and laced his skeleton with an unbreakable metal. Logan escaped this evil group and joined the X-Men, but he eventually left the team, believing that he didn't belong with idealistic peacekeepers.

That was three months ago...

SHOCK AND AWE

PART ONE OF TWO

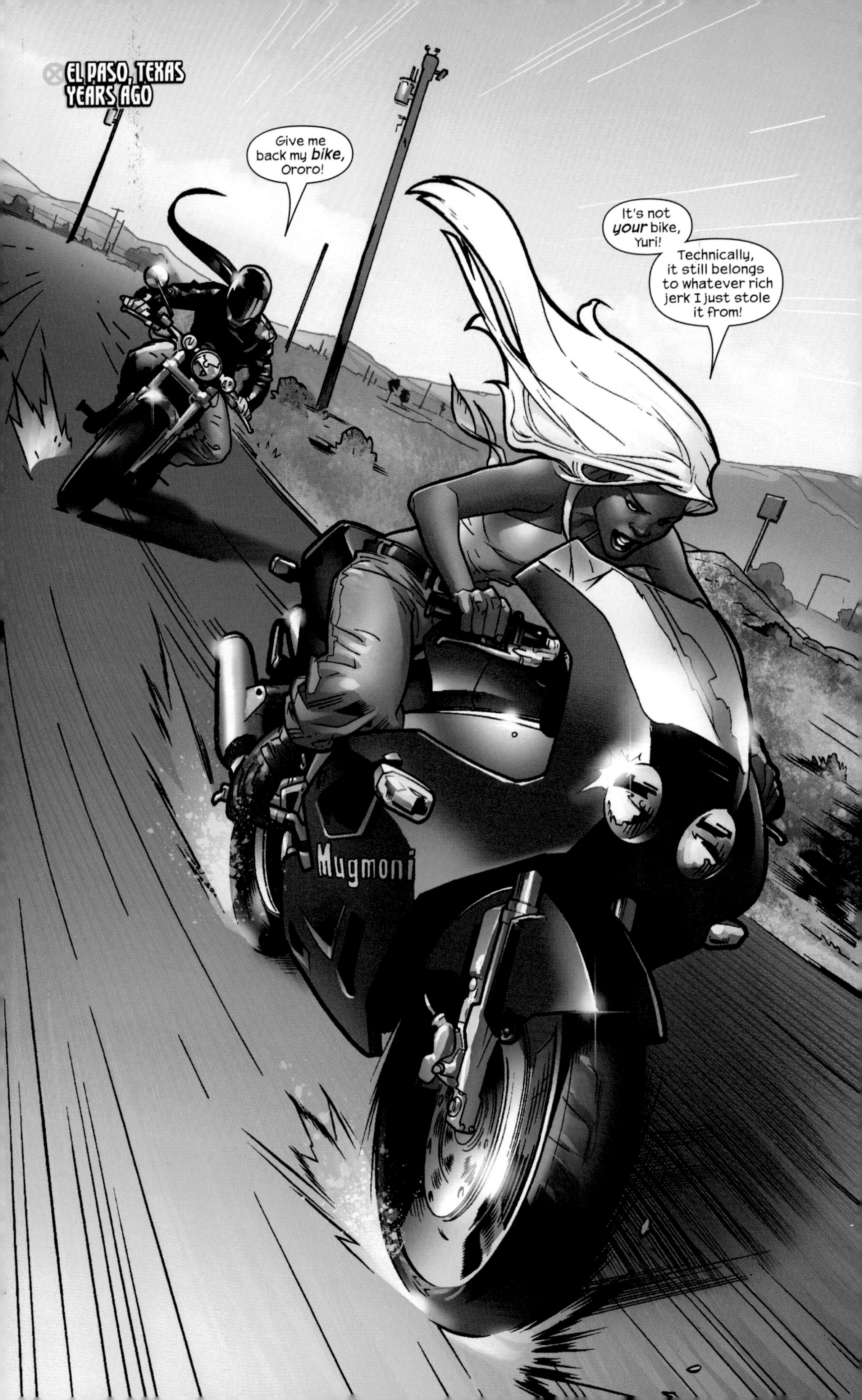
EL PASO, TEXAS
YEARS AGO
Give me back my bike, Ororo!
It's not your bike, Yuri!
Technically, it still belongs to whatever rich jerk I just stole it from!
Mugmoni

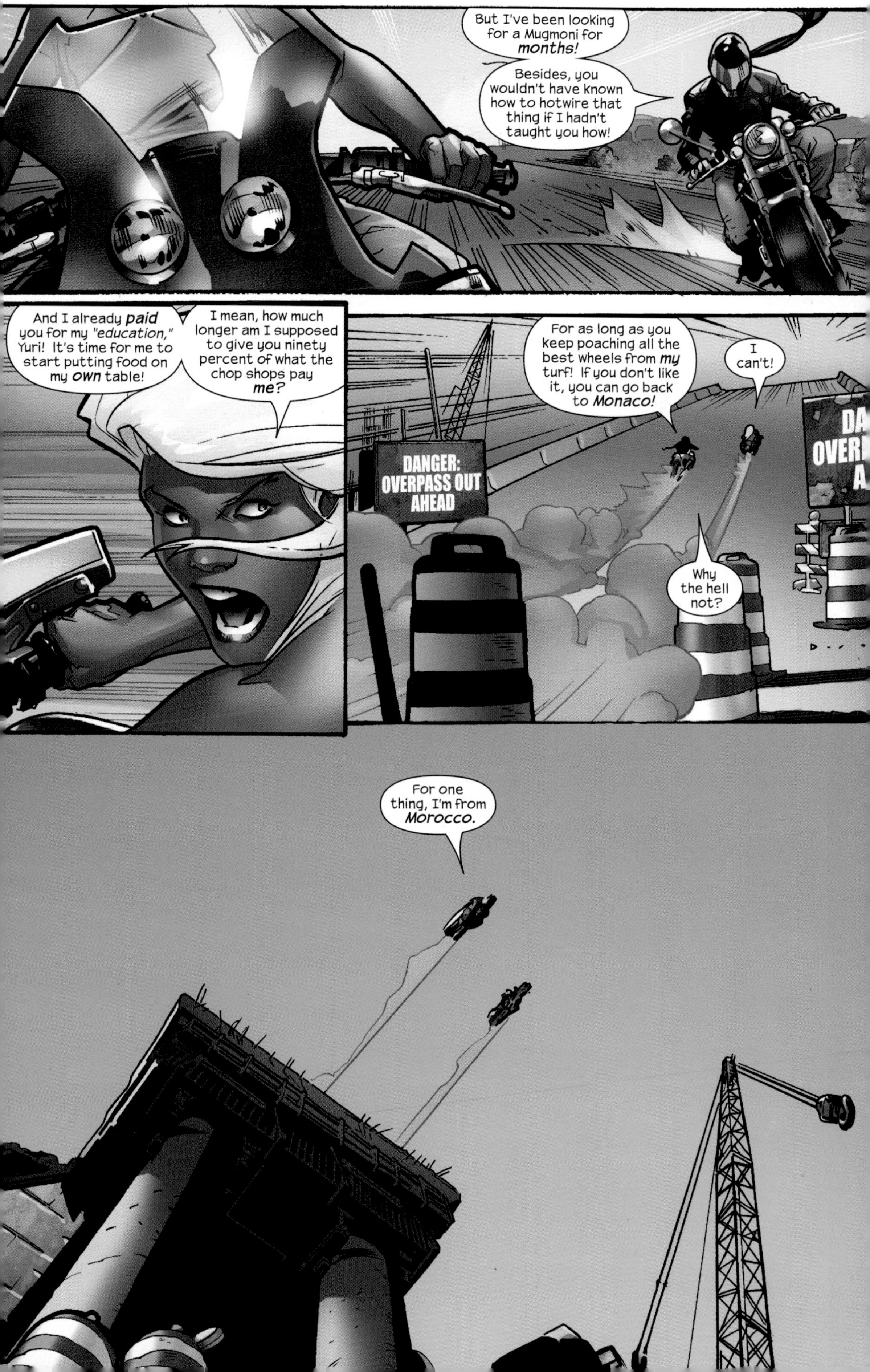
But I've been looking for a Mugmoni for *months!*
Besides, you wouldn't have known how to hotwire that thing if I hadn't taught you how!
And I already *paid* you for my *"education,"* Yuri! It's time for me to start putting food on my *own* table!
I mean, how much longer am I supposed to give you ninety percent of what the chop shops pay *me?*
DANGER: OVERPASS OUT AHEAD
For as long as you keep poaching all the best wheels from *my* turf! If you don't like it, you can go back to *Monaco!*
I can't!
Why the hell not?
For one thing, I'm from *Morocco.*

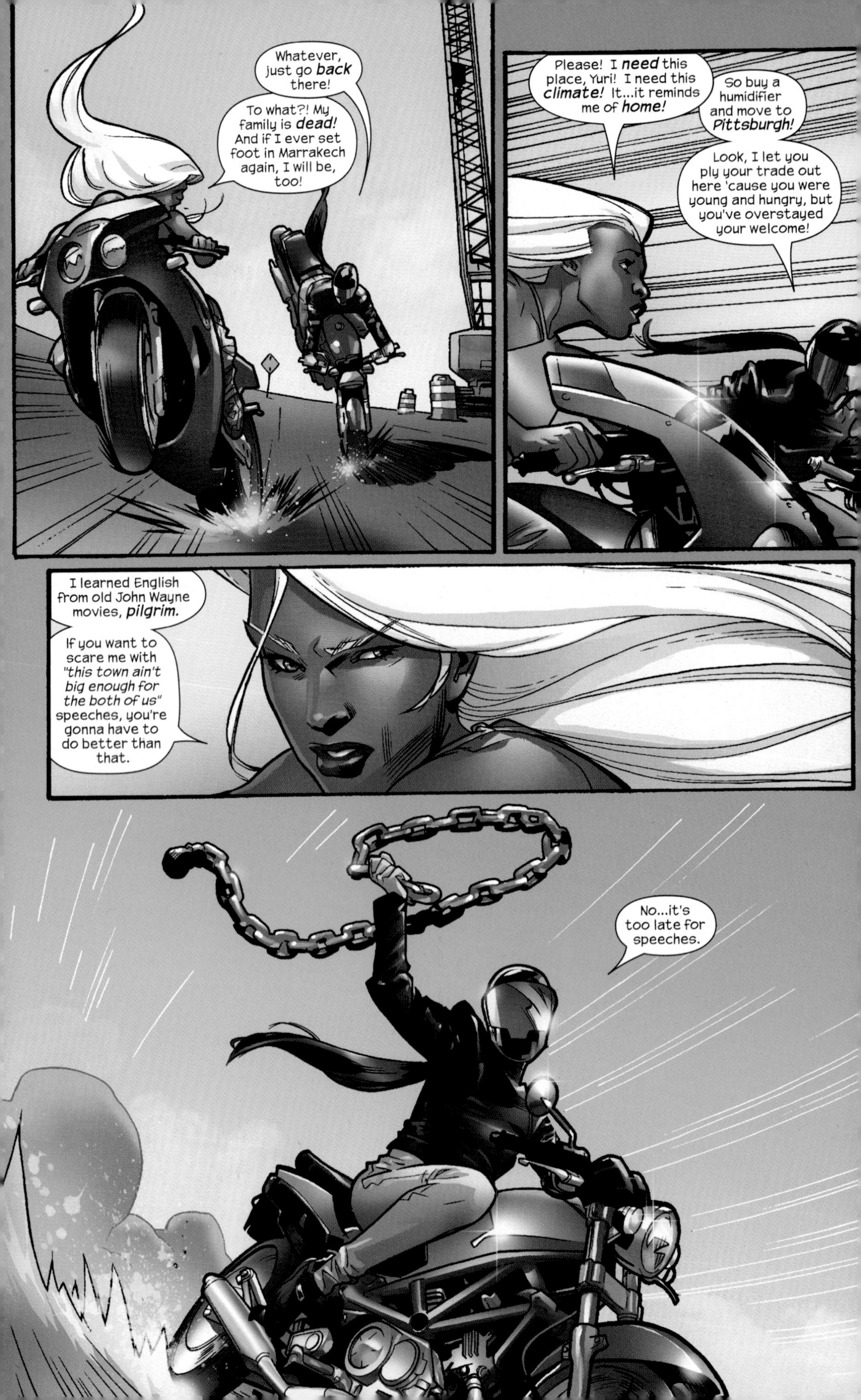

Whatever, just go back there!
To what?! My family is dead! And if I ever set foot in Marrakech again, I will be, too!
Please! I need this place, Yuri! I need this climate! It...it reminds me of home!
So buy a humidifier and move to Pittsburgh!
Look, I let you ply your trade out here 'cause you were young and hungry, but you've overstayed your welcome!
I learned English from old John Wayne movies, pilgrim.
If you want to scare me with "this town ain't big enough for the both of us" speeches, you're gonna have to do better than that.
No...it's too late for speeches.

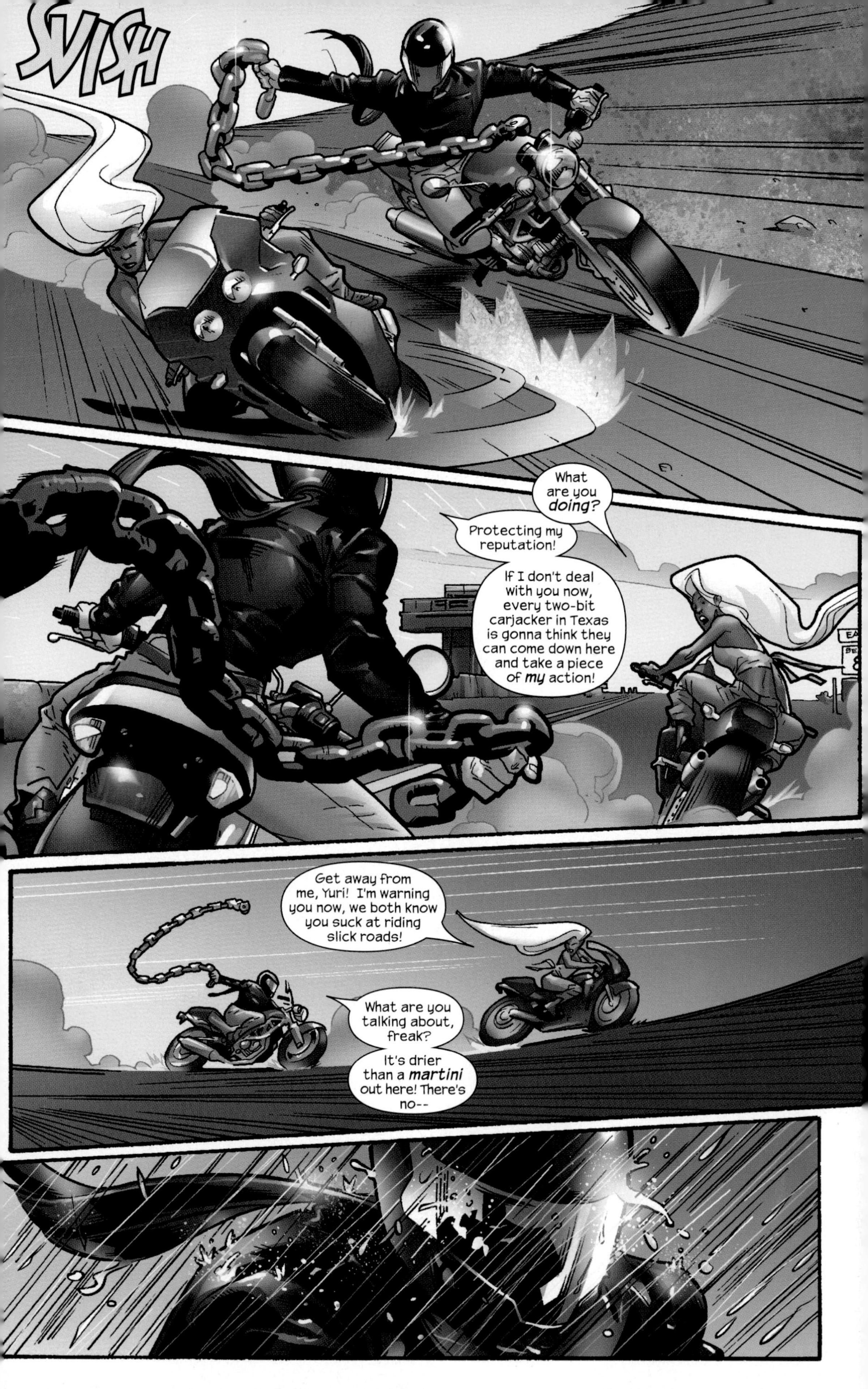
SWISH
What are you doing?
Protecting my reputation!
If I don't deal with you now, every two-bit carjacker in Texas is gonna think they can come down here and take a piece of my action!
Get away from me, Yuri! I'm warning you now, we both know you suck at riding slick roads!
What are you talking about, freak?
It's drier than a martini out here! There's no--

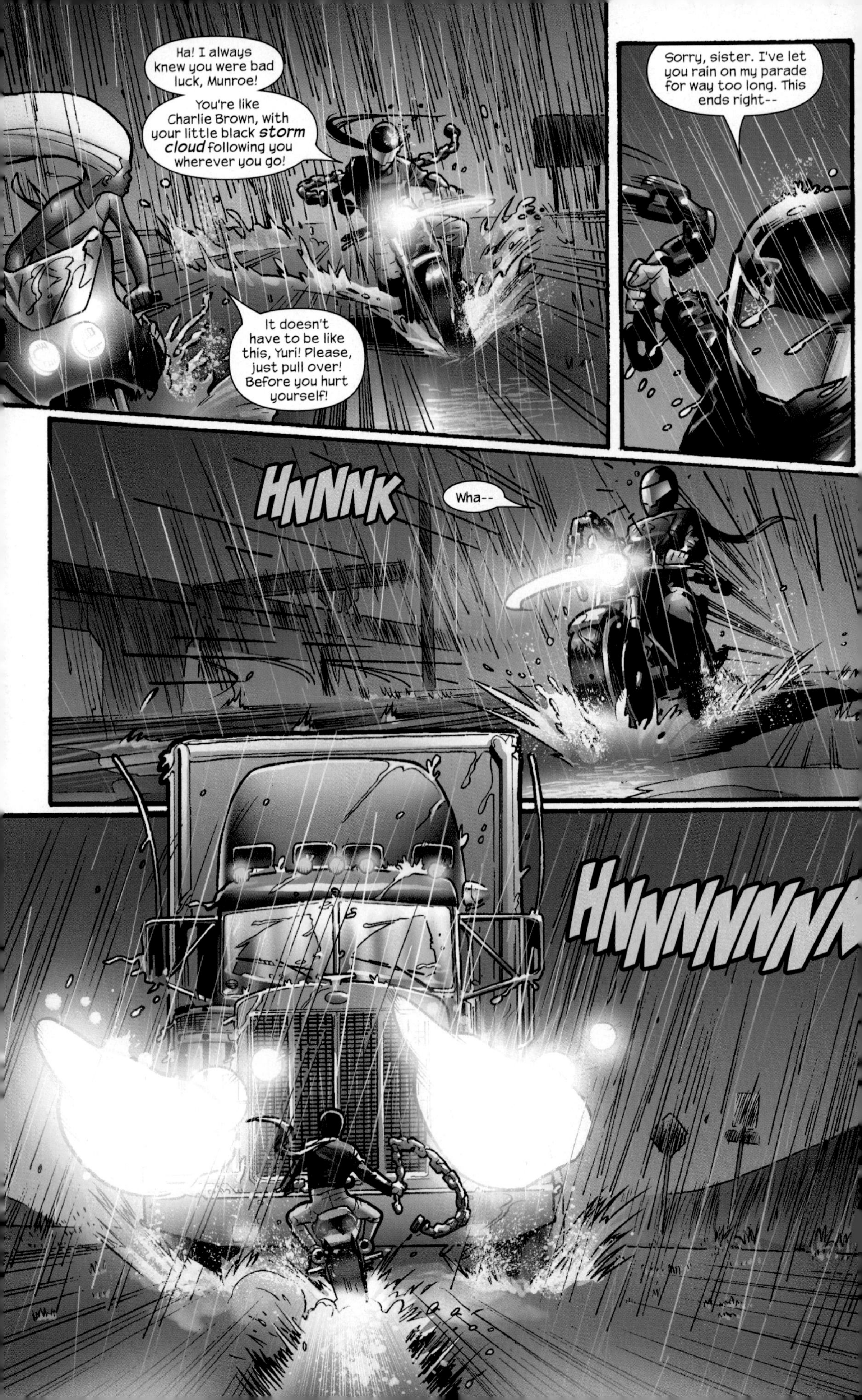
Ha! I always knew you were bad luck, Munroe!
You're like Charlie Brown, with your little black storm cloud following you wherever you go!
It doesn't have to be like this, Yuri! Please, just pull over! Before you hurt yourself!
Sorry, sister. I've let you rain on my parade for way too long. This ends right--
HNNNK
Wha--
HNNNNNNN

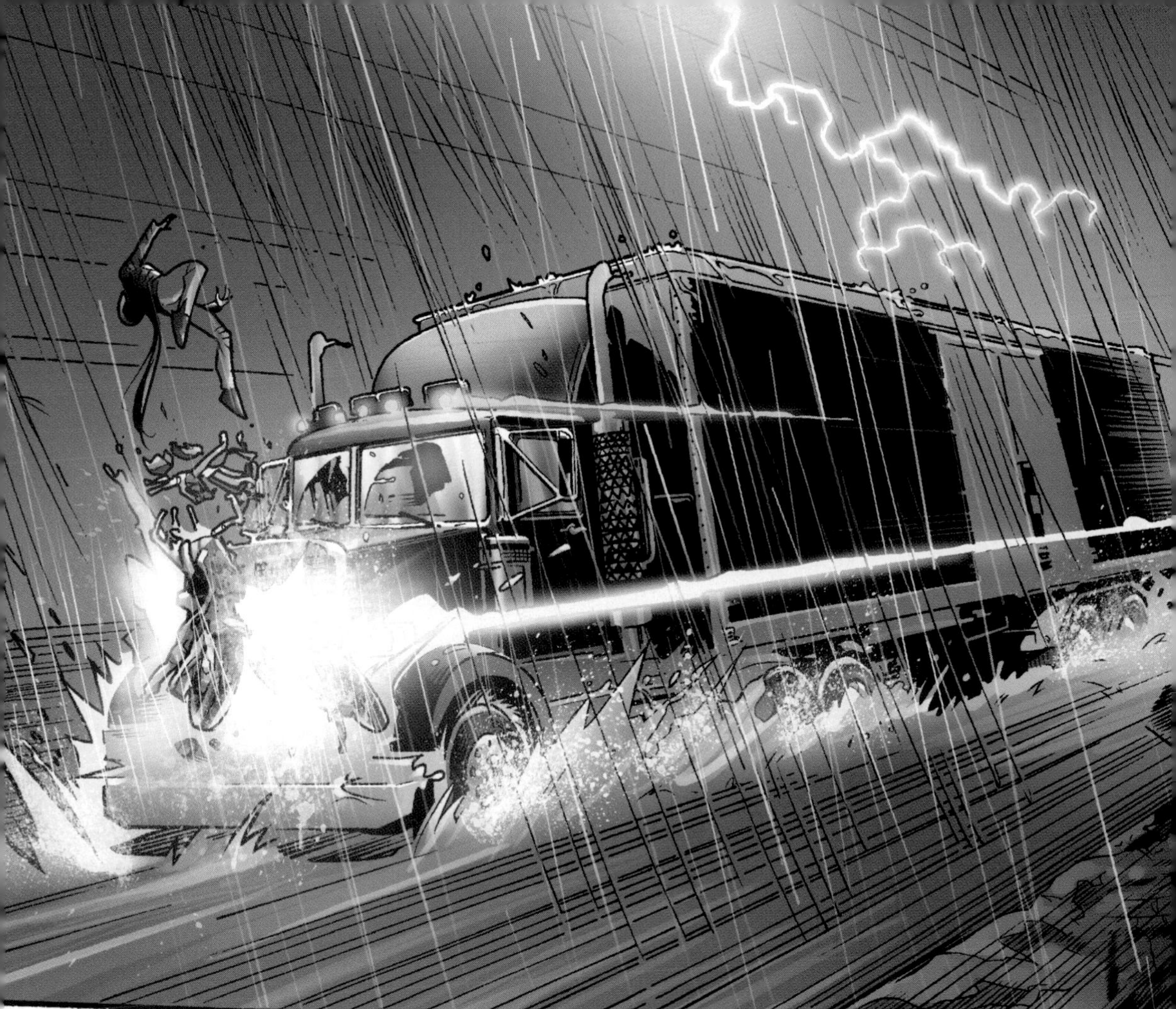

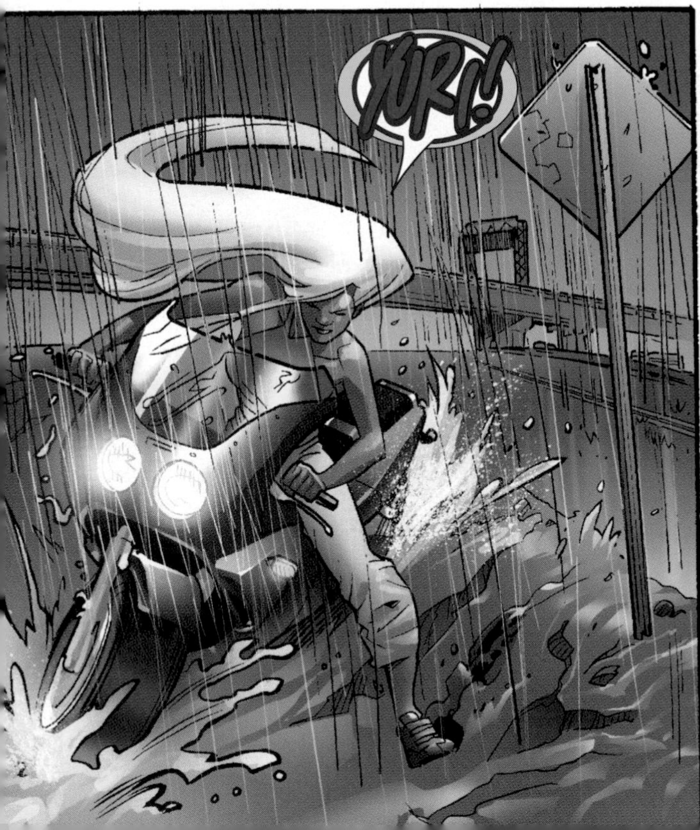
YURI!

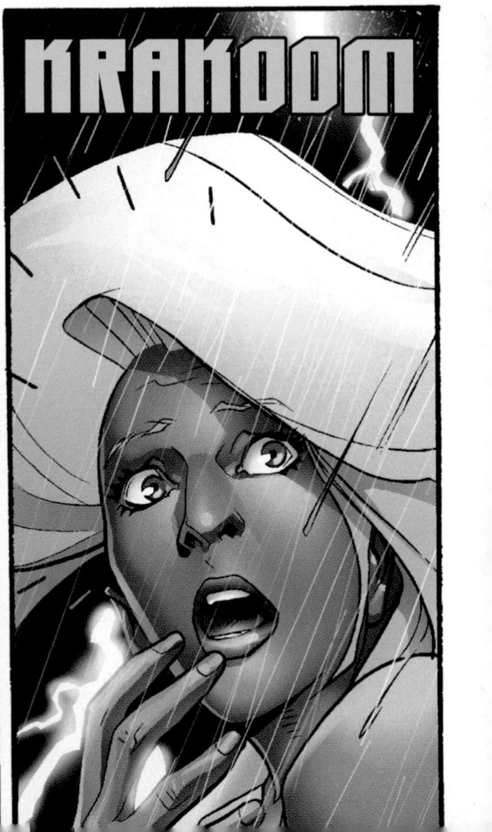
KRAKOOM

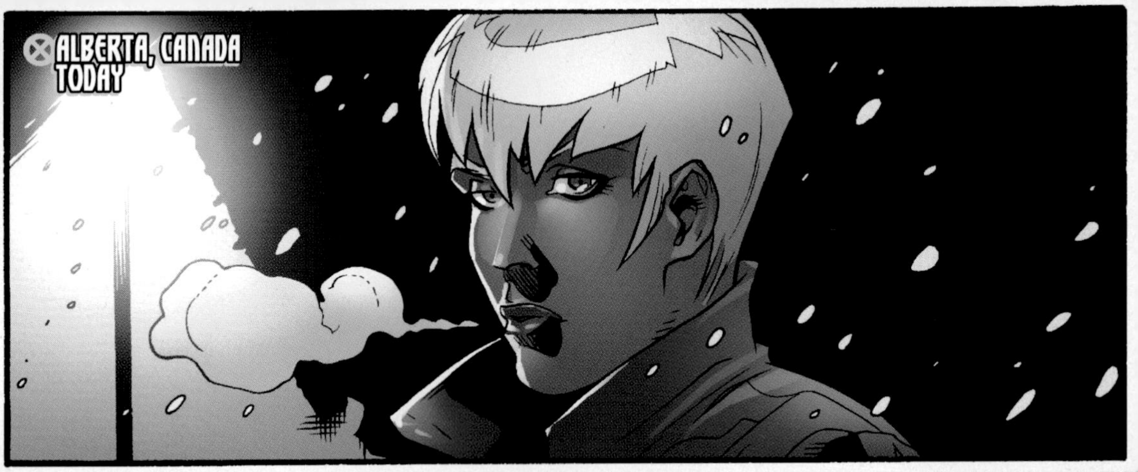
ALBERTA, CANADA
TODAY

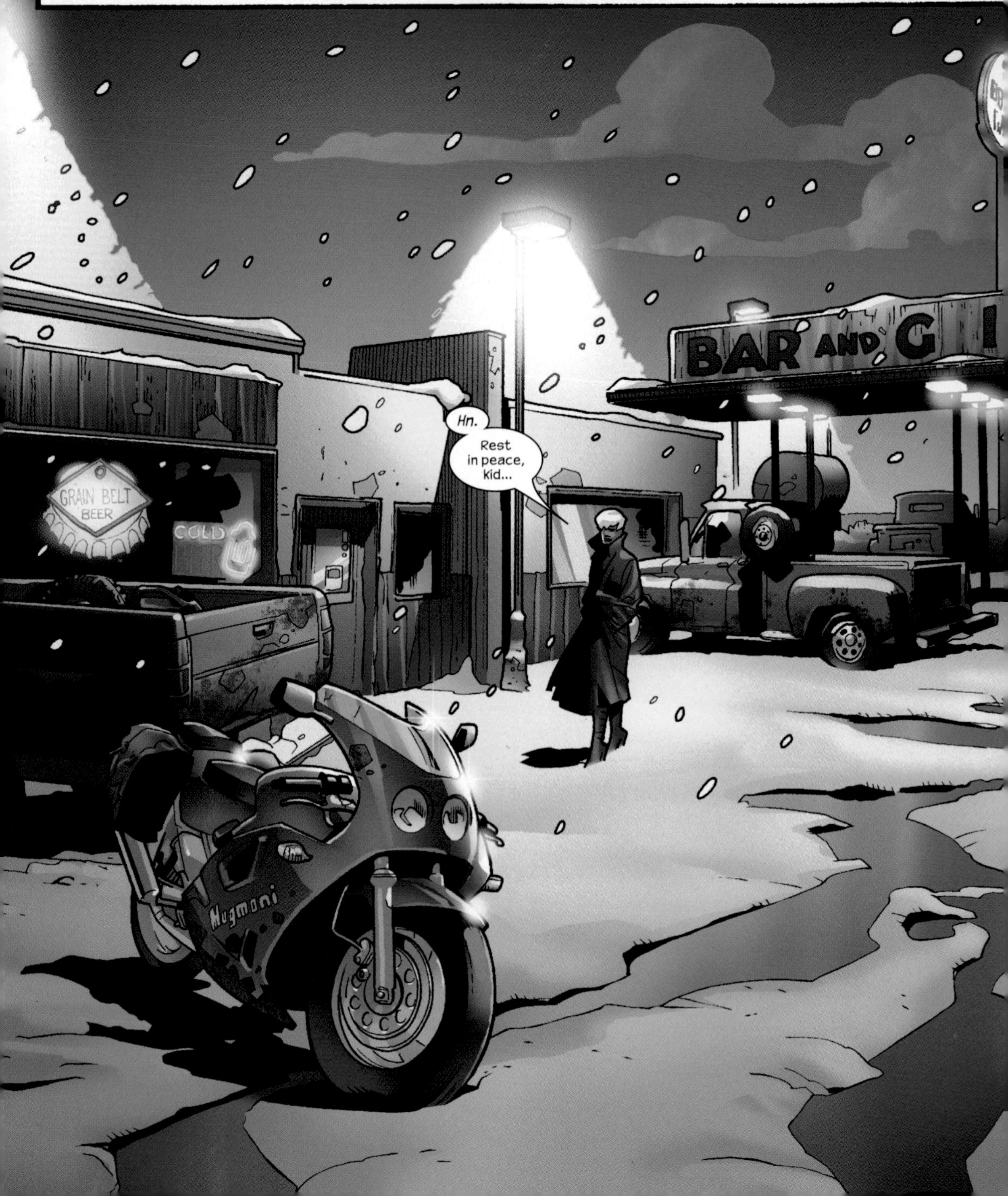
BAR AND G
GRAIN BELT BEER
COLD
Hn.
Rest in peace, kid...
Hugmoni

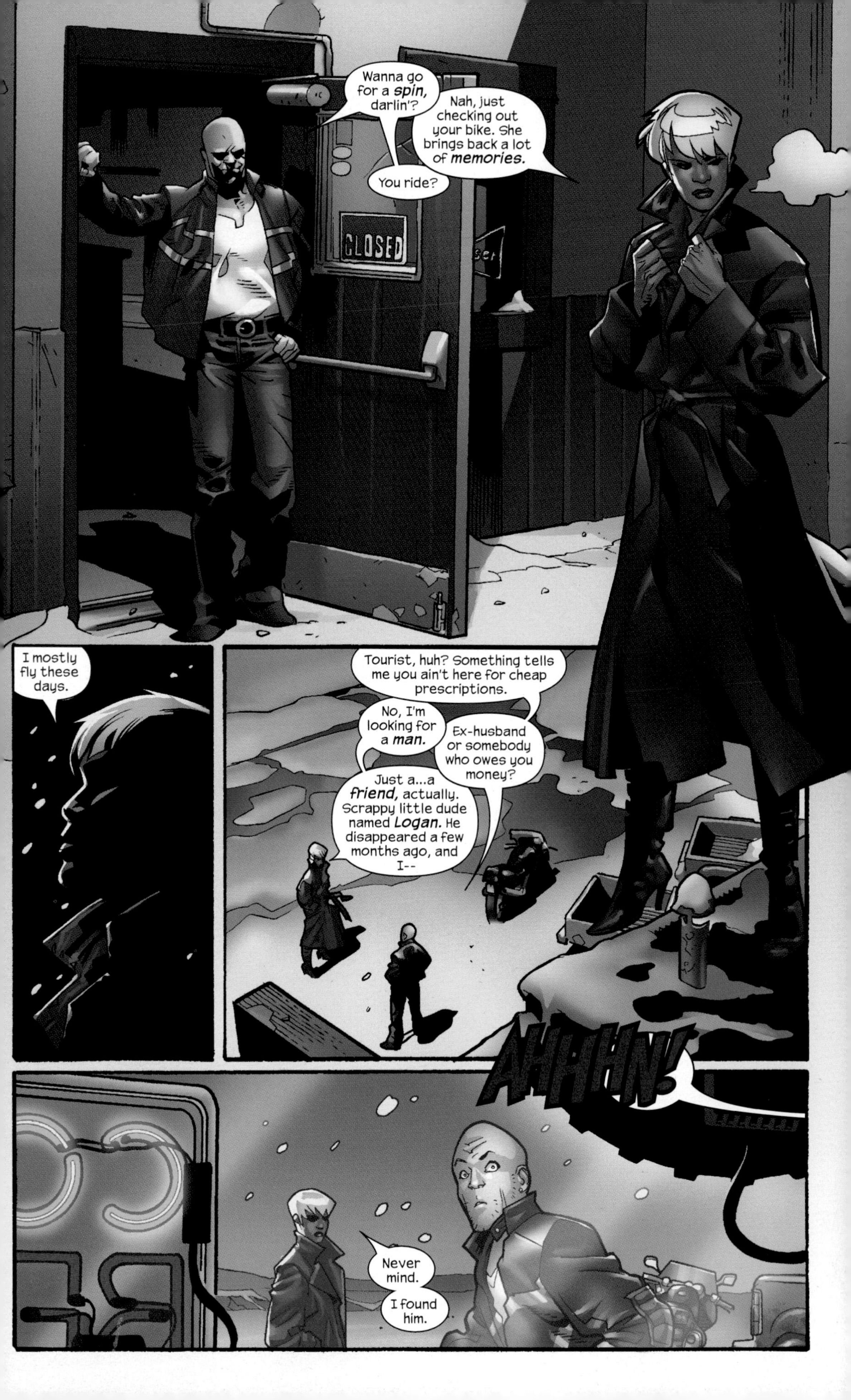
Wanna go for a spin, darlin'?
Nah, just checking out your bike. She brings back a lot of memories.
You ride?
CLOSED
I mostly fly these days.
Tourist, huh? Something tells me you ain't here for cheap prescriptions.
No, I'm looking for a man.
Ex-husband or somebody who owes you money?
Just a...a friend, actually. Scrappy little dude named Logan. He disappeared a few months ago, and I--
AHHHN!
Never mind.
I found him.

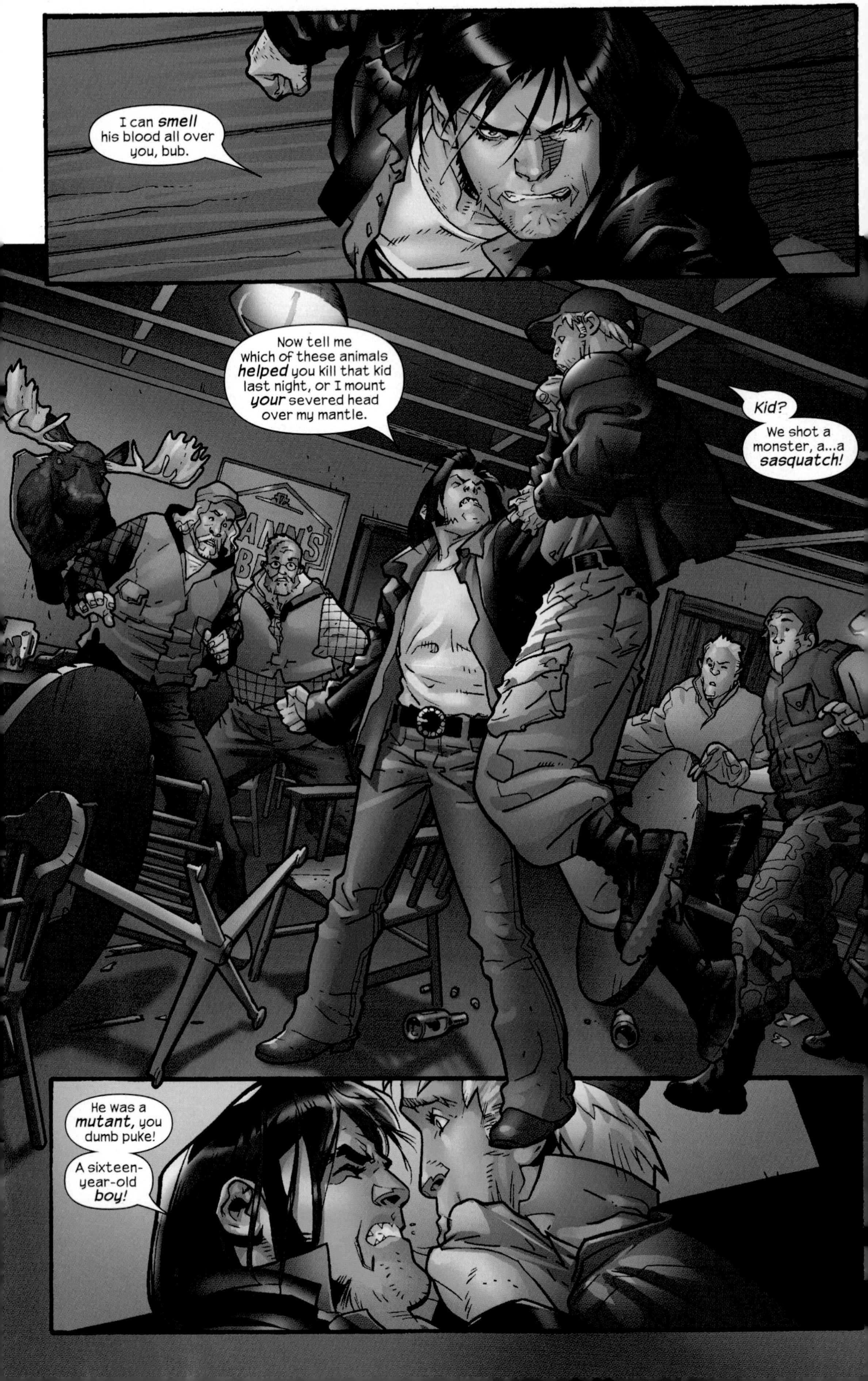
I can *smell* his blood all over you, bub.
Now tell me which of these animals *helped* you kill that kid last night, or I mount *your* severed head over my mantle.
Kid?
We shot a monster, a...a *sasquatch!*
He was a *mutant,* you dumb puke!
A sixteen-year-old *boy!*

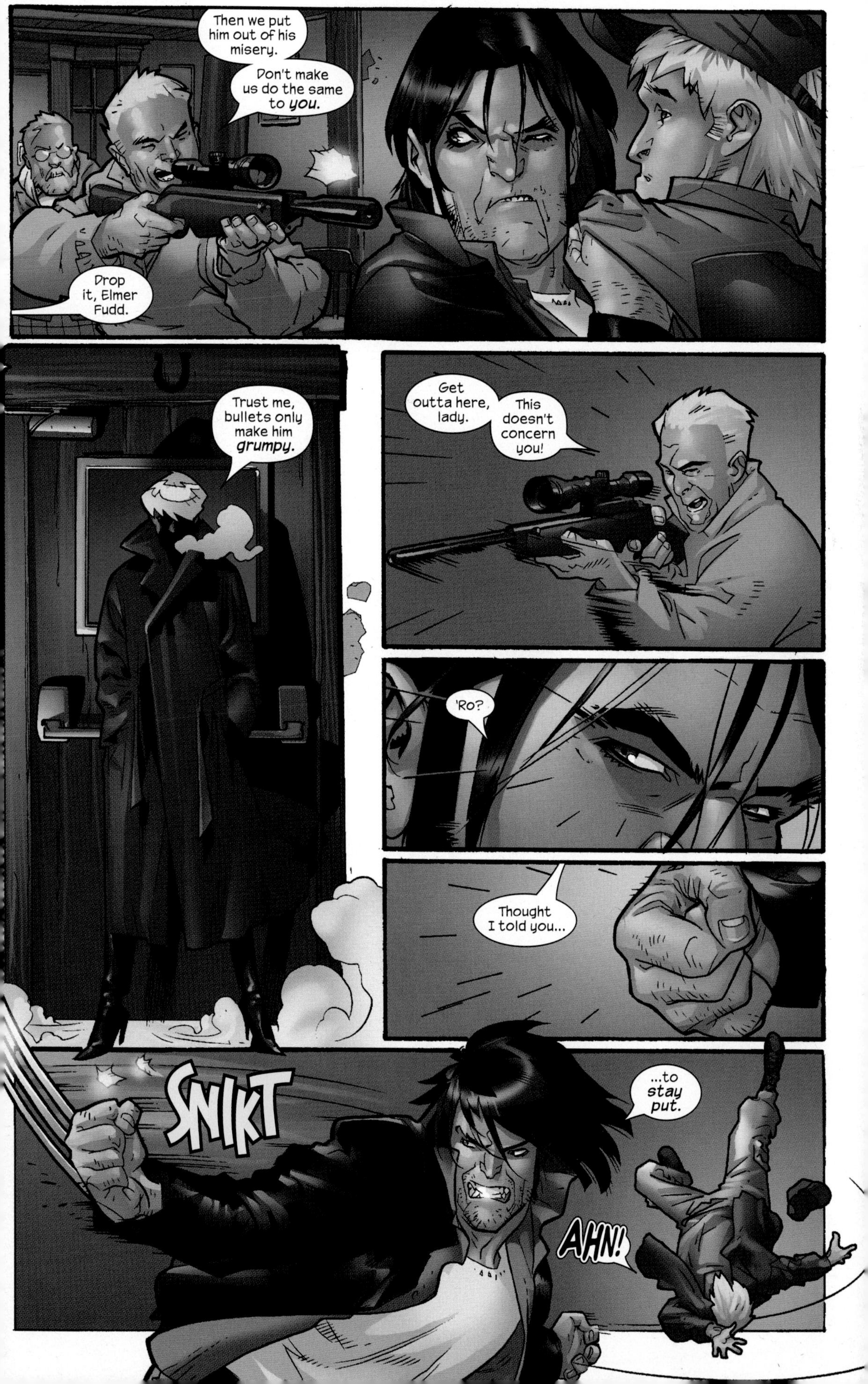
Then we put him out of his misery.
Don't make us do the same to *you.*
Drop it, Elmer Fudd.
Trust me, bullets only make him *grumpy.*
Get outta here, lady.
This doesn't concern you!
'Ro?
Thought I told you...
SNIKT
...to *stay put.*
AHN!

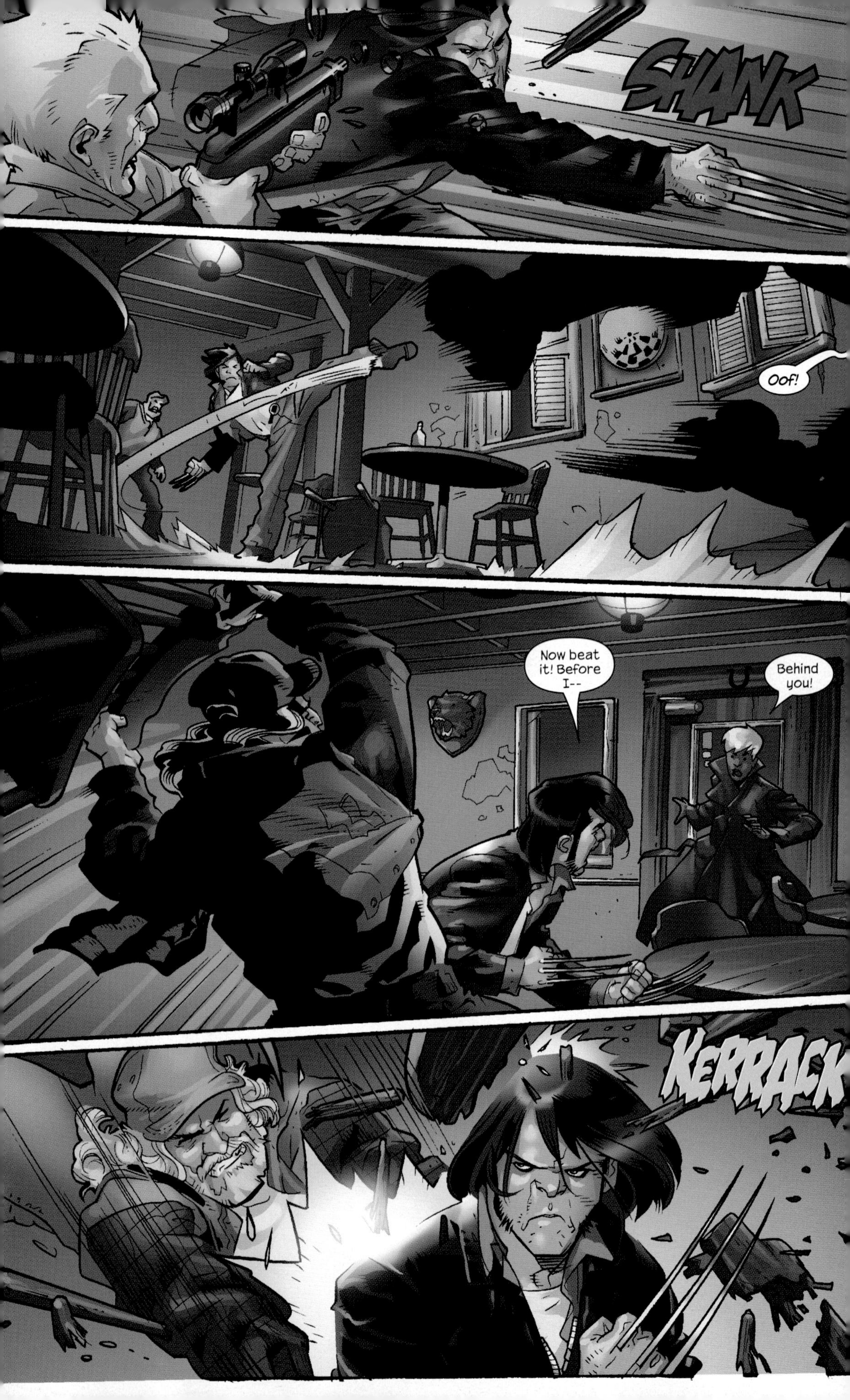
SHANK
Oof!
Now beat it! Before I--
Behind you!
KERRACK

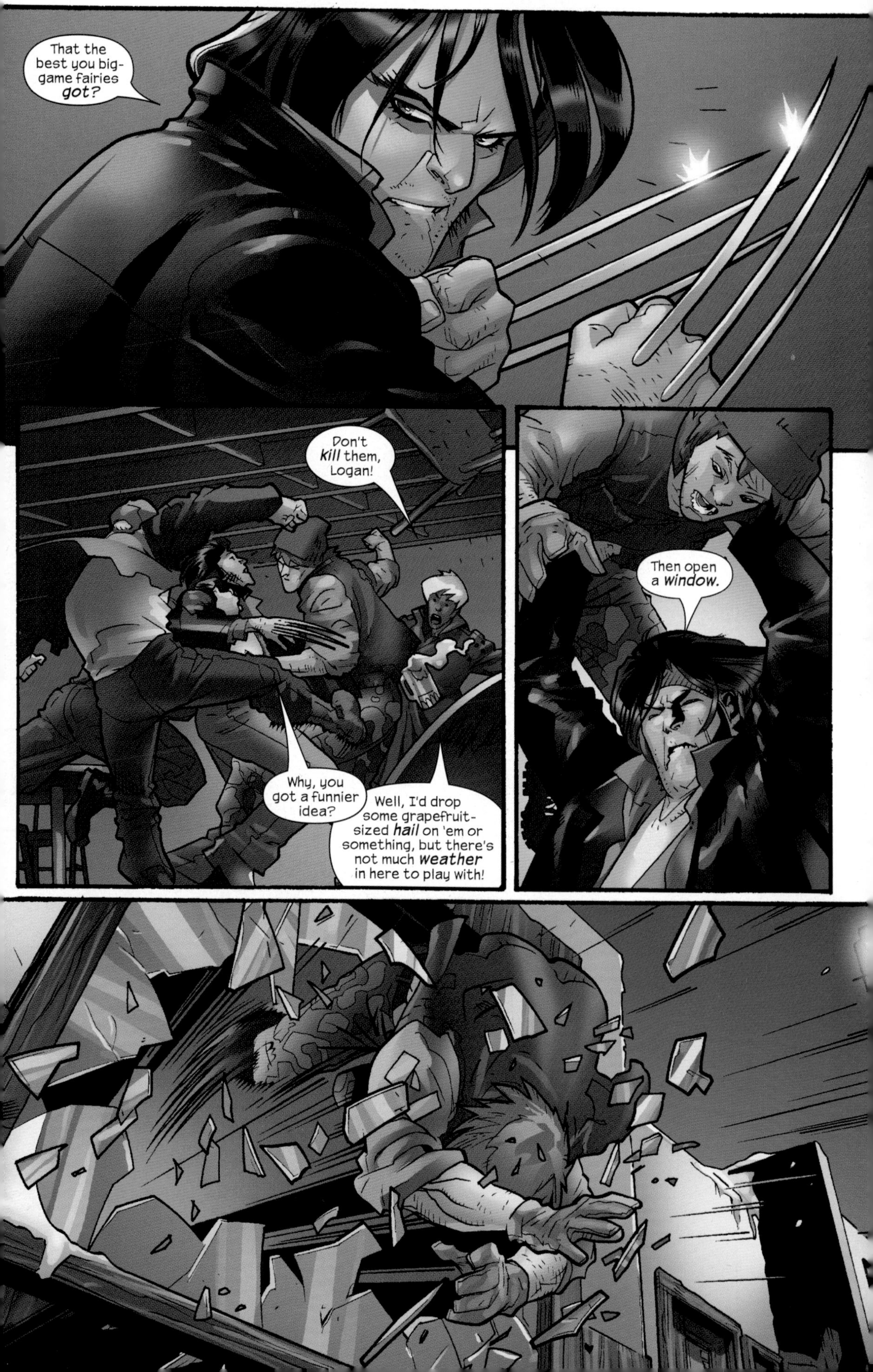
That the best you big-game fairies got?
Don't kill them, Logan!
Why, you got a funnier idea?
Well, I'd drop some grapefruit-sized hail on 'em or something, but there's not much weather in here to play with!
Then open a window.

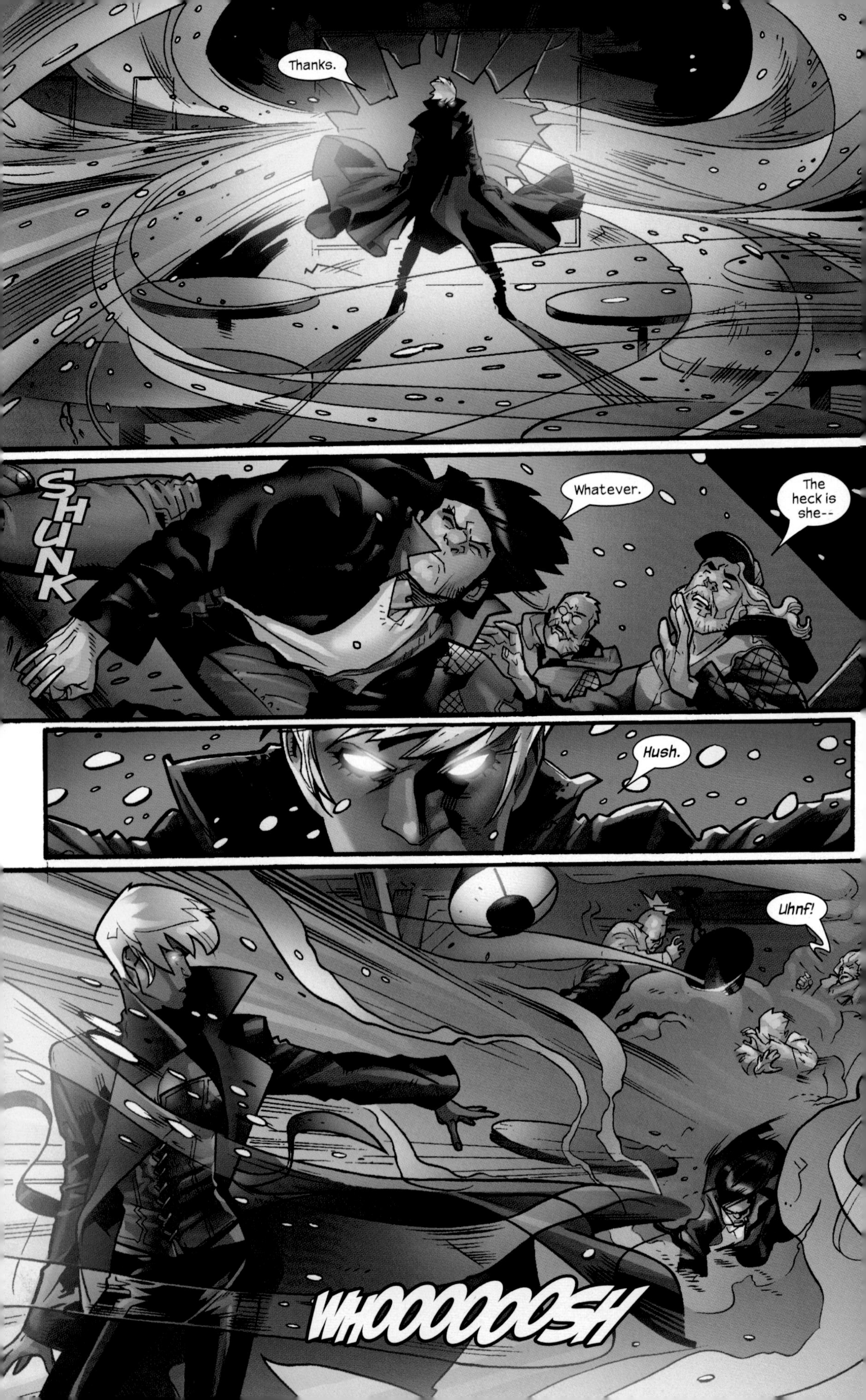
Thanks.
SHUNK
Whatever.
The heck is she--
Hush.
Uhnf!
WHOOOOOOOSH

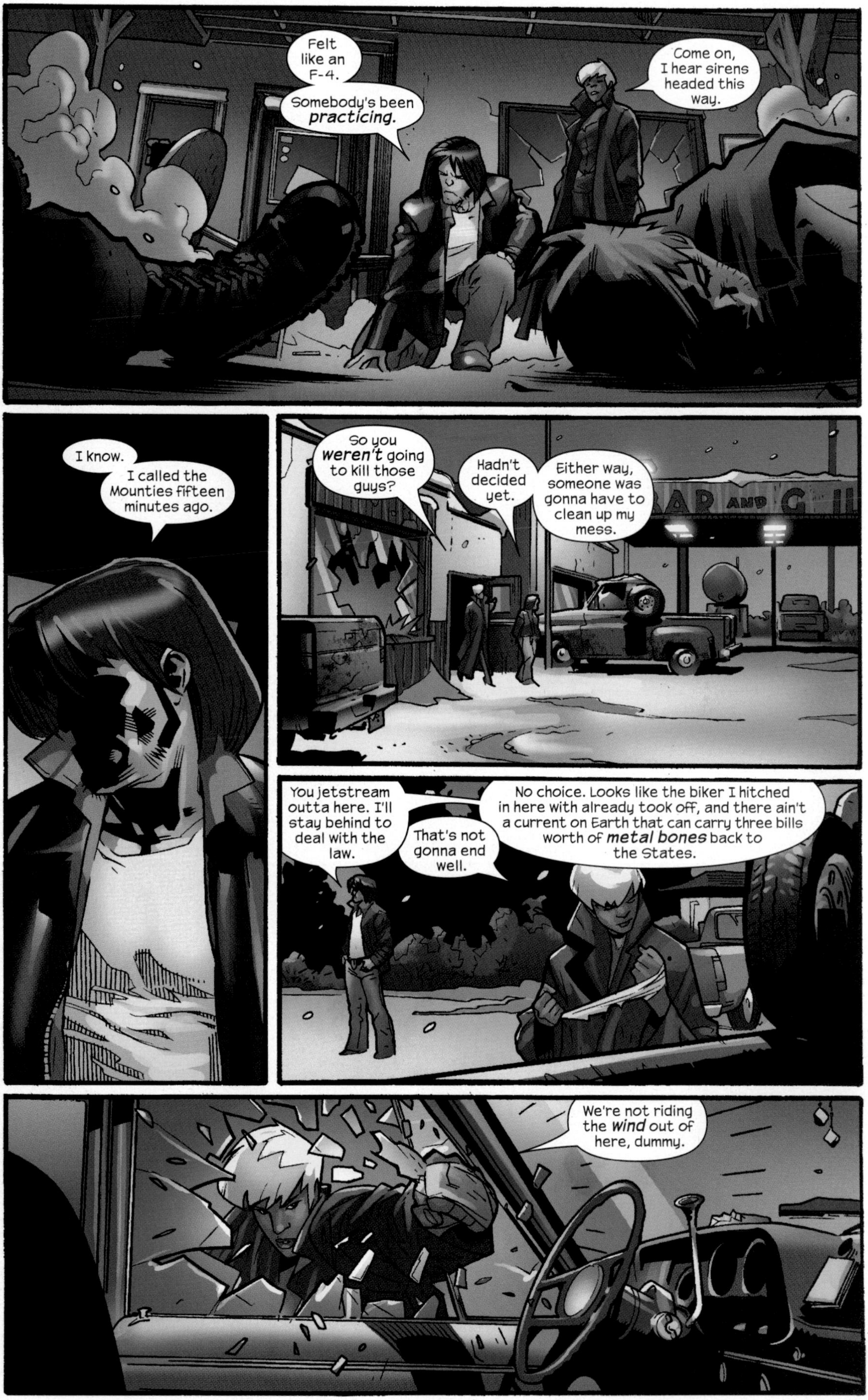

Felt like an F-4.
Somebody's been *practicing.*
Come on, I hear sirens headed this way.
I know.
I called the Mounties fifteen minutes ago.
So you *weren't* going to kill those guys?
Hadn't decided yet.
Either way, someone was gonna have to clean up my mess.
You jetstream outta here. I'll stay behind to deal with the law.
That's not gonna end well.
No choice. Looks like the biker I hitched in here with already took off, and there ain't a current on Earth that can carry three bills worth of *metal bones* back to the States.
We're not riding the *wind* out of here, dummy.

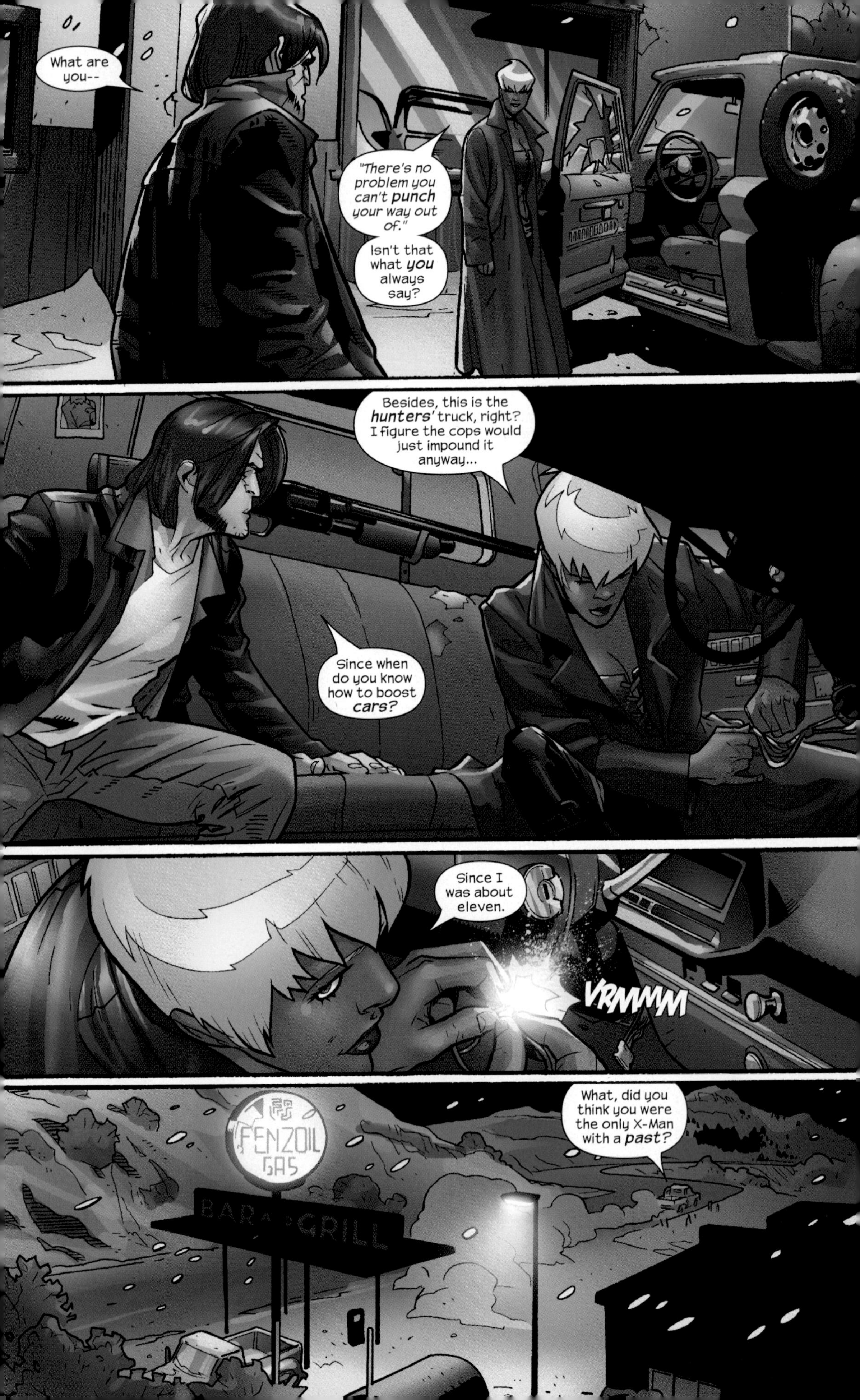
What are you--
"There's no problem you can't **punch** your way out of."
Isn't that what ***you*** always say?
Besides, this is the ***hunters'*** truck, right? I figure the cops would just impound it anyway...
Since when do you know how to boost ***cars?***
Since I was about eleven.
VRMMM
FENZOIL GAS
BAR GRILL
What, did you think you were the only X-Man with a ***past?***

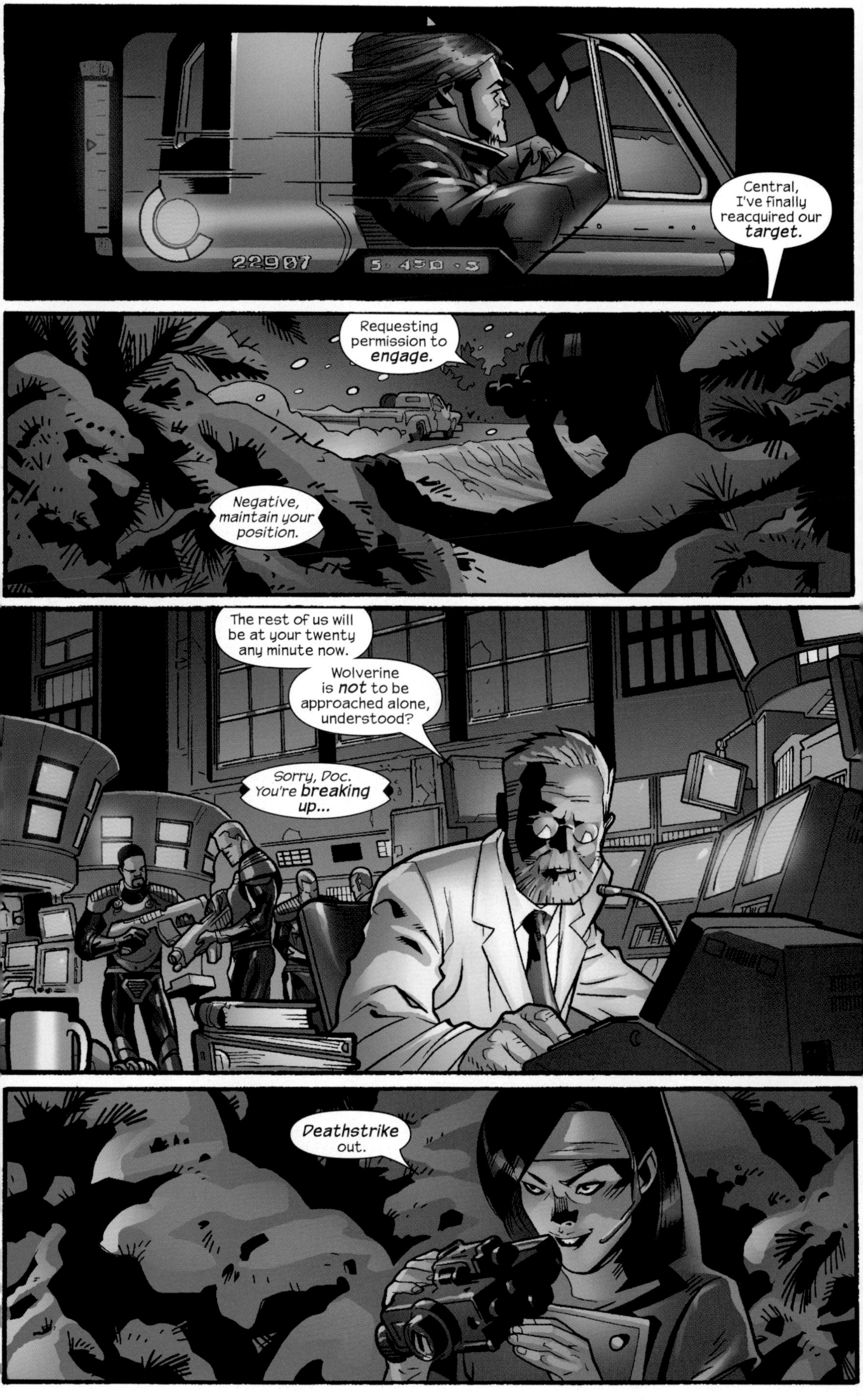

Central, I've finally reacquired our *target.*
Requesting permission to *engage.*
Negative, maintain your position.
The rest of us will be at your twenty any minute now.
Wolverine is *not* to be approached alone, understood?
Sorry, Doc. You're **breaking up...**
Deathstrike out.

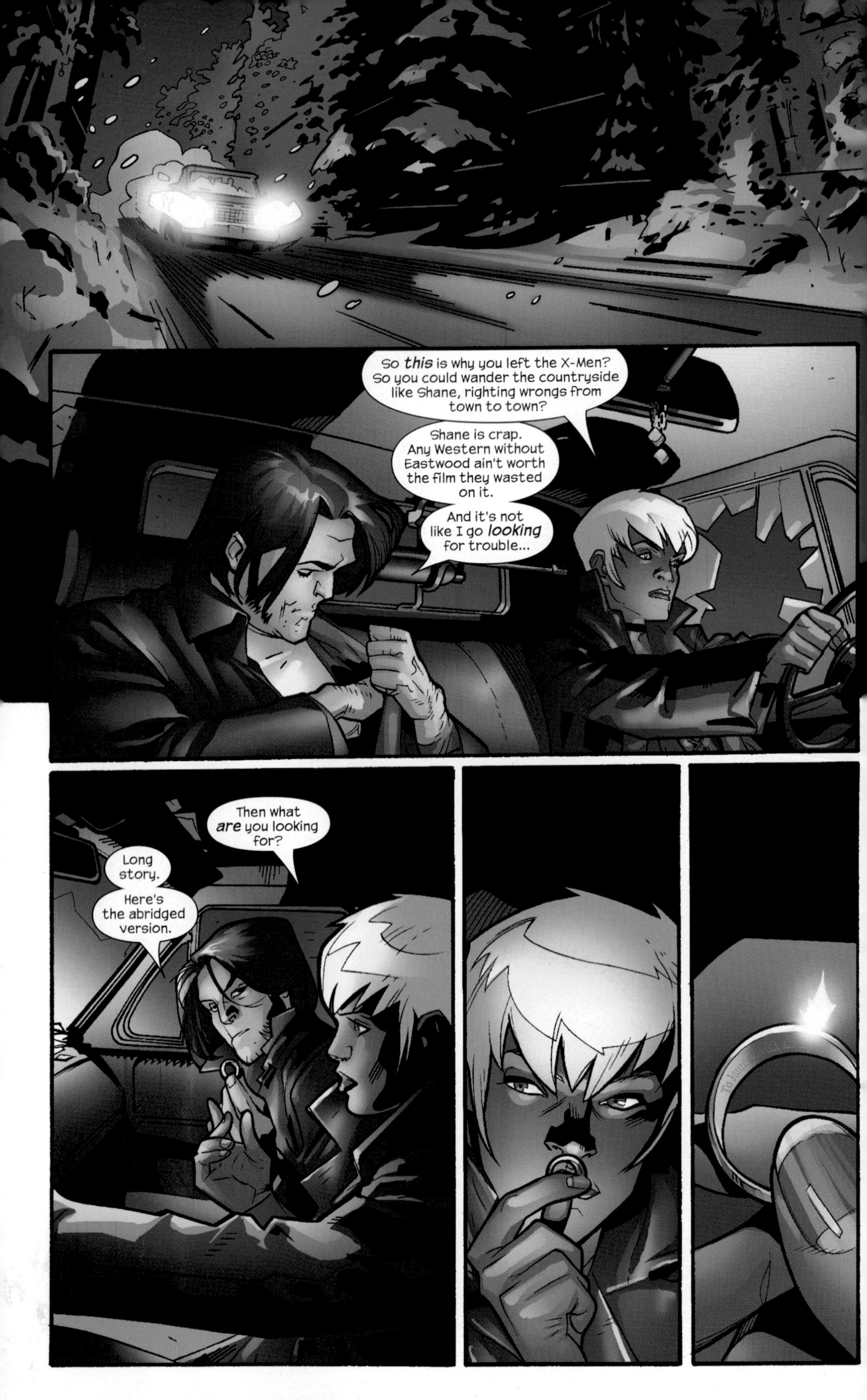
So this is why you left the X-Men? So you could wander the countryside like Shane, righting wrongs from town to town?
Shane is crap. Any Western without Eastwood ain't worth the film they wasted on it.
And it's not like I go looking for trouble...
Then what are you looking for?
Long story.
Here's the abridged version.

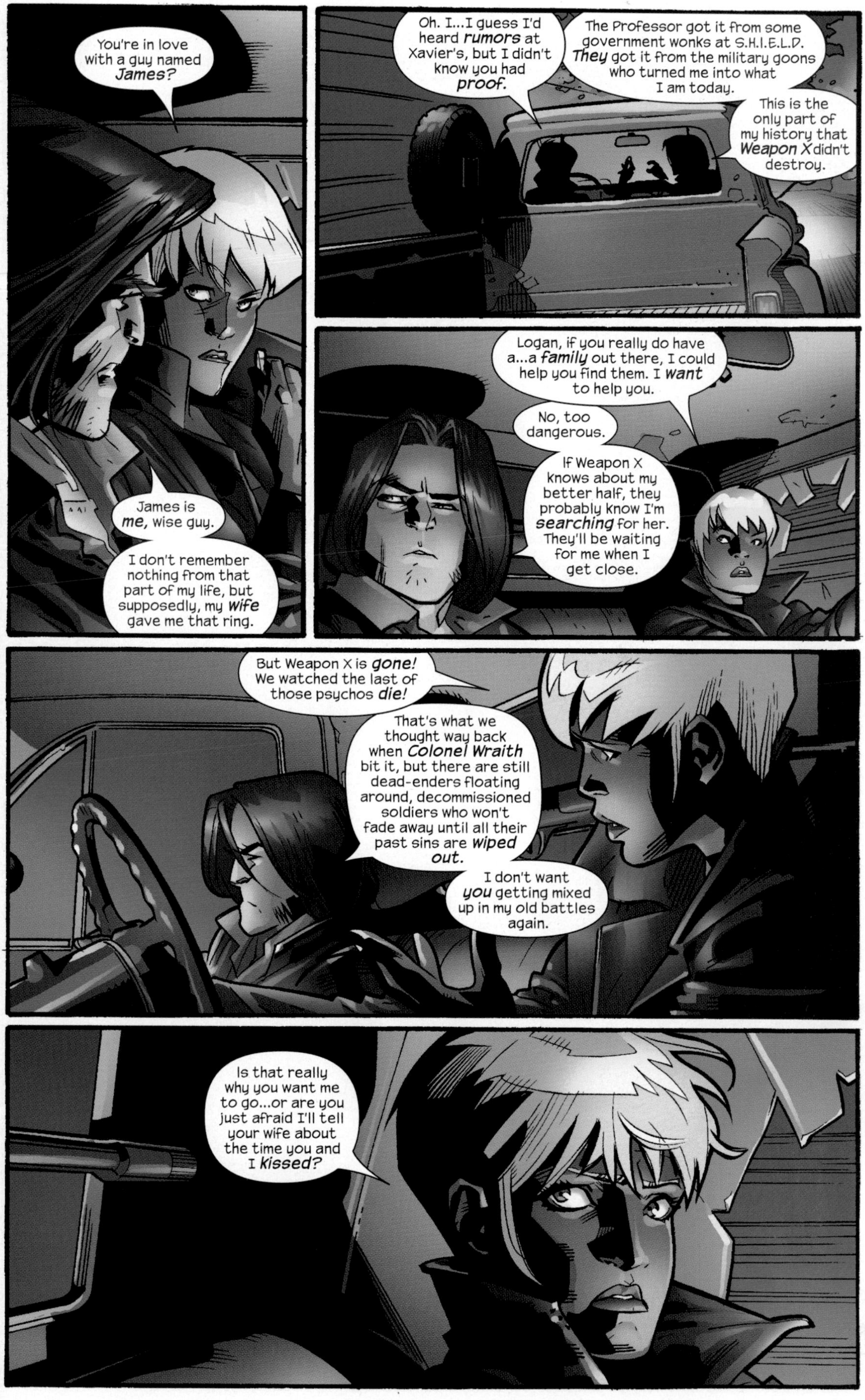
You're in love with a guy named James?
Oh. I...I guess I'd heard rumors at Xavier's, but I didn't know you had proof.
The Professor got it from some government wonks at S.H.I.E.L.D. They got it from the military goons who turned me into what I am today.
This is the only part of my history that Weapon X didn't destroy.
James is me, wise guy.
I don't remember nothing from that part of my life, but supposedly, my wife gave me that ring.
Logan, if you really do have a...a family out there, I could help you find them. I want to help you.
No, too dangerous.
If Weapon X knows about my better half, they probably know I'm searching for her. They'll be waiting for me when I get close.
But Weapon X is gone! We watched the last of those psychos die!
That's what we thought way back when Colonel Wraith bit it, but there are still dead-enders floating around, decommissioned soldiers who won't fade away until all their past sins are wiped out.
I don't want you getting mixed up in my old battles again.
Is that really why you want me to go...or are you just afraid I'll tell your wife about the time you and I kissed?

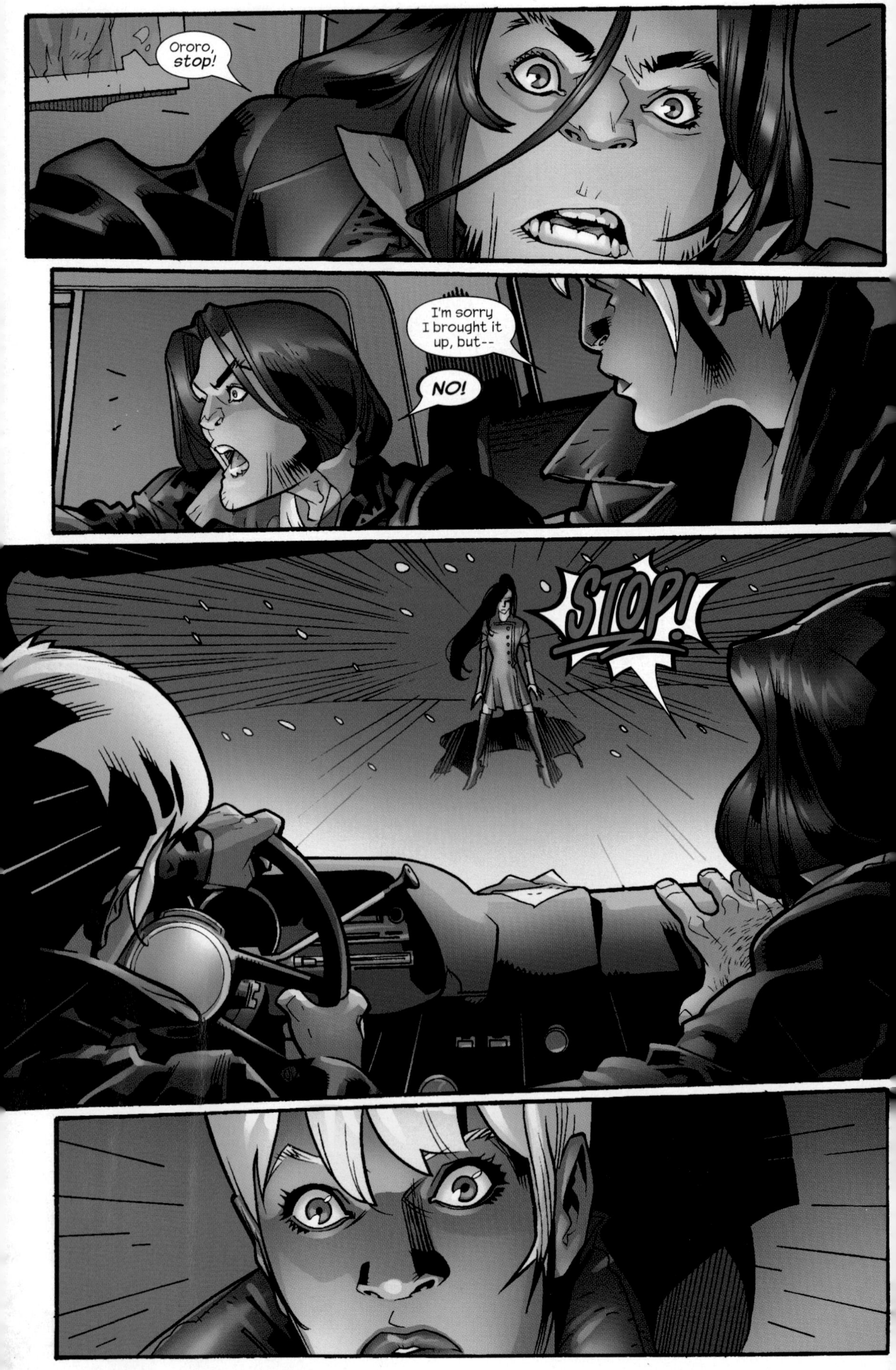
Ororo, stop!
I'm sorry I brought it up, but--
NO!
STOP!

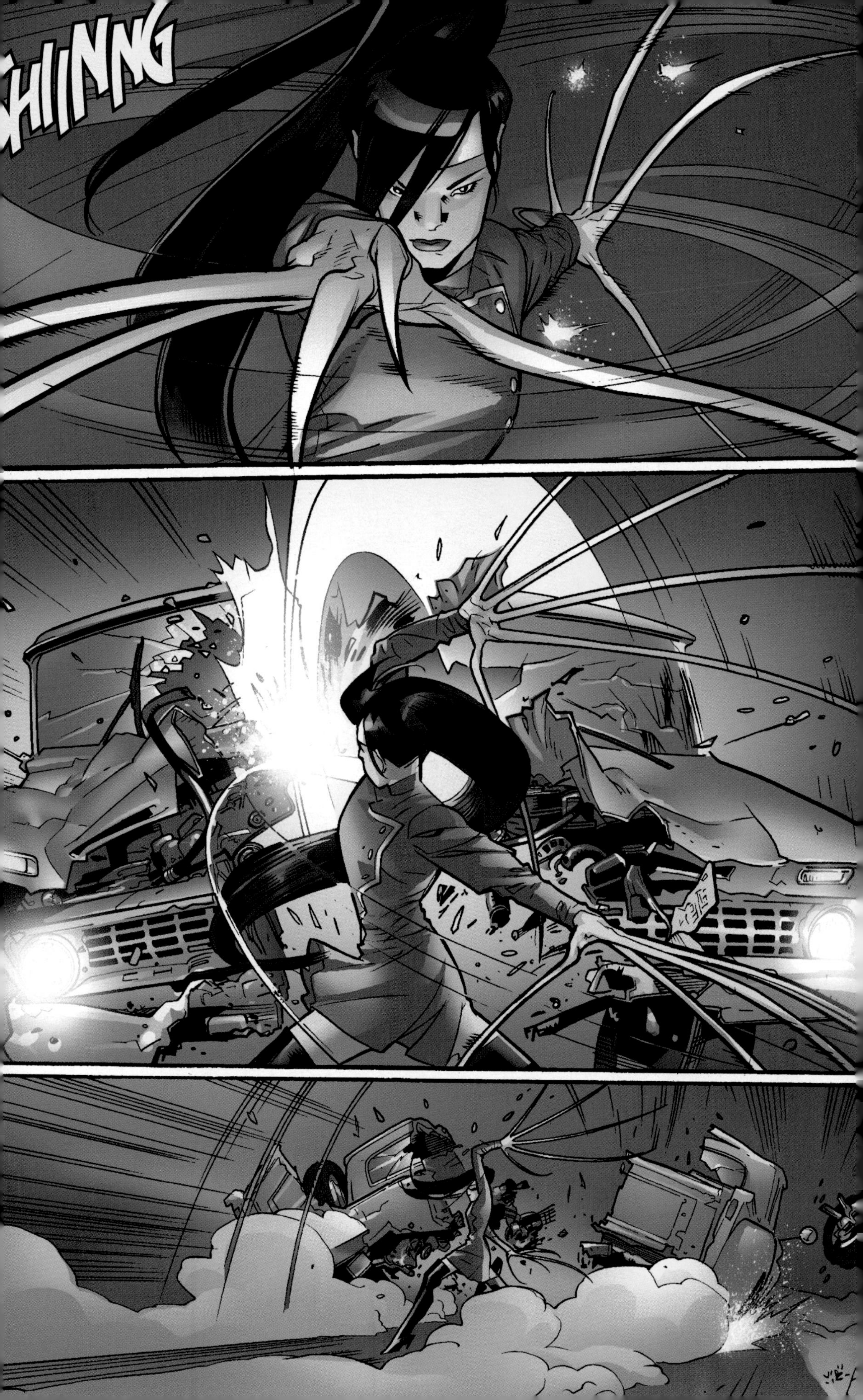
HIINNG

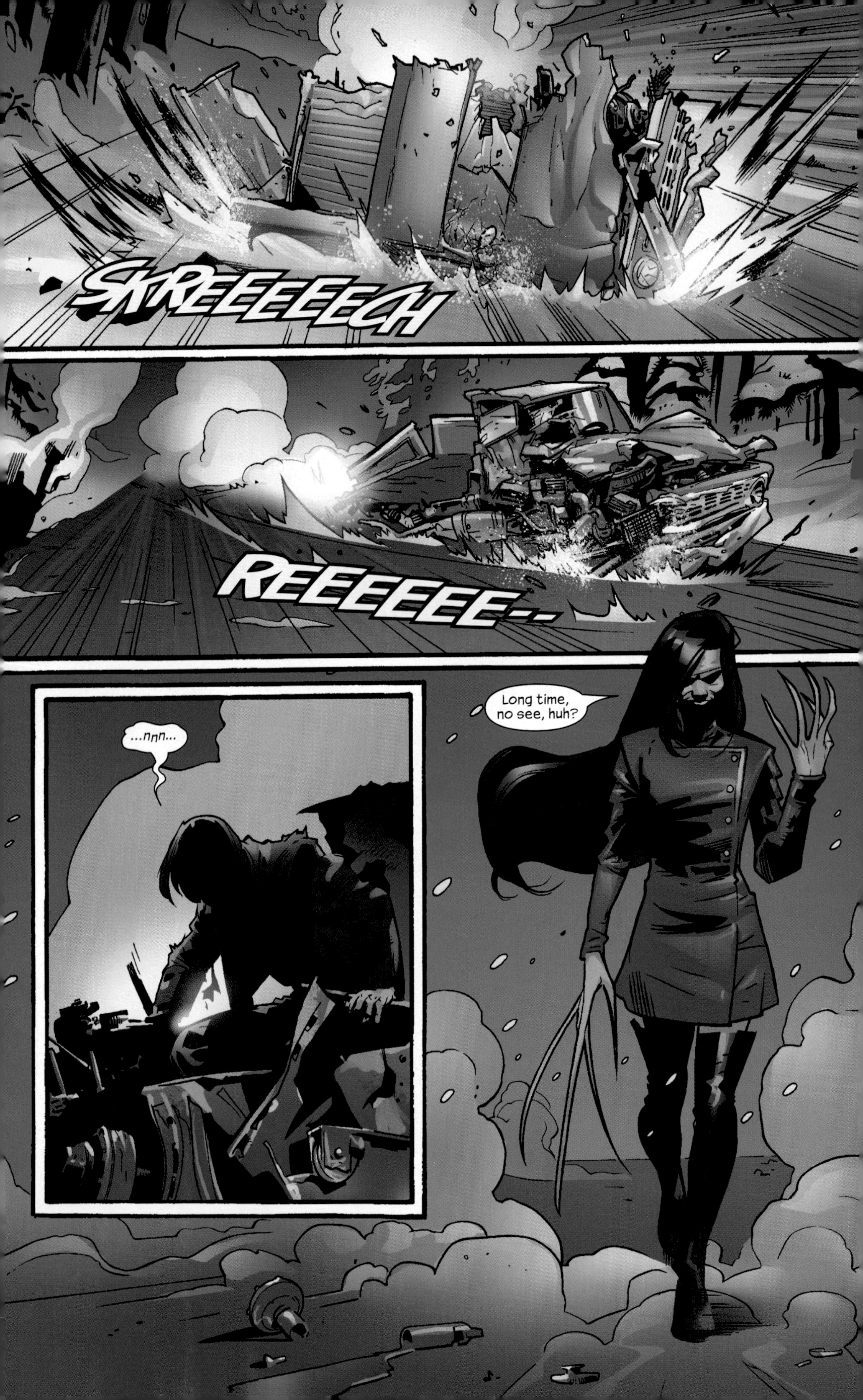
SKREEEEEECH
REEEEEEE...
Long time, no see, huh?
...nnn...

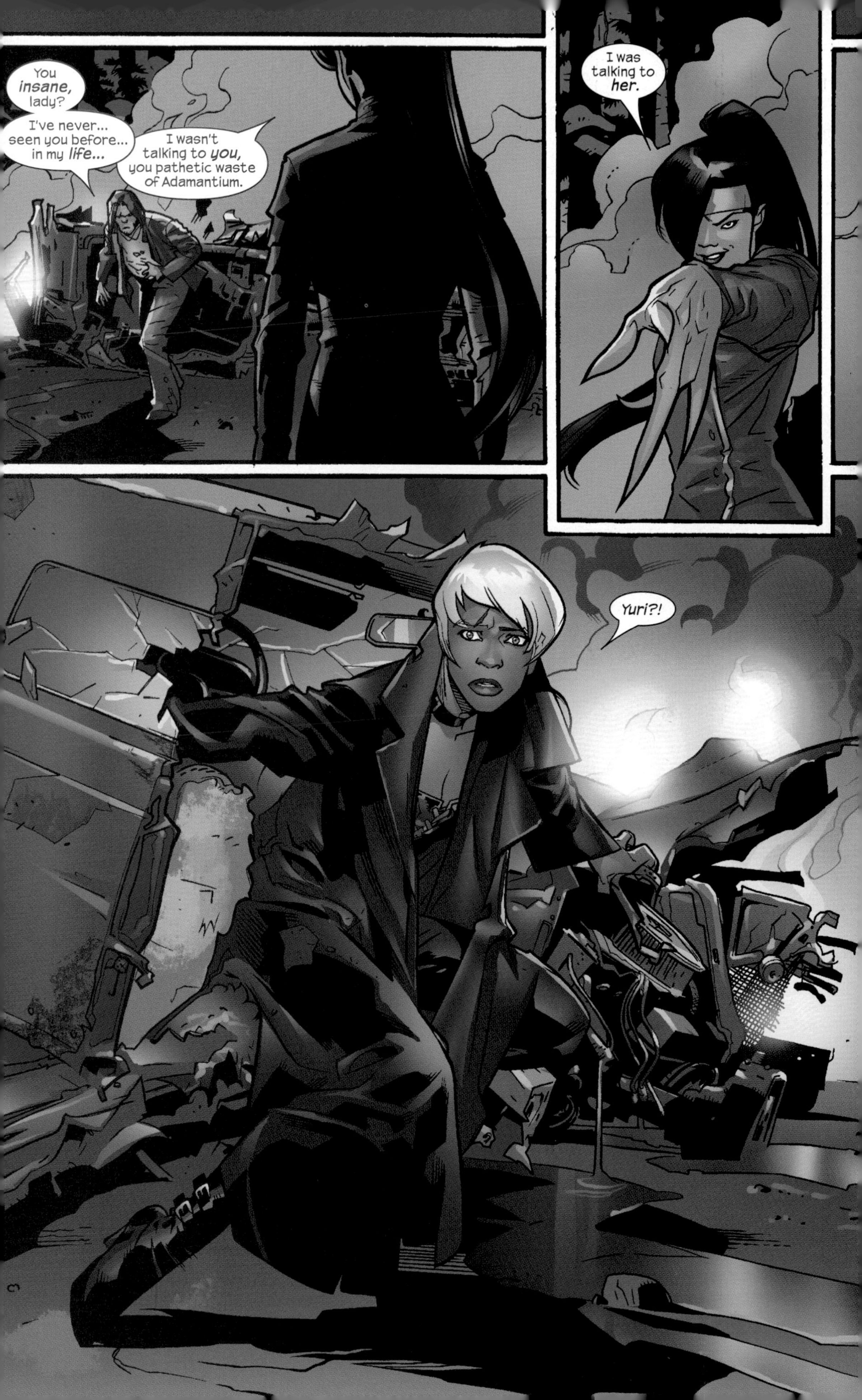
You *insane,* lady?
I've never... seen you before... in my *life...*
I wasn't talking to *you,* you pathetic waste of Adamantium.
I was talking to *her.*
Yuri?!

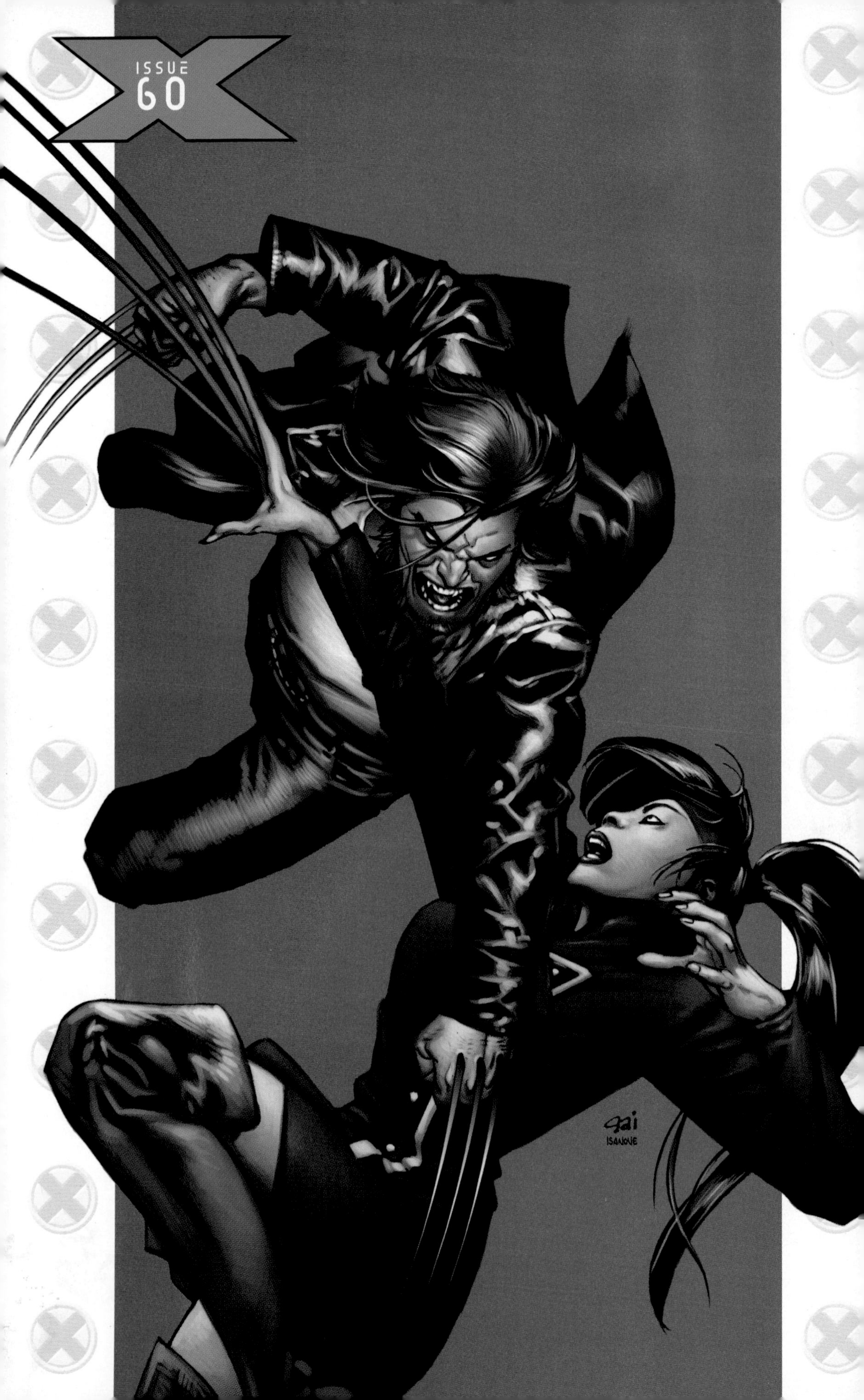
ISSUE
60

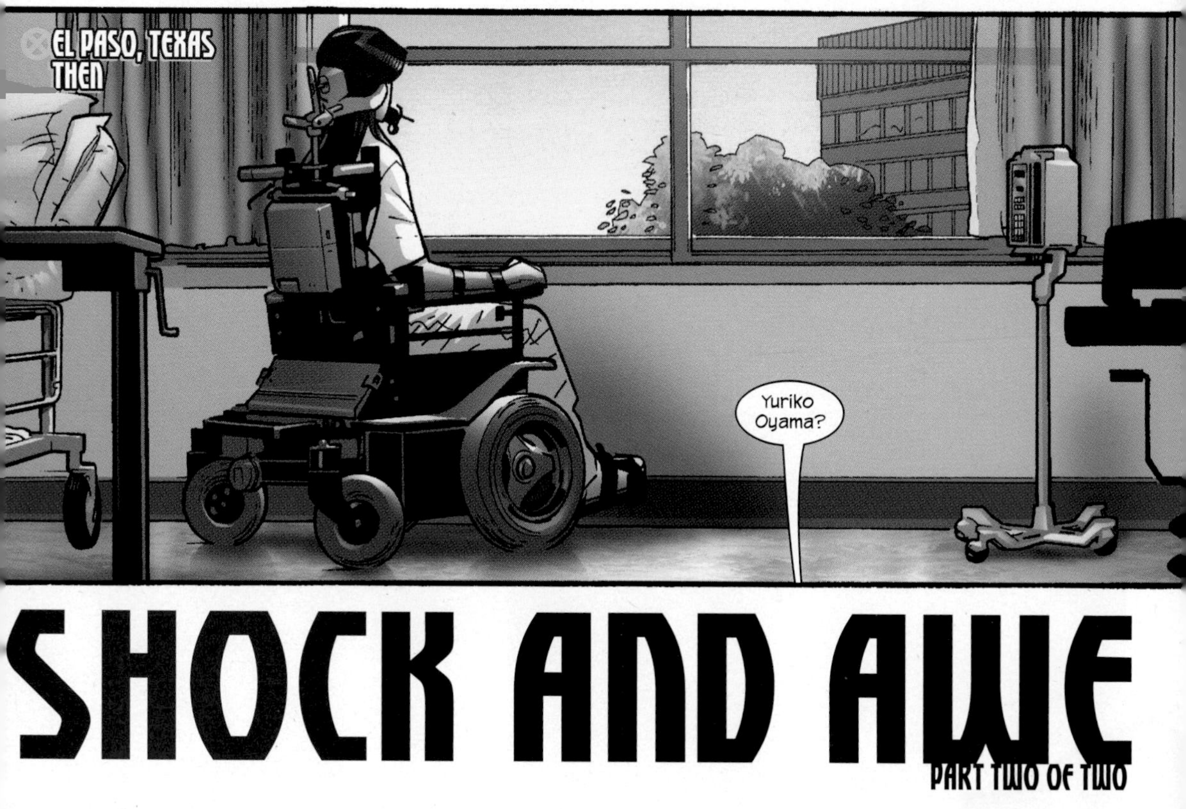
EL PASO, TEXAS
THEN
Yuriko Oyama?

SHOCK AND AWE

PART TWO OF TWO

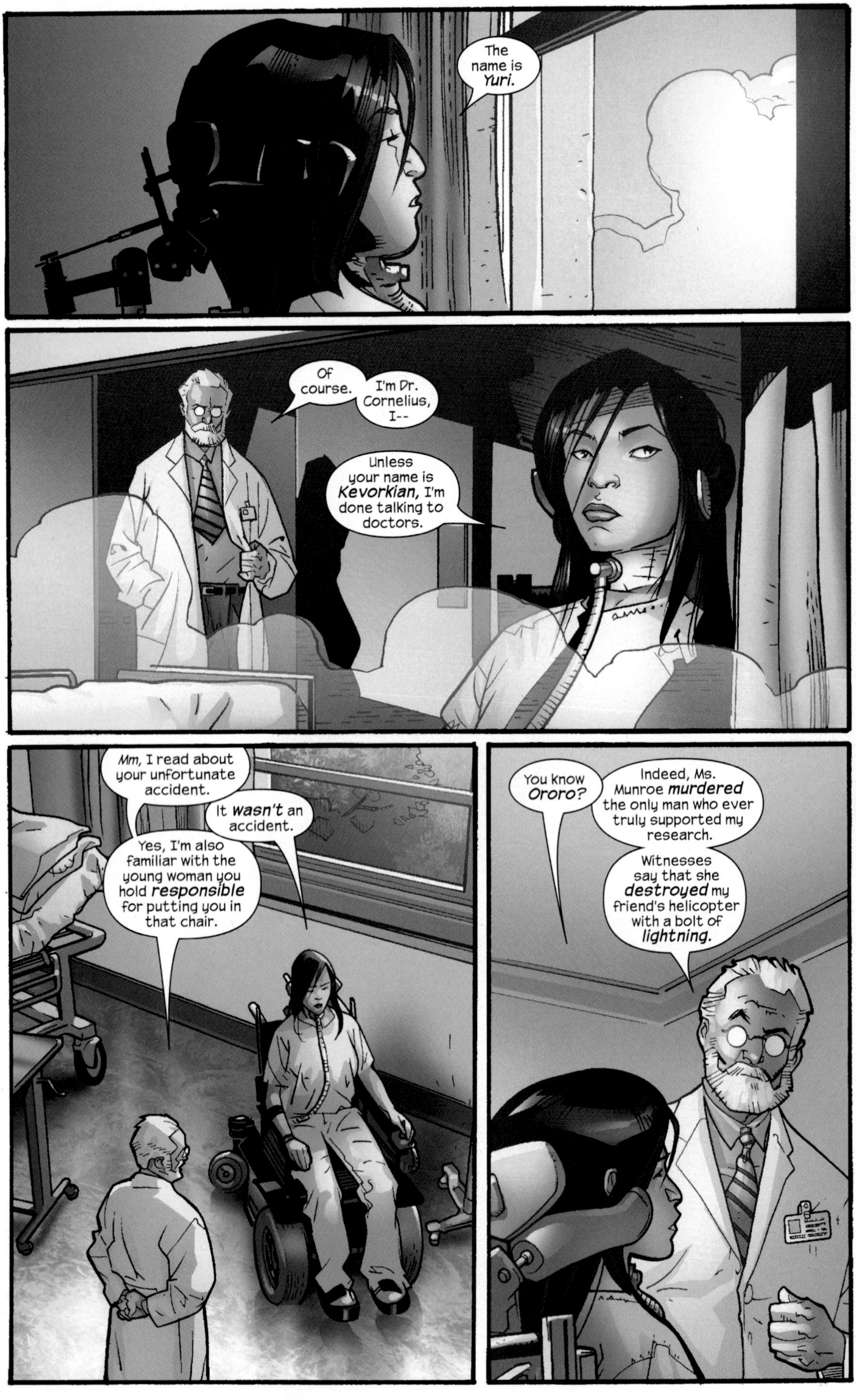
The name is *Yuri.*
Of course.
I'm Dr. Cornelius, I--
Unless your name is **Kevorkian,** I'm done talking to doctors.
Mm, I read about your unfortunate accident.
It ***wasn't*** an accident.
Yes, I'm also familiar with the young woman you hold ***responsible*** for putting you in that chair.
You know *Ororo?*
Indeed, Ms. Munroe ***murdered*** the only man who ever truly supported my research.
Witnesses say that she ***destroyed*** my friend's helicopter with a bolt of ***lightning.***

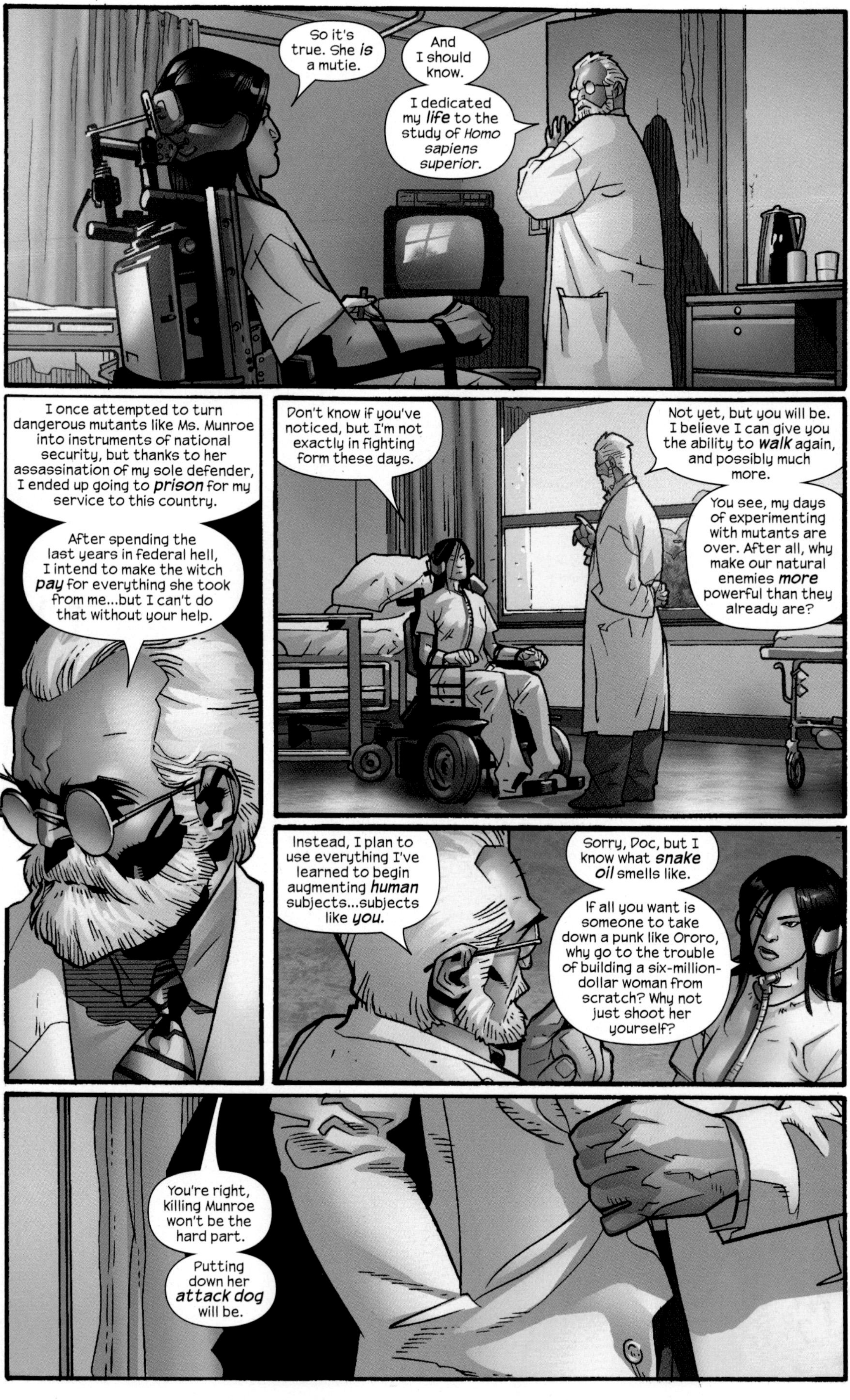
So it's true. She *is* a mutie.
And I should know.
I dedicated my *life* to the study of *Homo sapiens superior.*
I once attempted to turn dangerous mutants like Ms. Munroe into instruments of national security, but thanks to her assassination of my sole defender, I ended up going to *prison* for my service to this country.
After spending the last years in federal hell, I intend to make the witch *pay* for everything she took from me...but I can't do that without your help.
Don't know if you've noticed, but I'm not exactly in fighting form these days.
Not yet, but you will be. I believe I can give you the ability to *walk* again, and possibly much more.
You see, my days of experimenting with mutants are over. After all, why make our natural enemies *more* powerful than they already are?
Instead, I plan to use everything I've learned to begin augmenting *human* subjects...subjects like *you.*
Sorry, Doc, but I know what *snake oil* smells like.
If all you want is someone to take down a punk like Ororo, why go to the trouble of building a six-million-dollar woman from scratch? Why not just shoot her yourself?
You're right, killing Munroe won't be the hard part.
Putting down her *attack dog* will be.

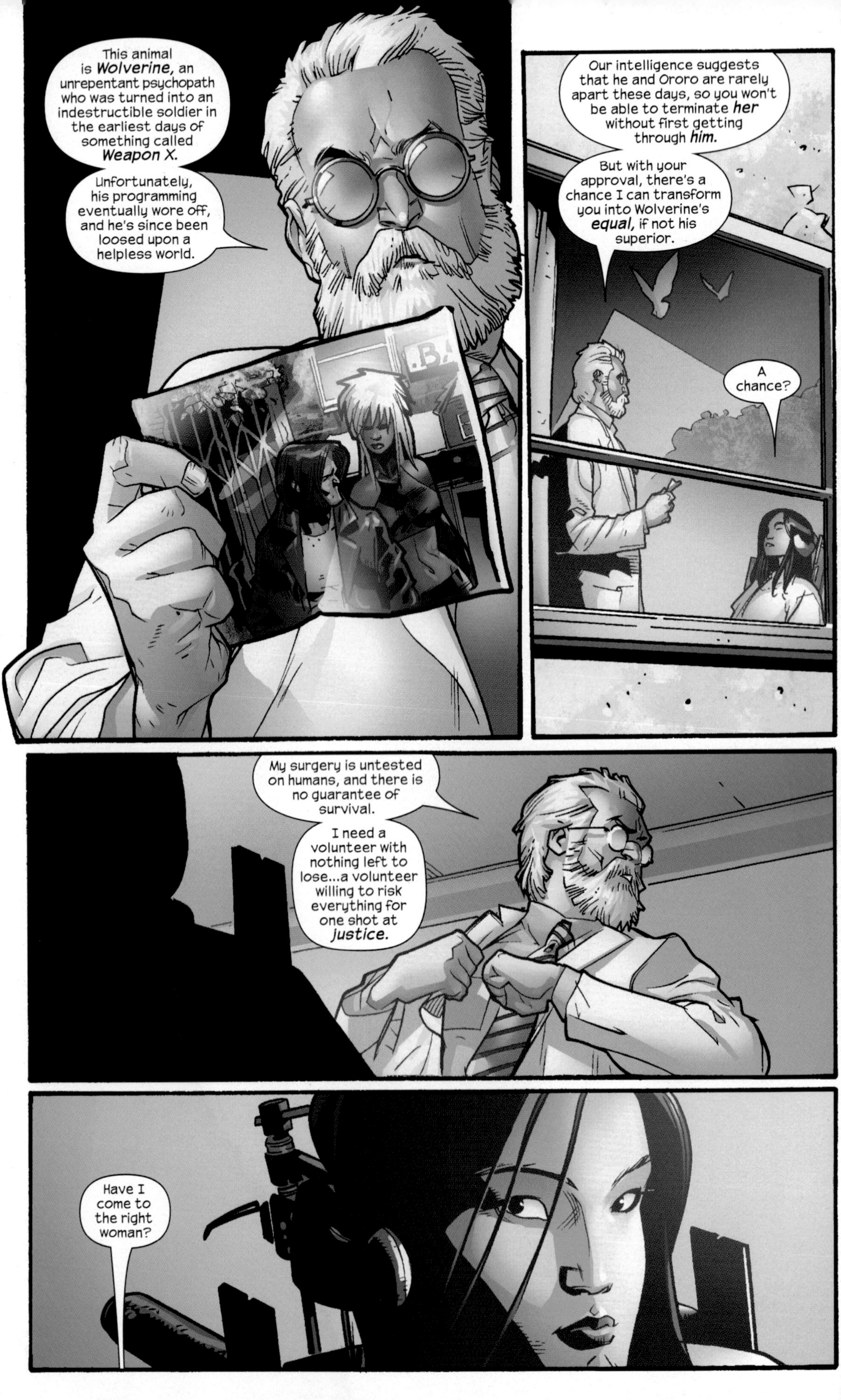
This animal is Wolverine, an unrepentant psychopath who was turned into an indestructible soldier in the earliest days of something called Weapon X.
Unfortunately, his programming eventually wore off, and he's since been loosed upon a helpless world.
Our intelligence suggests that he and Ororo are rarely apart these days, so you won't be able to terminate her without first getting through him.
But with your approval, there's a chance I can transform you into Wolverine's equal, if not his superior.
A chance?
My surgery is untested on humans, and there is no guarantee of survival.
I need a volunteer with nothing left to lose...a volunteer willing to risk everything for one shot at justice.
Have I come to the right woman?

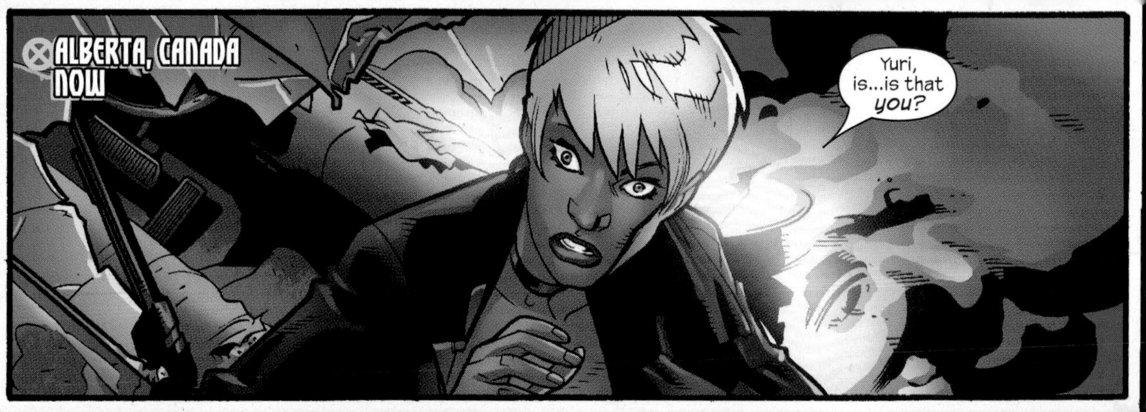
ALBERTA, CANADA
NOW
Yuri, is...is that *you?*

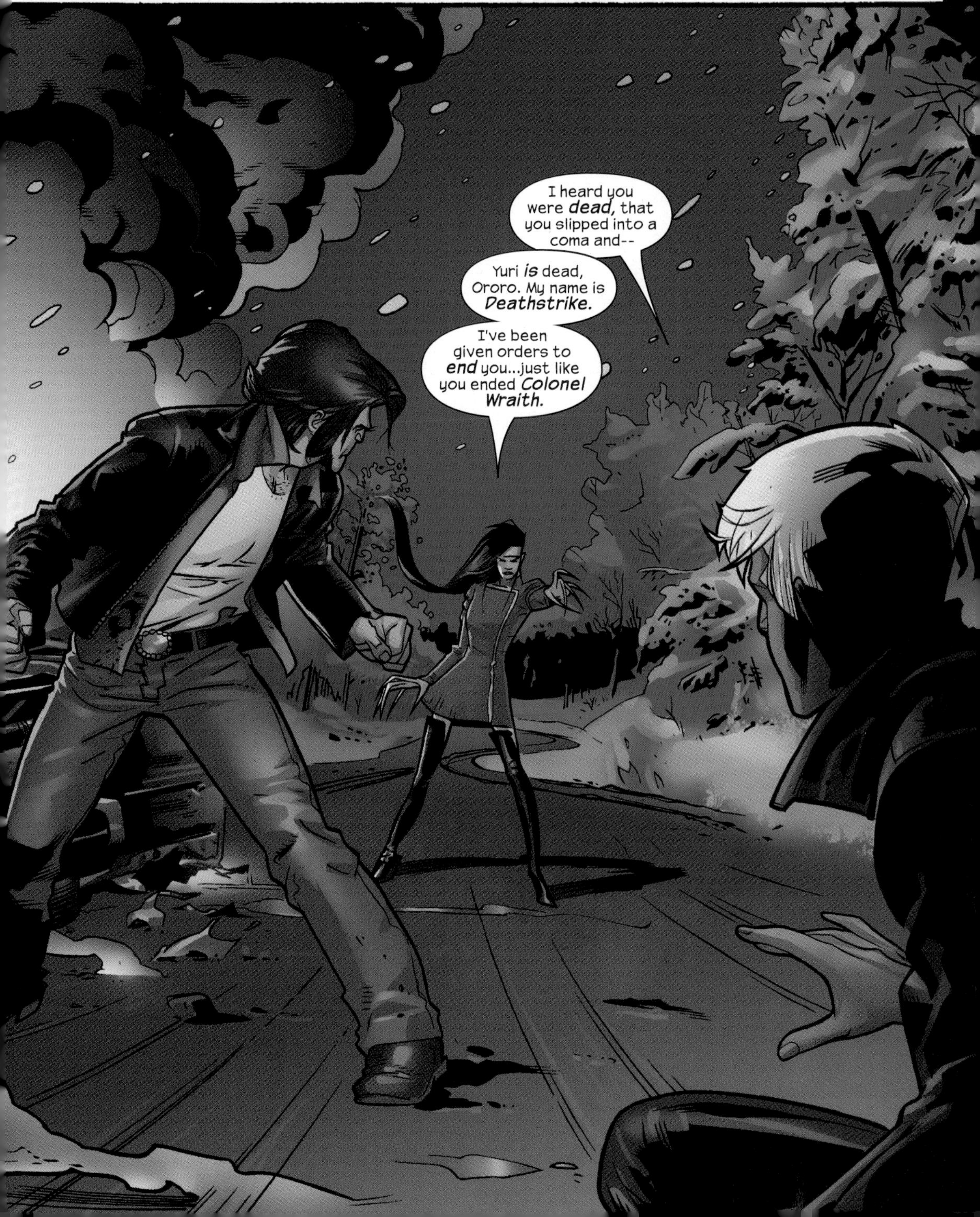
I heard you were *dead,* that you slipped into a coma and--
Yuri *is* dead, Ororo. My name is *Deathstrike.*
I've been given orders to *end* you...just like you ended *Colonel Wraith.*

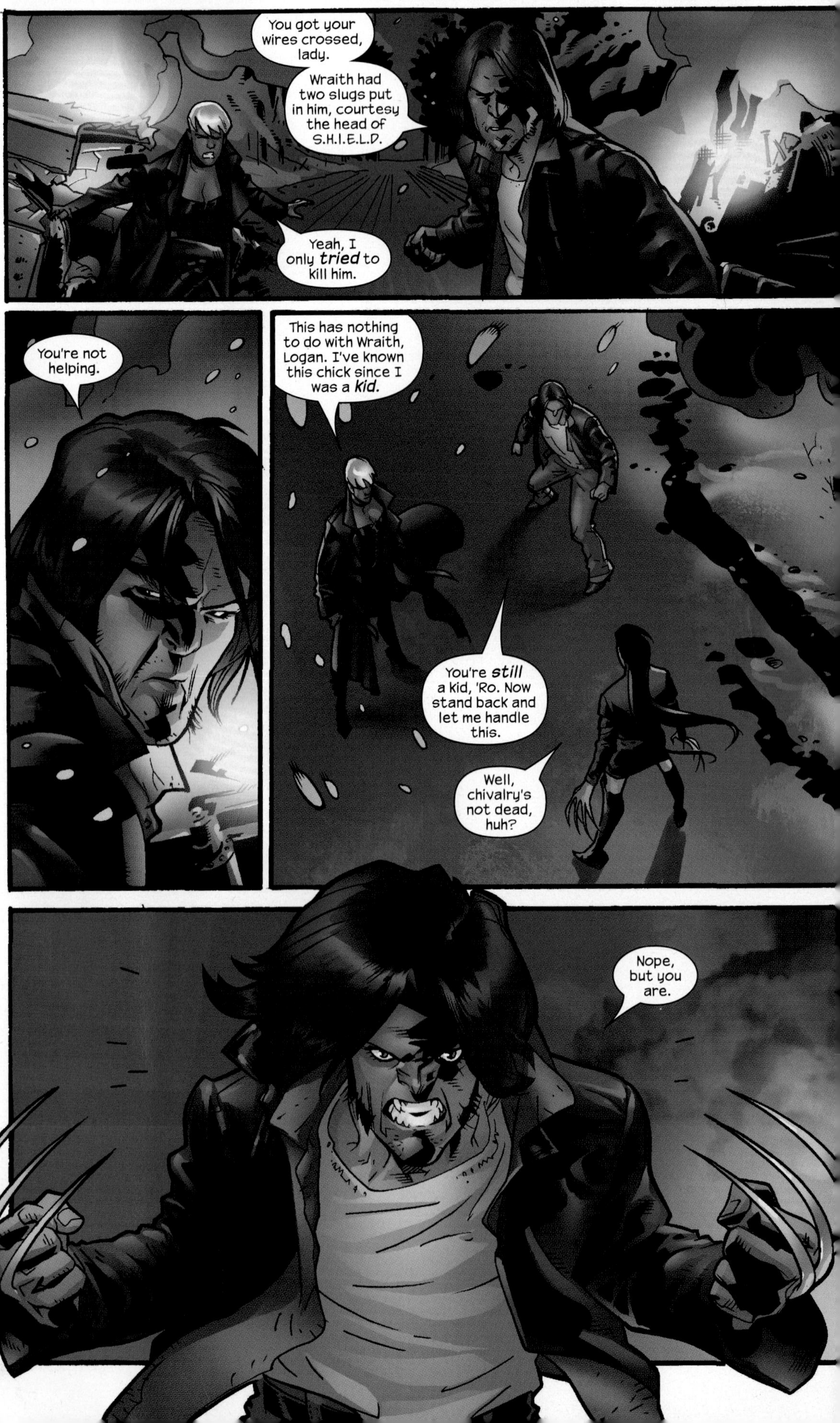
You got your wires crossed, lady.
Wraith had two slugs put in him, courtesy the head of S.H.I.E.L.D.
Yeah, I only *tried* to kill him.
You're not helping.
This has nothing to do with Wraith, Logan. I've known this chick since I was a *kid.*
You're *still* a kid, 'Ro. Now stand back and let me handle this.
Well, chivalry's not dead, huh?
Nope, but you are.

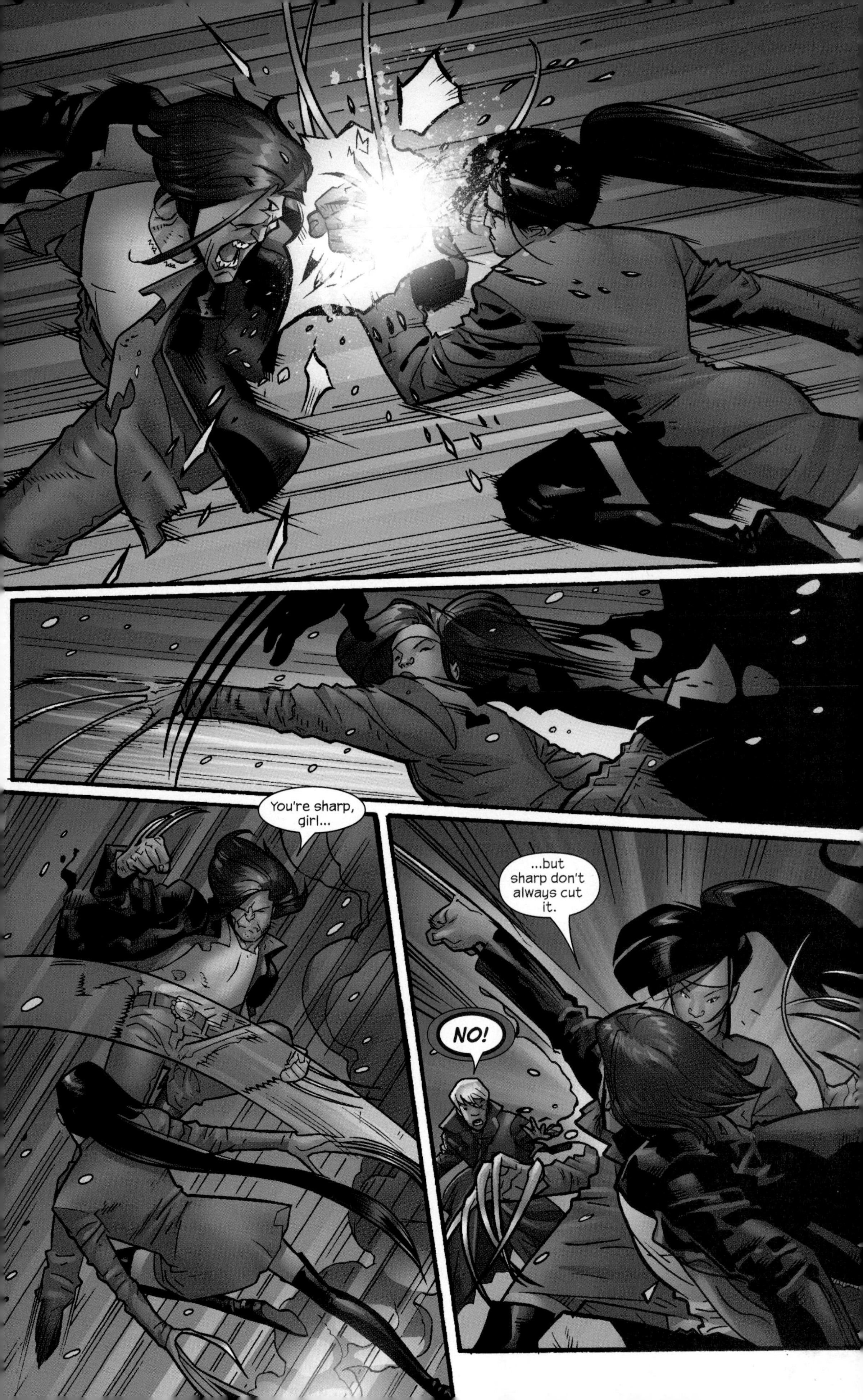
You're sharp, girl...
...but sharp don't always cut it.
NO!

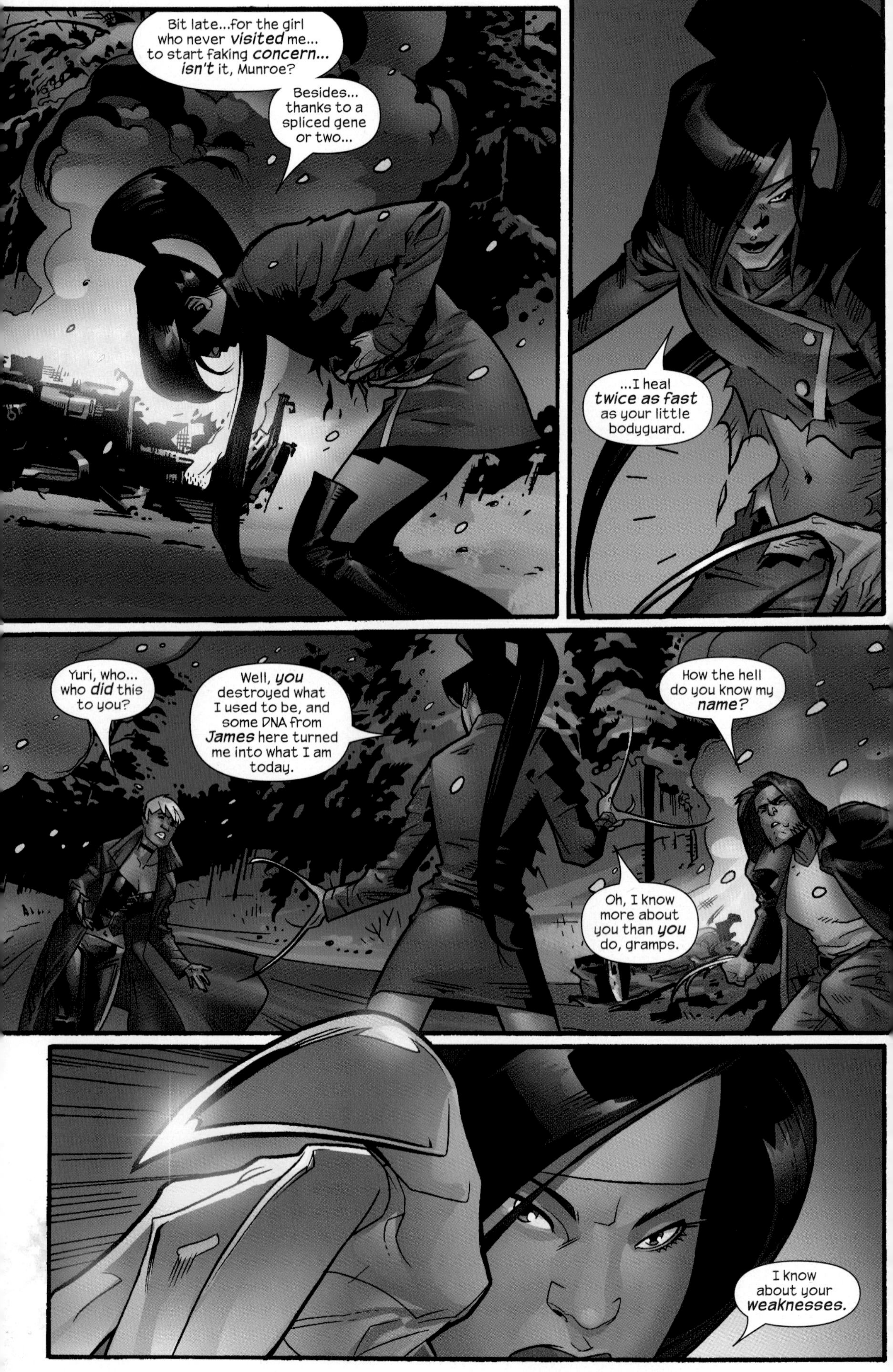
Bit late...for the girl who never visited me... to start faking concern... isn't it, Munroe?
Besides... thanks to a spliced gene or two...
...I heal twice as fast as your little bodyguard.
Yuri, who... who did this to you?
Well, you destroyed what I used to be, and some DNA from James here turned me into what I am today.
How the hell do you know my name?
Oh, I know more about you than you do, gramps.
I know about your weaknesses.

AHHN!

STOP IT!

Chill, Stormy. He's not dead... yet.

See, this guy's *xiphoid* still hadn't ossified when Adamantium was bonded to his skeleton, so now it's the only fragile bone in his body. Break it just right, and his whole nervous system *shuts down*.

You dropped out of *eighth grade*. When did you become a *biology major*?

I learned a few tricks from a guy named Cornelius, same egghead who turned your old pal Hank into a furry blue *freak*.

Oh, sorry... that freak's a *corpse* now, isn't he?

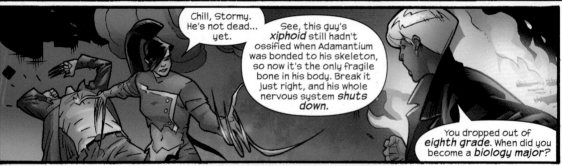

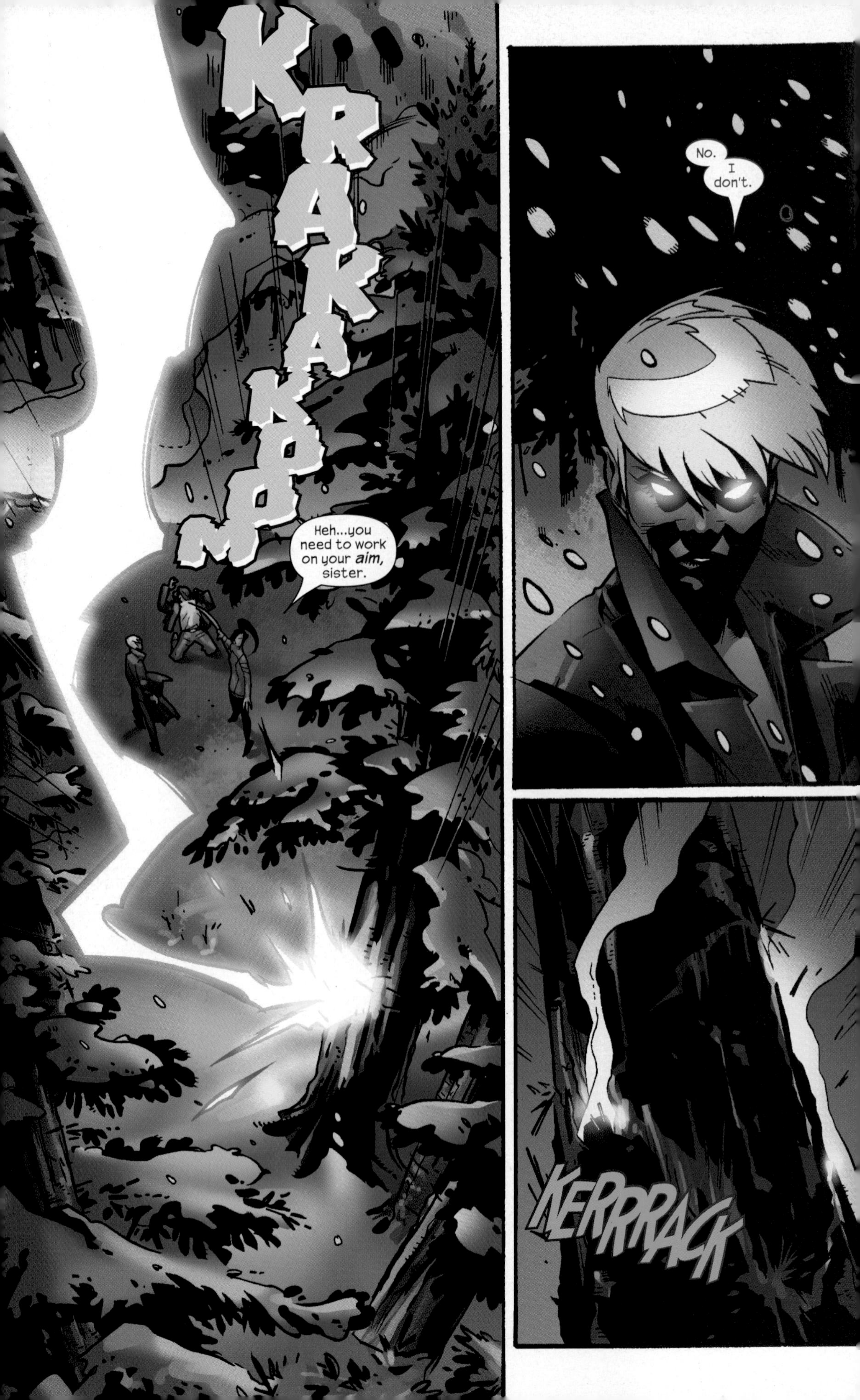
KRAKAKOOM
Heh...you need to work on your *aim,* sister.
No. I don't.
KERRRACK

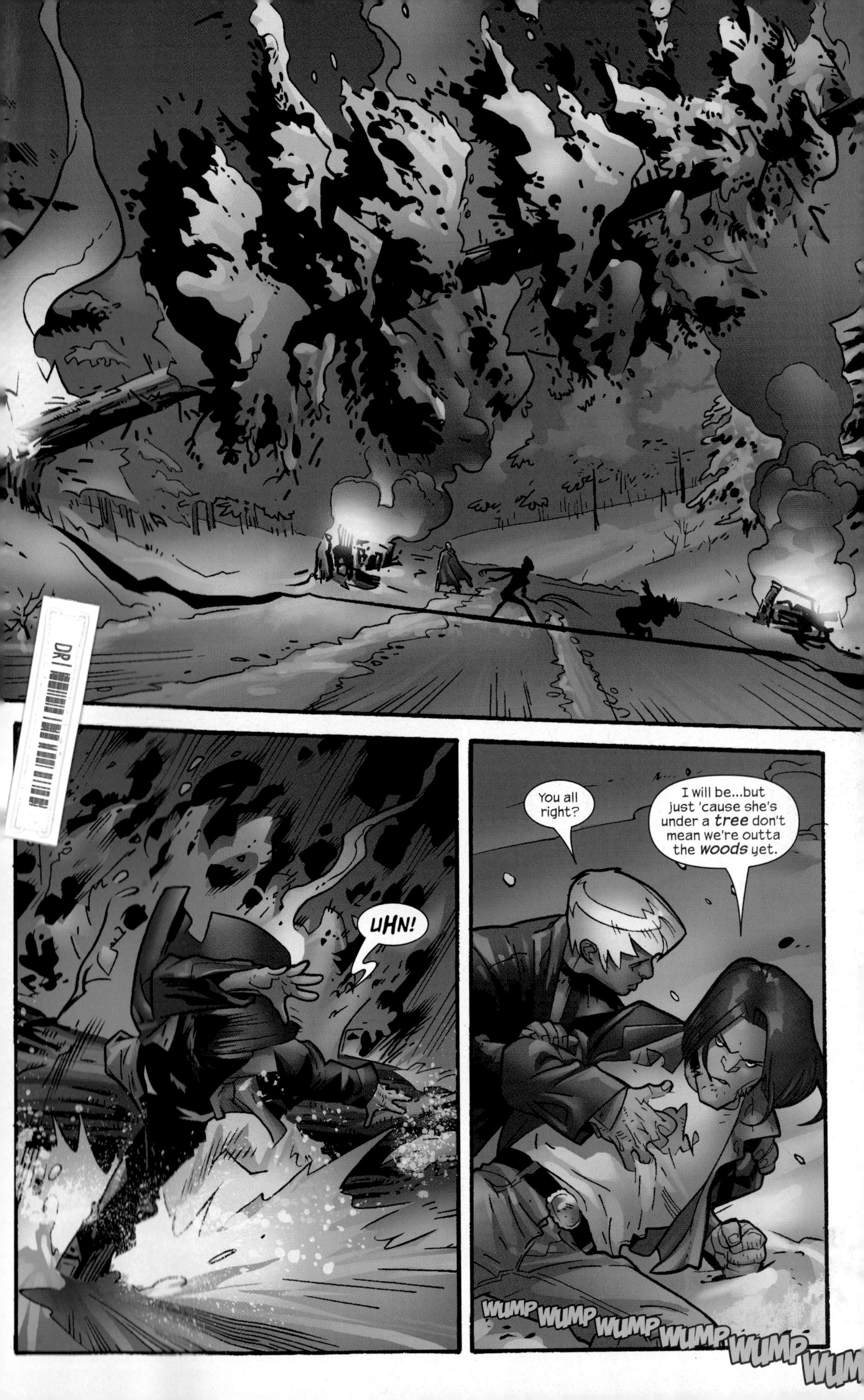
UHN!
You all right?
I will be...but just 'cause she's under a tree don't mean we're outta the woods yet.
WUMP WUMP WUMP WUMP WUMP

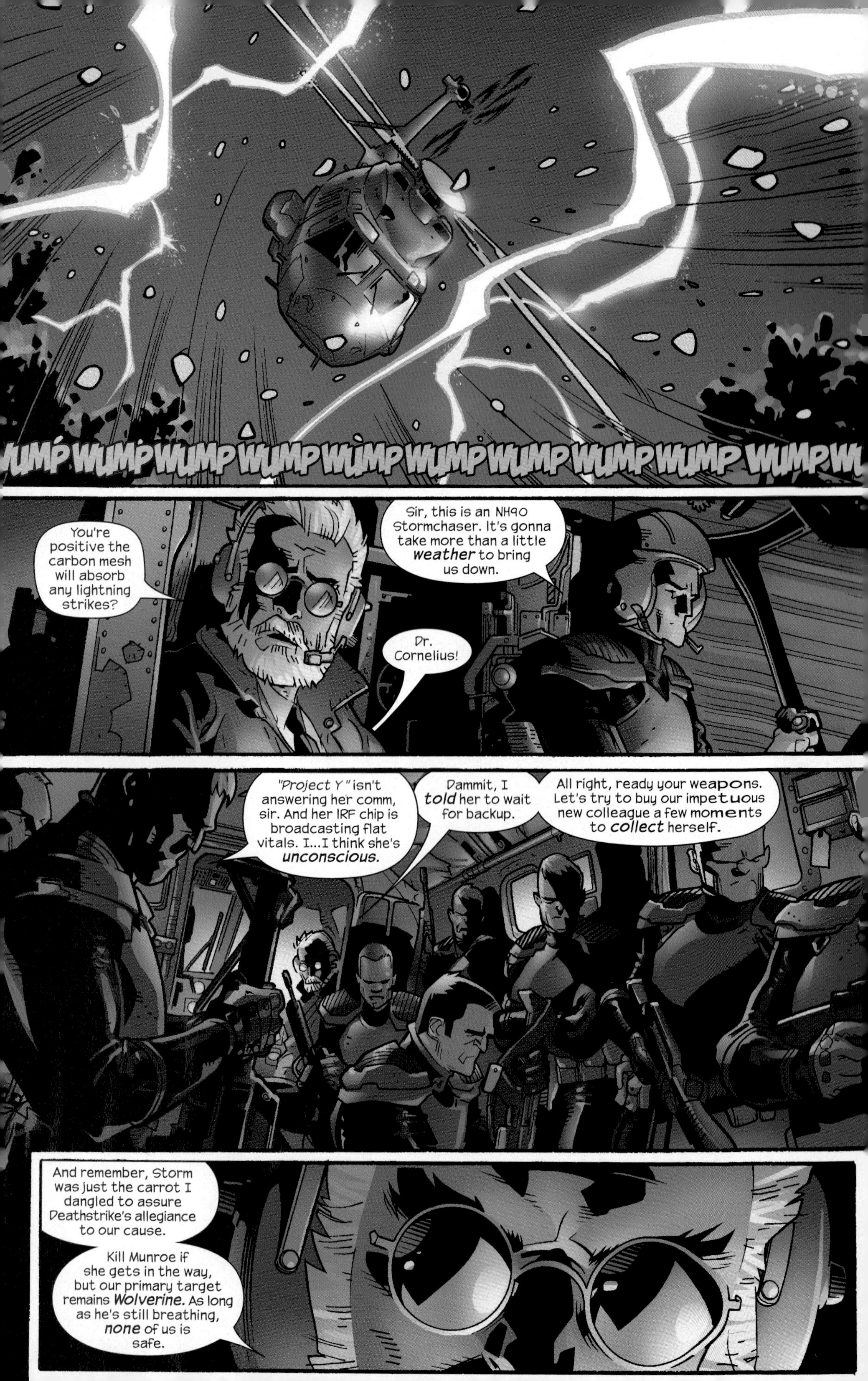
WUMP WUMP WUMP WUMP WUMP WUMP WUMP WUMP WUMP
You're positive the carbon mesh will absorb any lightning strikes?
Sir, this is an NH90 Stormchaser. It's gonna take more than a little *weather* to bring us down.
Dr. Cornelius!
"Project Y" isn't answering her comm, sir. And her IRF chip is broadcasting flat vitals. I...I think she's *unconscious.*
Dammit, I *told* her to wait for backup.
All right, ready your weapons. Let's try to buy our impetuous new colleague a few moments to *collect* herself.
And remember, Storm was just the carrot I dangled to assure Deathstrike's allegiance to our cause.
Kill Munroe if she gets in the way, but our primary target remains *Wolverine.* As long as he's still breathing, *none* of us is safe.

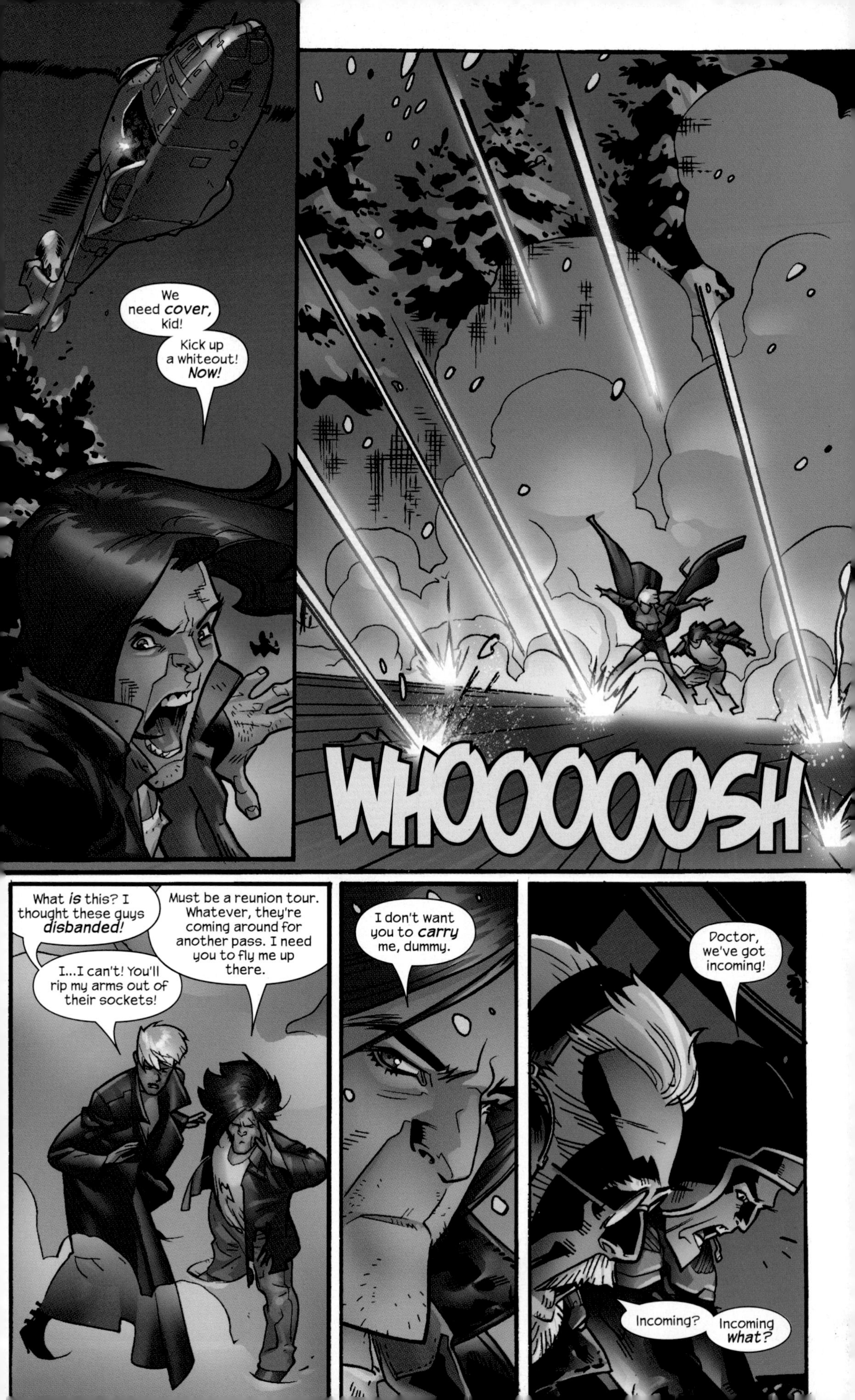
We need *cover,* kid!
Kick up a whiteout! *Now!*
WHOOOOOOSH
What *is* this? I thought these guys *disbanded!*
Must be a reunion tour. Whatever, they're coming around for another pass. I need you to fly me up there.
I...I can't! You'll rip my arms out of their sockets!
I don't want you to *carry* me, dummy.
Doctor, we've got incoming!
Incoming?
Incoming *what?*

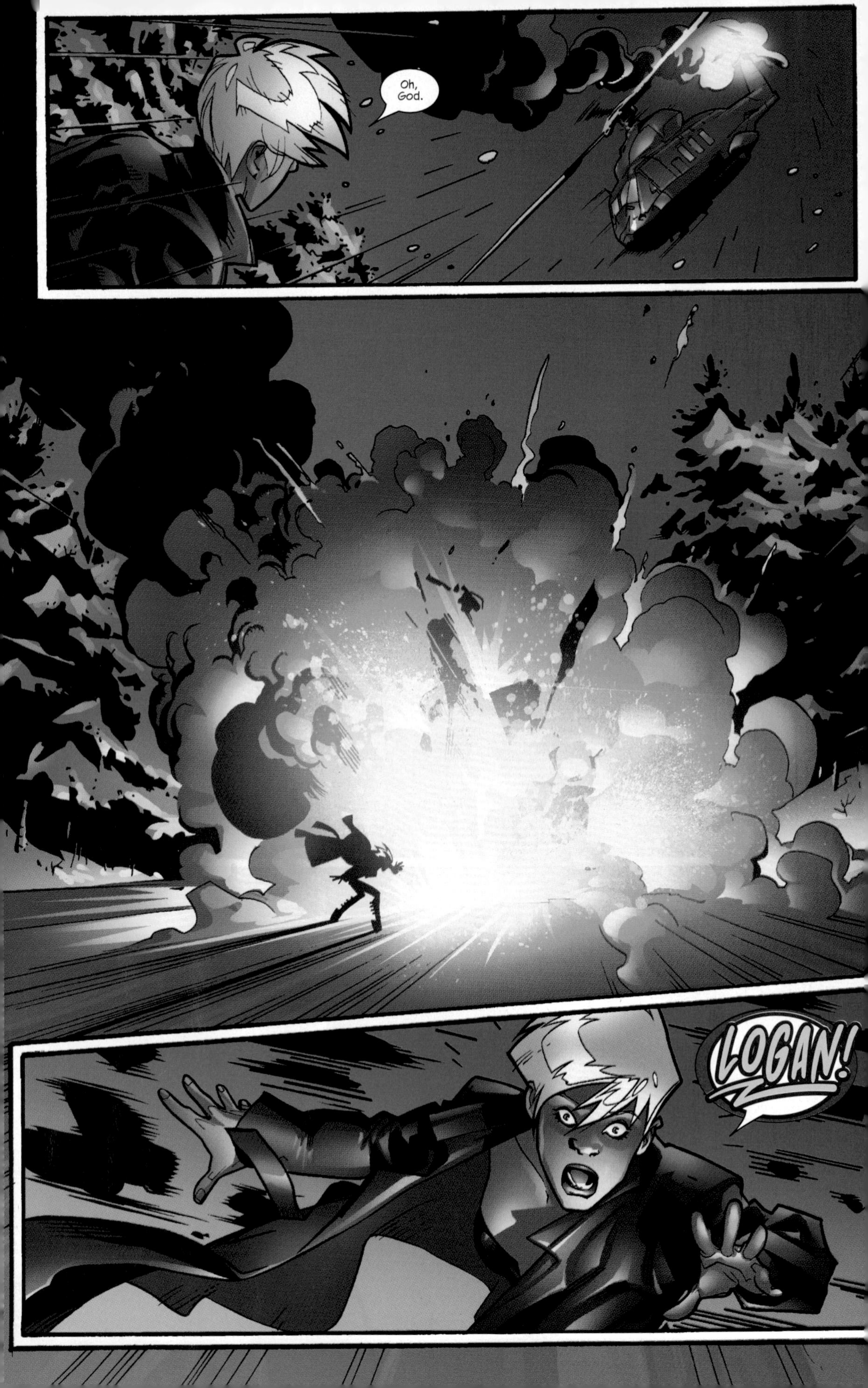
Oh, God.
LOGAN!

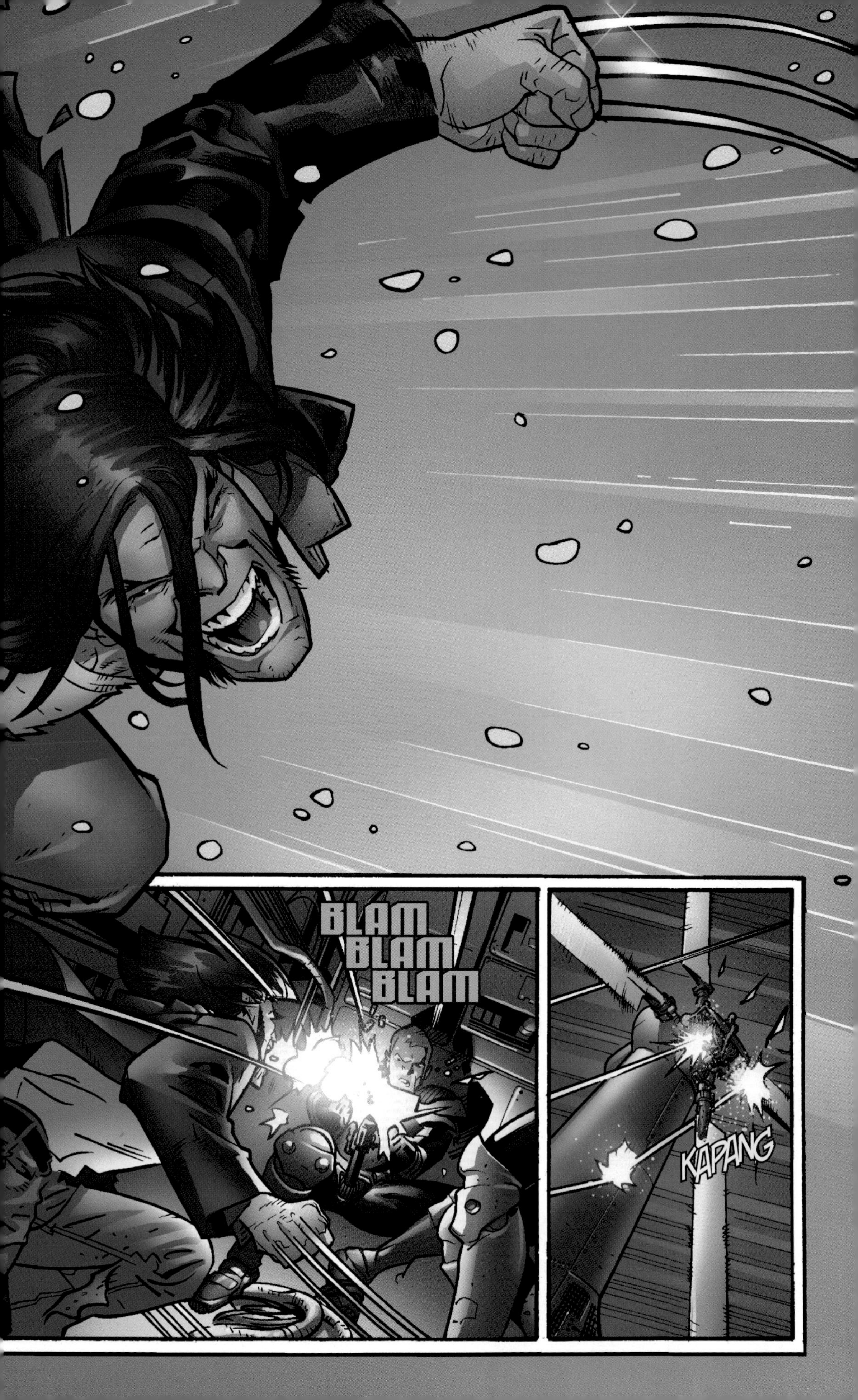
BLAM
BLAM
BLAM
KAPANG

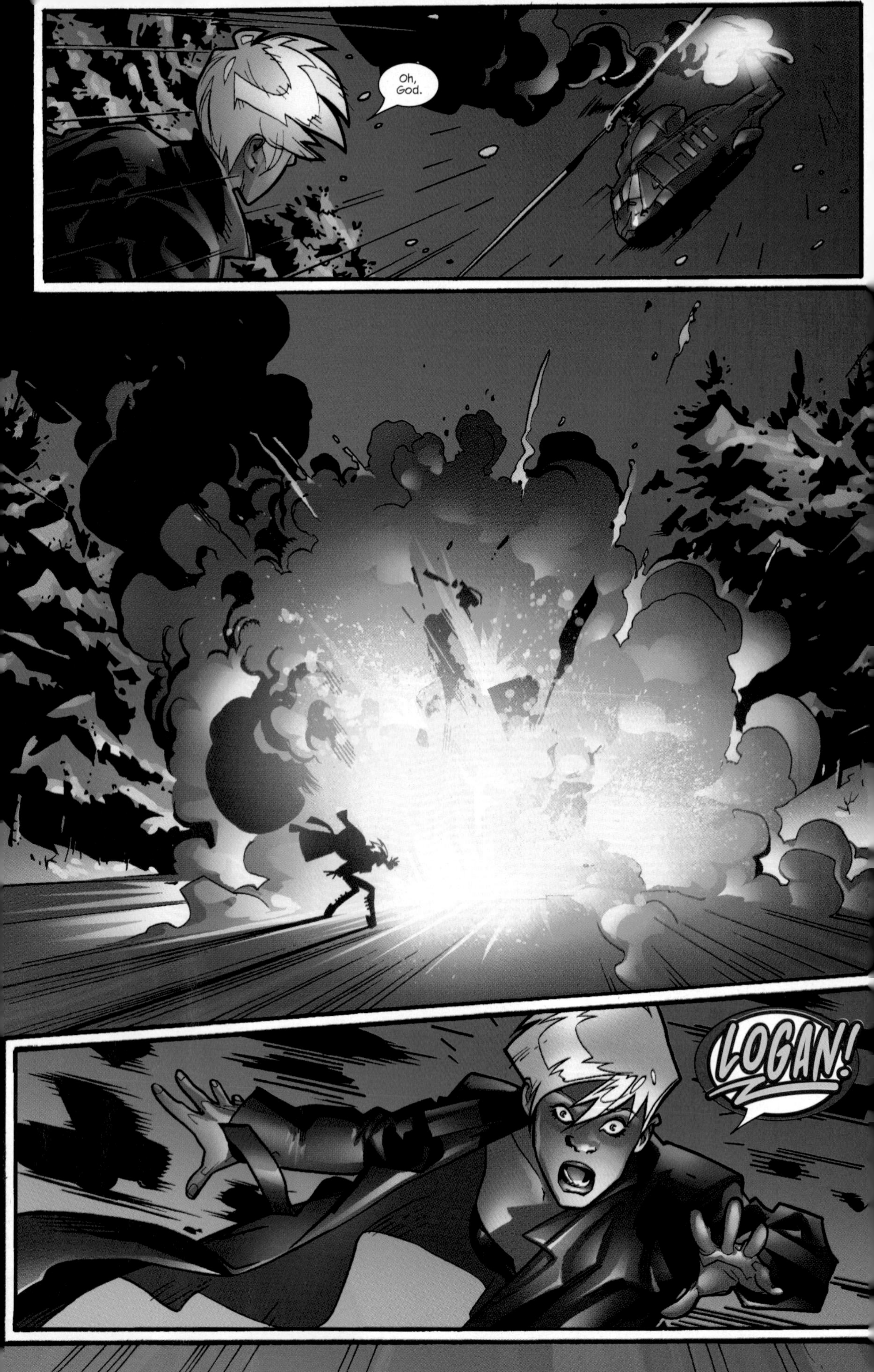
Oh, God.
LOGAN!

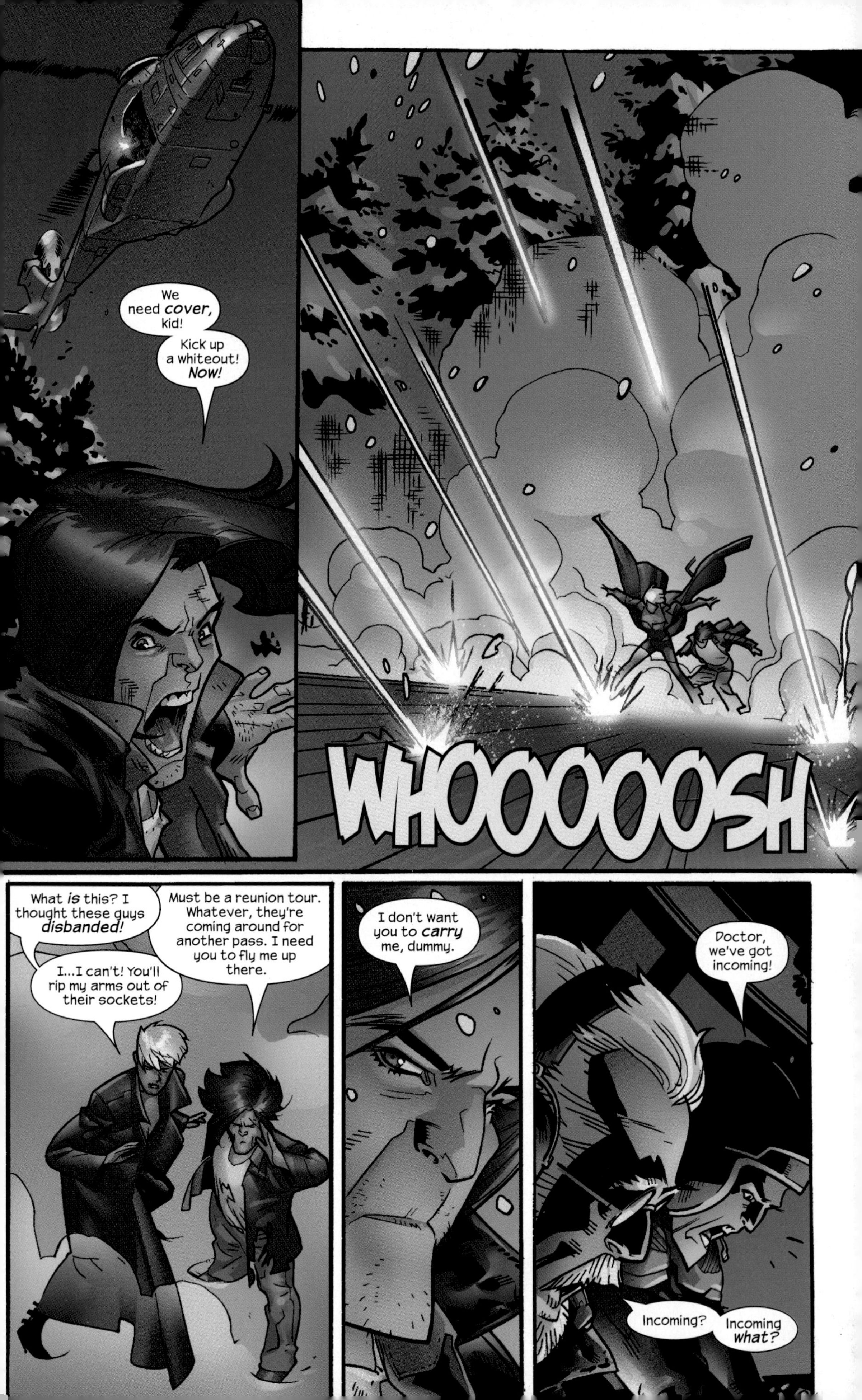
We need *cover,* kid!
Kick up a whiteout! *Now!*
WHOOOOOOSH
What *is* this? I thought these guys *disbanded!*
Must be a reunion tour. Whatever, they're coming around for another pass. I need you to fly me up there.
I...I can't! You'll rip my arms out of their sockets!
I don't want you to *carry* me, dummy.
Doctor, we've got incoming!
Incoming?
Incoming *what?*

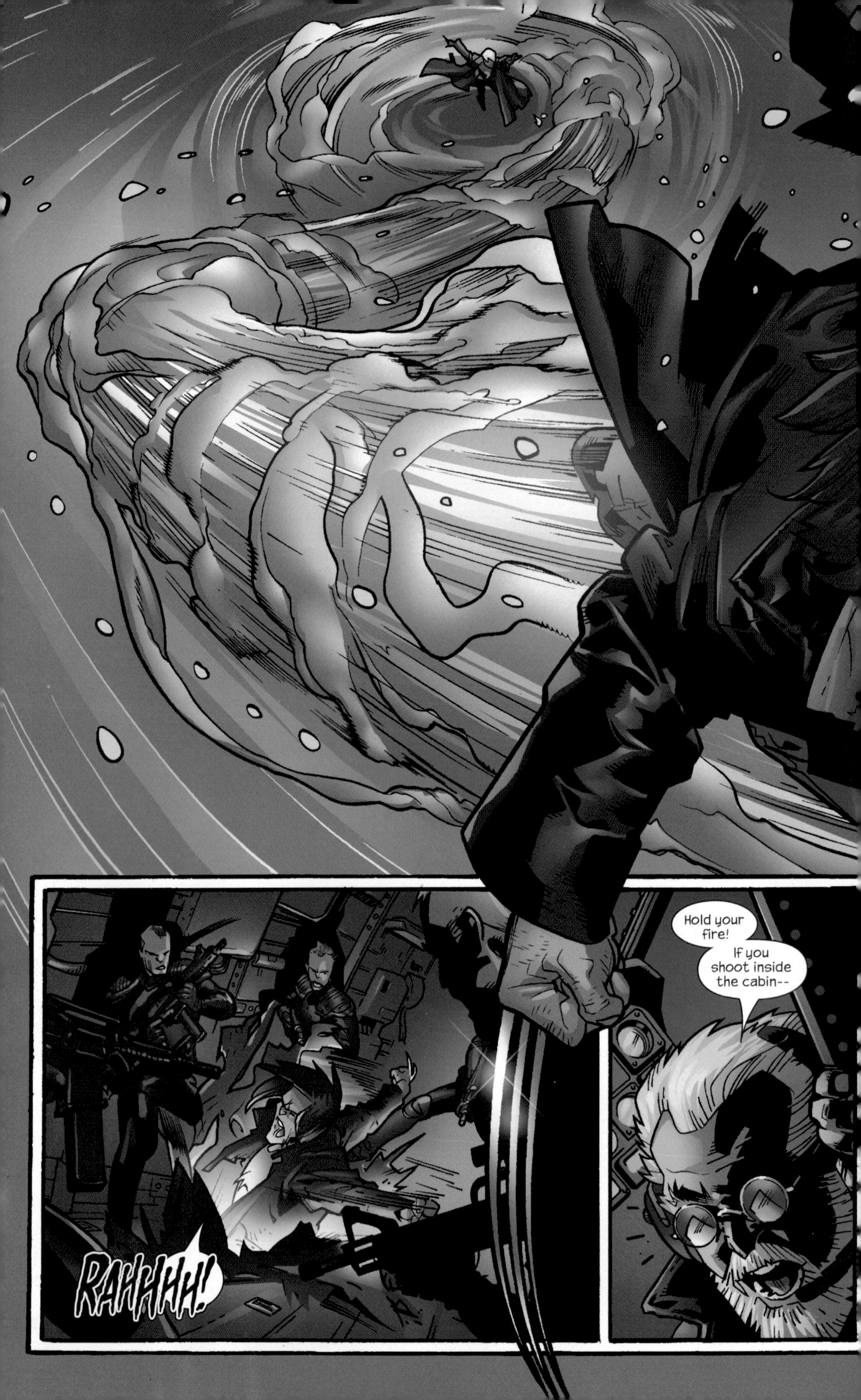
RAHHHH!
Hold your fire!
If you shoot inside the cabin--

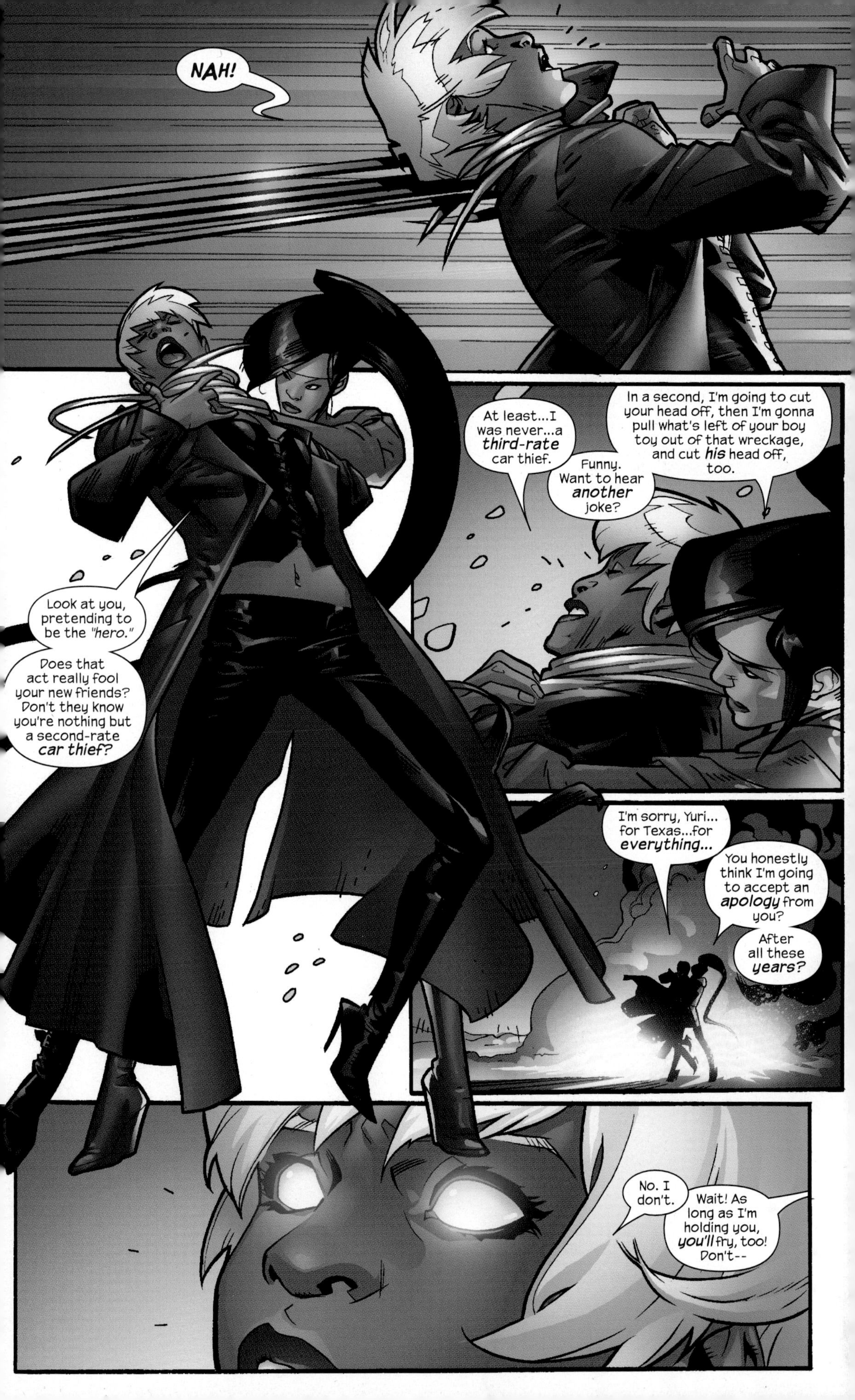
NAH!
Look at you, pretending to be the "hero."
Does that act really fool your new friends? Don't they know you're nothing but a second-rate car thief?
At least...I was never...a third-rate car thief.
Funny. Want to hear another joke?
In a second, I'm going to cut your head off, then I'm gonna pull what's left of your boy toy out of that wreckage, and cut his head off, too.
I'm sorry, Yuri... for Texas...for everything...
You honestly think I'm going to accept an apology from you?
After all these years?
No. I don't.
Wait! As long as I'm holding you, you'll fry, too! Don't--

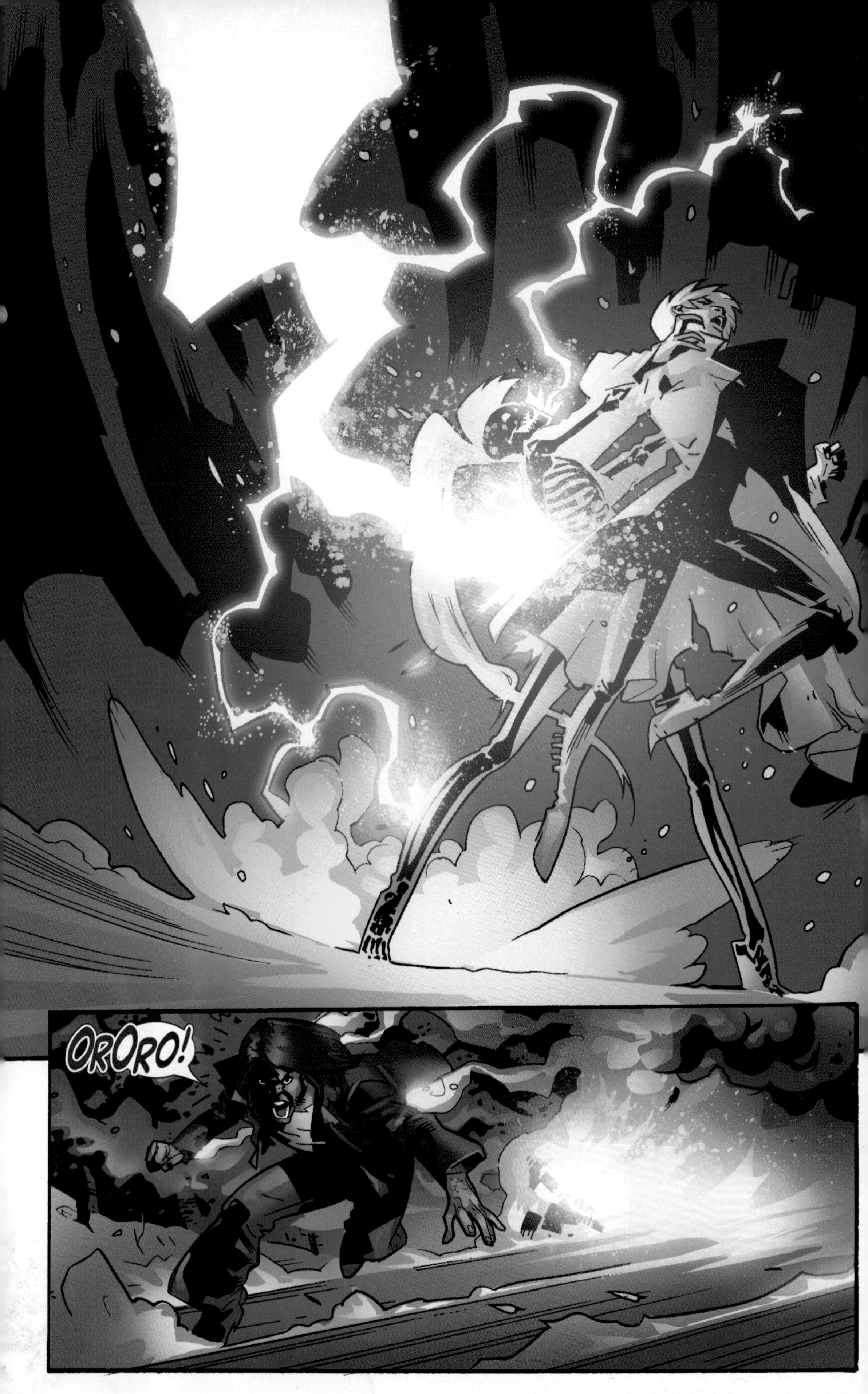
ORORO!

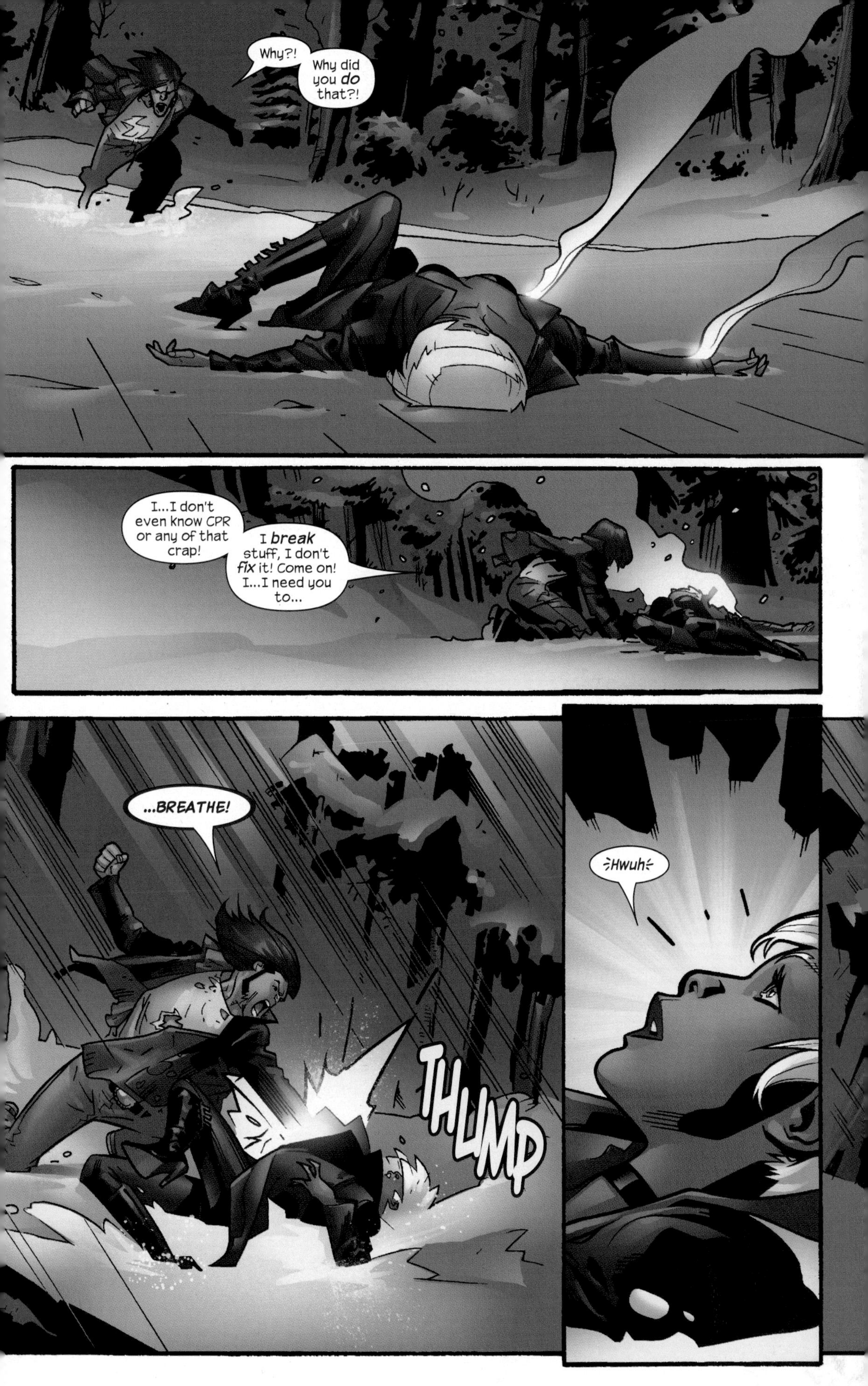
Why?!
Why did you *do* that?!
I...I don't even know CPR or any of that crap!
I *break* stuff, I don't *fix* it! Come on! I...I need you to...
...BREATHE!
THUMP
Hwuh

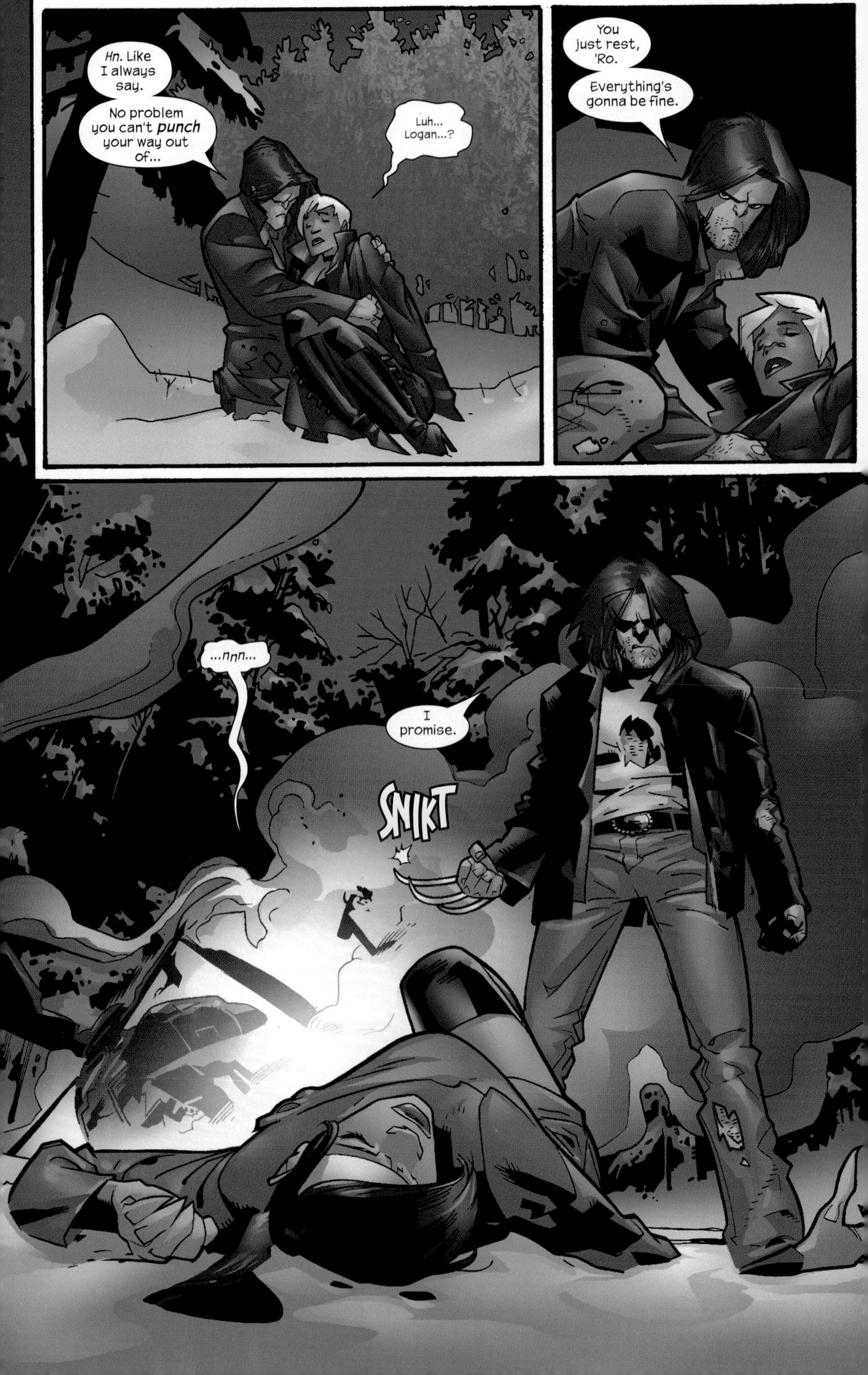

Hn. Like I always say.
No problem you can't punch your way out of...
Luh... Logan...?
You just rest, 'Ro.
Everything's gonna be fine.
...nnn...
I promise.
SNIKT

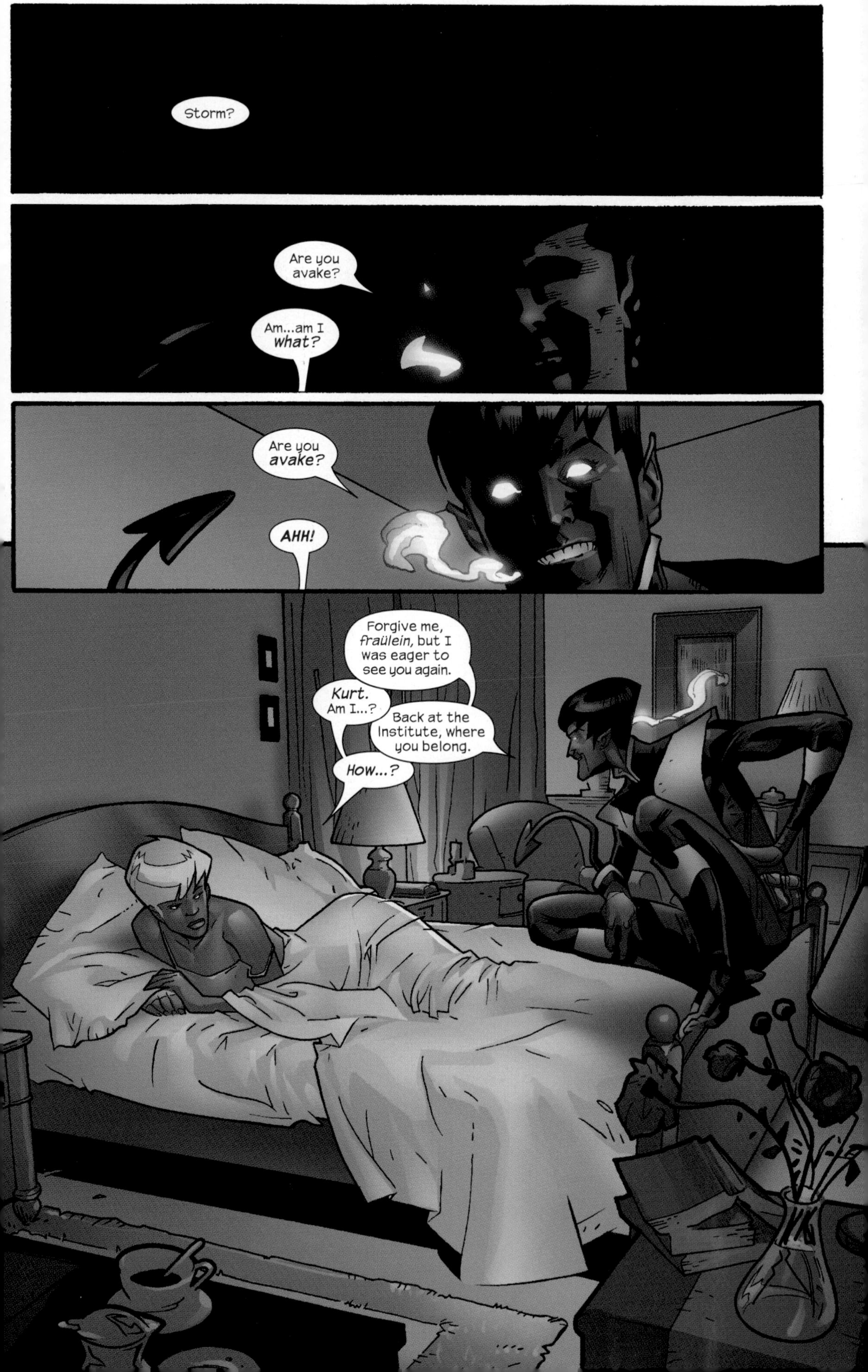
Storm?
Are you avake?
Am...am I what?
Are you avake?
AHH!
Forgive me, fraülein, but I was eager to see you again.
Kurt. Am I...?
Back at the Institute, where you belong.
HOW...?

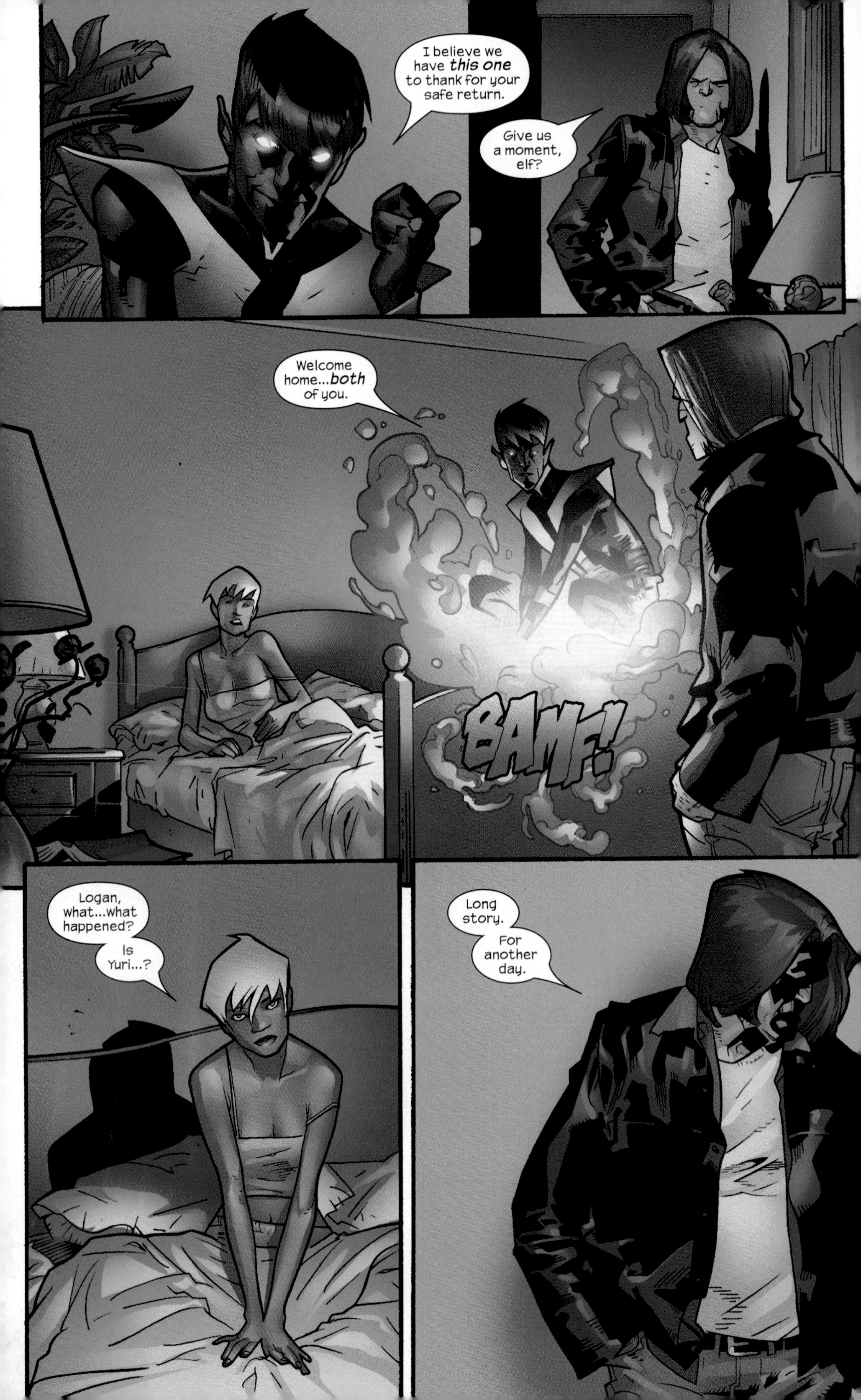
I believe we have ***this one*** to thank for your safe return.
Give us a moment, elf?
Welcome home...***both*** of you.
BAMF!
Logan, what...what happened?
Is Yuri...?
Long story.
For another day.

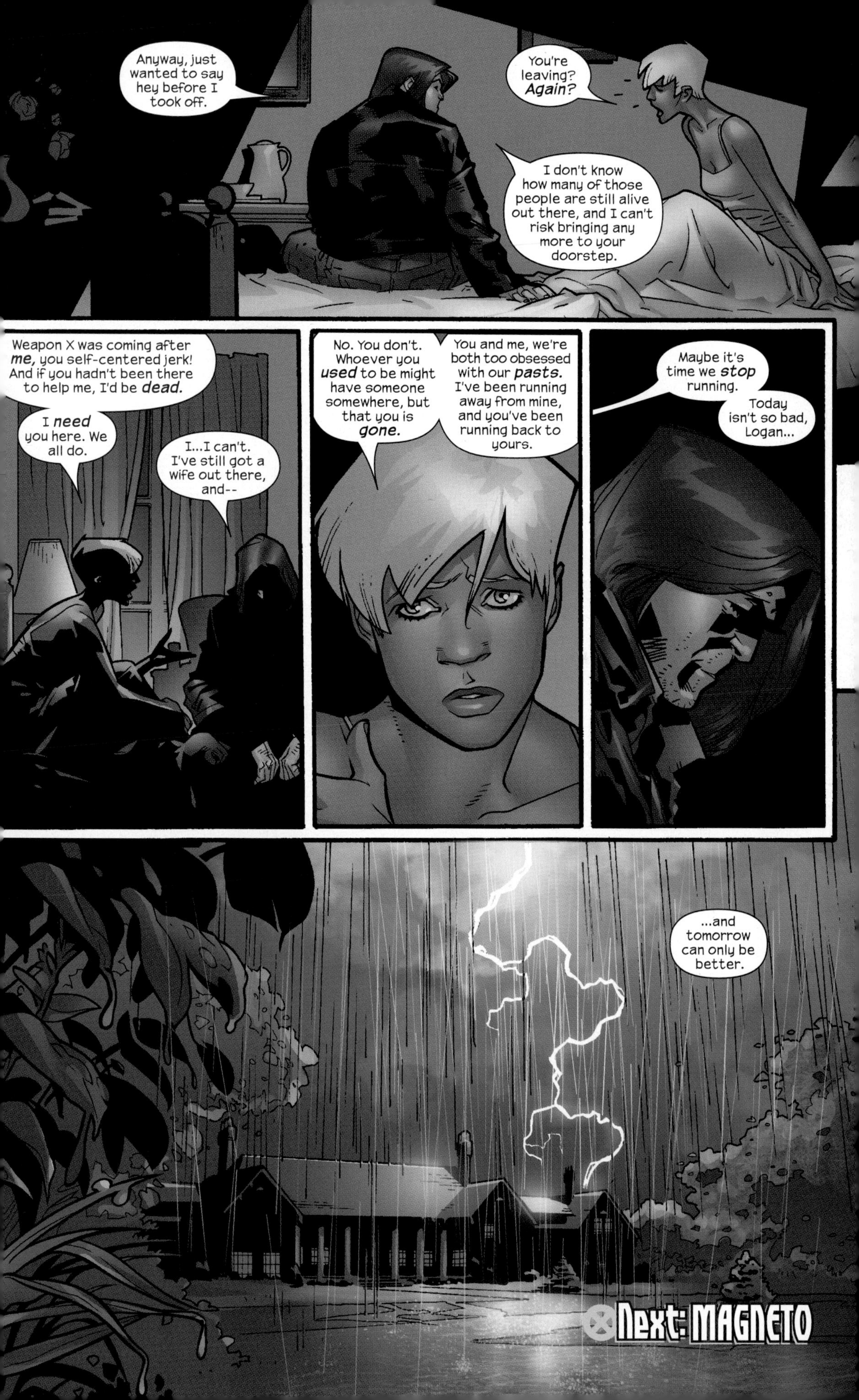

Anyway, just wanted to say hey before I took off.
You're leaving? *Again?*
I don't know how many of those people are still alive out there, and I can't risk bringing any more to your doorstep.
Weapon X was coming after *me,* you self-centered jerk! And if you hadn't been there to help me, I'd be *dead.*
I *need* you here. We all do.
I...I can't. I've still got a wife out there, and--
No. You don't. Whoever you *used* to be might have someone somewhere, but that you is *gone.*
You and me, we're both too obsessed with our *pasts.* I've been running away from mine, and you've been running back to yours.
Maybe it's time we *stop* running.
Today isn't so bad, Logan...
...and tomorrow can only be better.
Next: MAGNETO

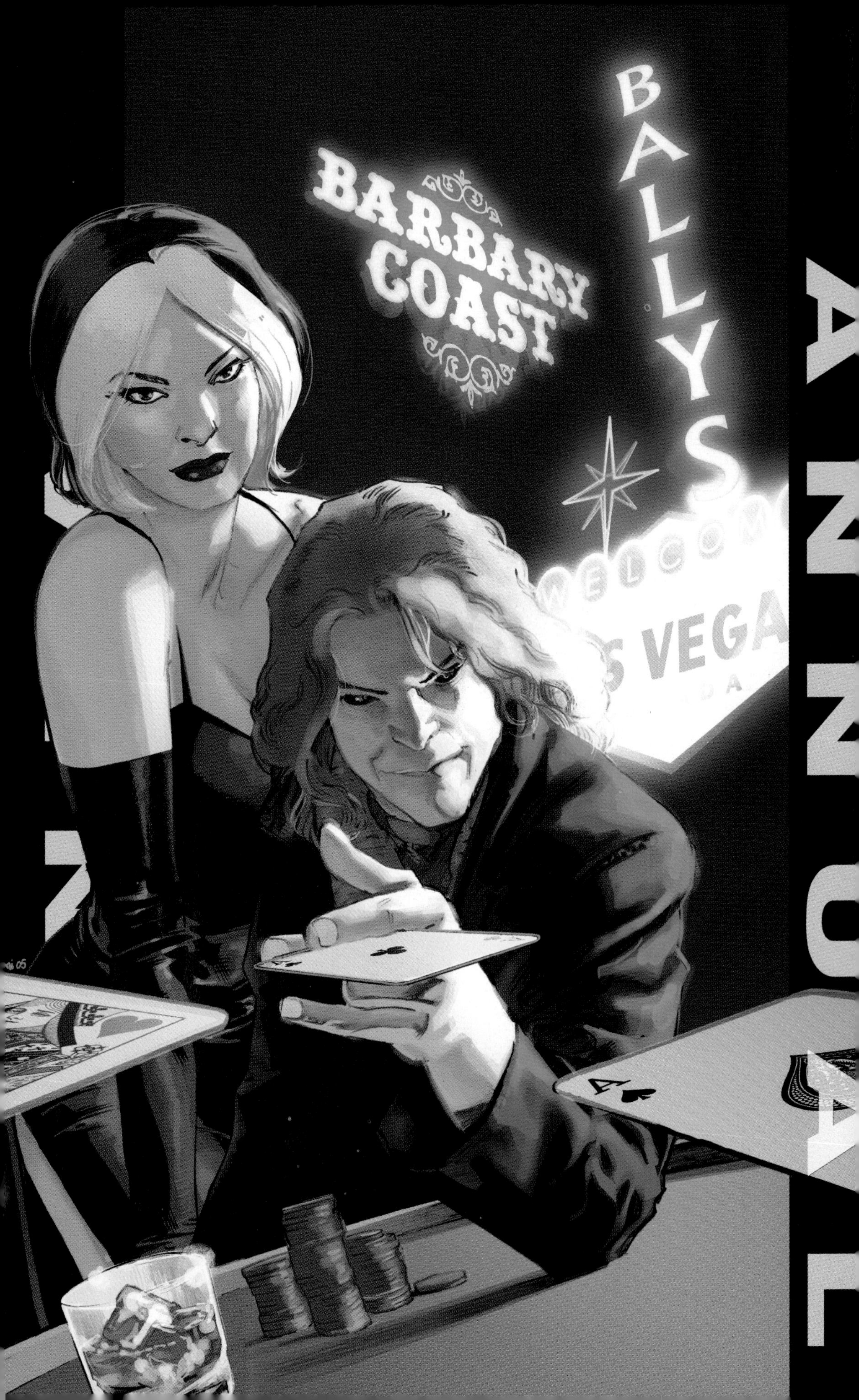
BARBARY COAST
BALLYS

PREVIOUSLY IN ULTIMATE X-MEN:

Born with strange and amazing abilities, the X-Men are young mutant heroes,
sworn to protect a world that fears and hates them.

One of their recent recruits is Rogue, a teenage girl and reformed acolyte of the mutant terrorist
Magneto. forced to absorb the memories and abilities of whomever she touches, Rogue has
always had a difficult time getting close to others.

But after being manipulated by the billionaire industrialists known as fenris, Rogue decided to run
off with a dashing mutant thief named Gambit, who convinced the young woman to leave her
teammates and pursue her own destiny.

Congratulations,
X-Men.

You have the
honor of being
escorted into
oblivion by none
other than...*the
Green Goblin.*

ULTIMATE SACRIFICE

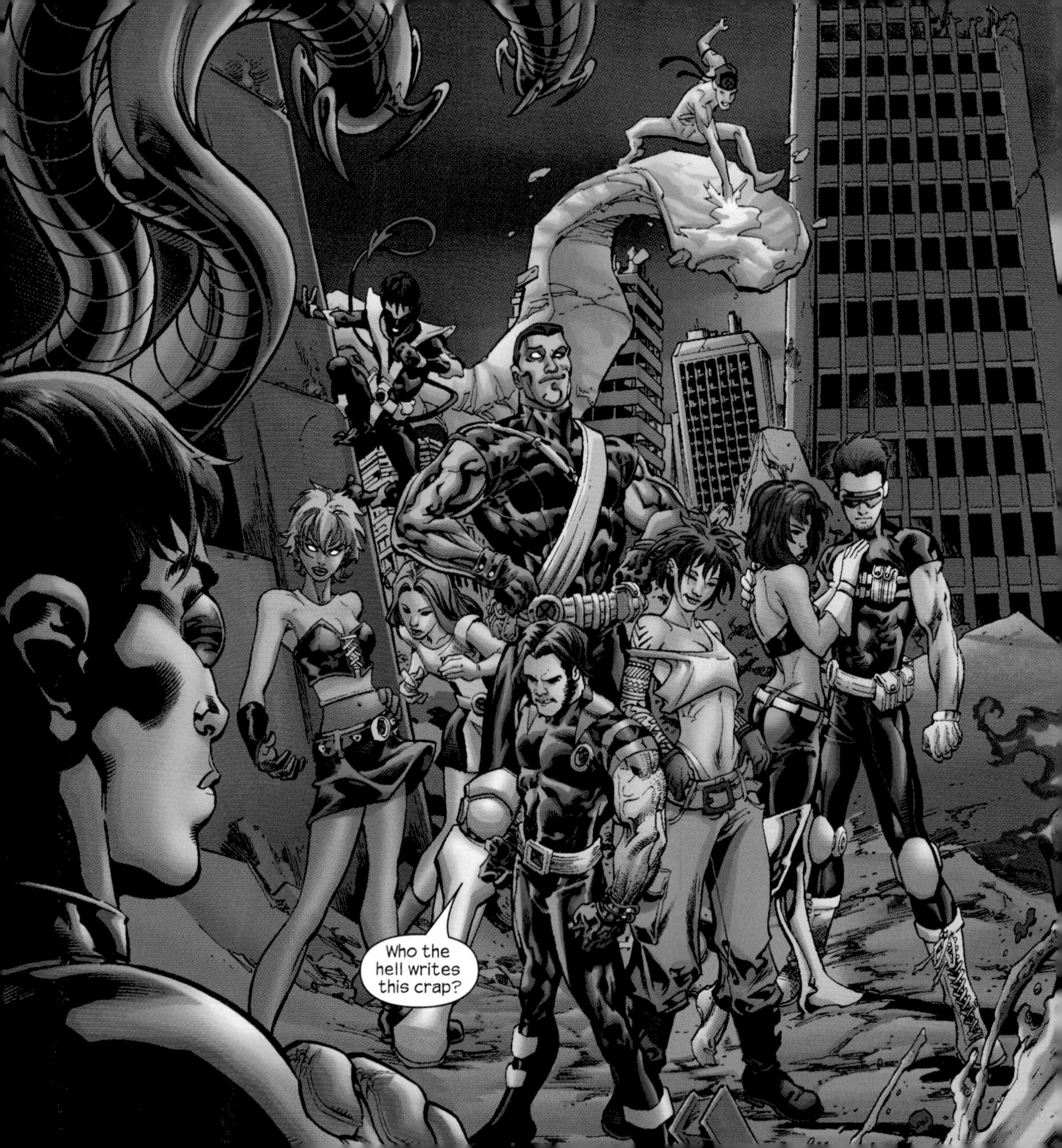
Who the hell writes this crap?

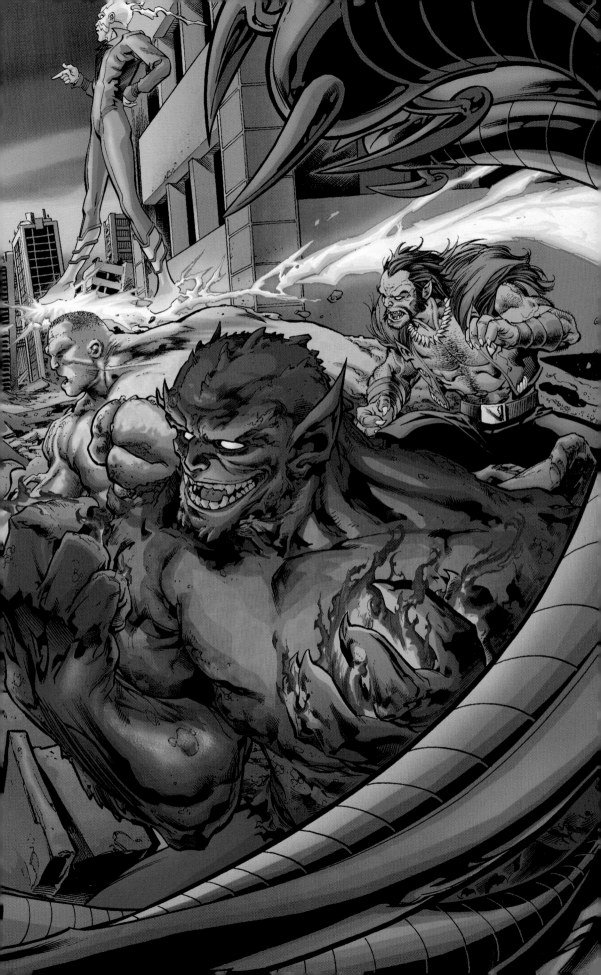

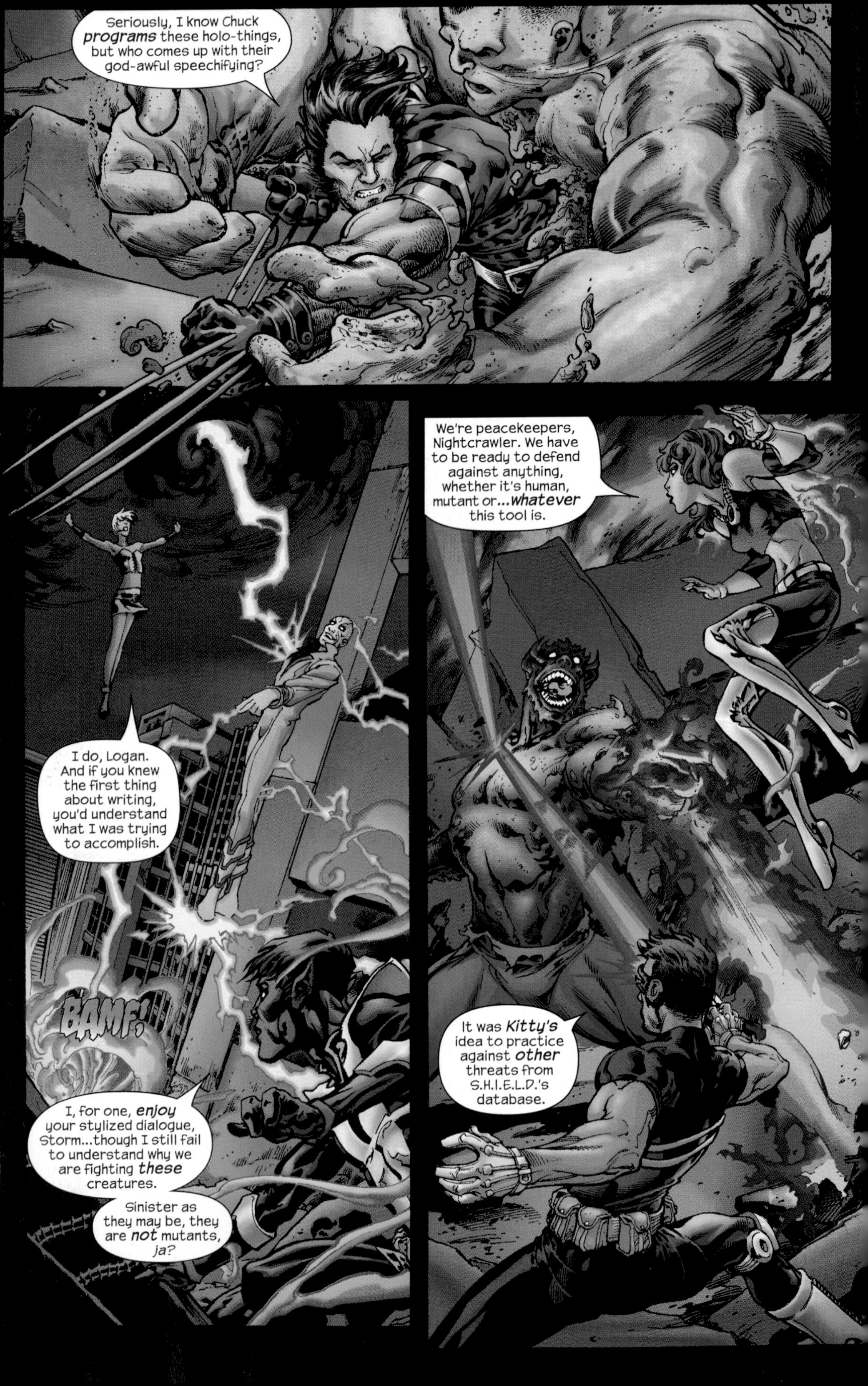
Seriously, I know Chuck *programs* these holo-things, but who comes up with their god-awful speechifying?
I do, Logan. And if you knew the first thing about writing, you'd understand what I was trying to accomplish.
BAMF!
I, for one, *enjoy* your stylized dialogue, Storm...though I still fail to understand why we are fighting *these* creatures.
Sinister as they may be, they are *not* mutants, *ja?*
We're peacekeepers, Nightcrawler. We have to be ready to defend against anything, whether it's human, mutant or...*whatever* this tool is.
It was *Kitty's* idea to practice against *other* threats from S.H.I.E.L.D.'s database.

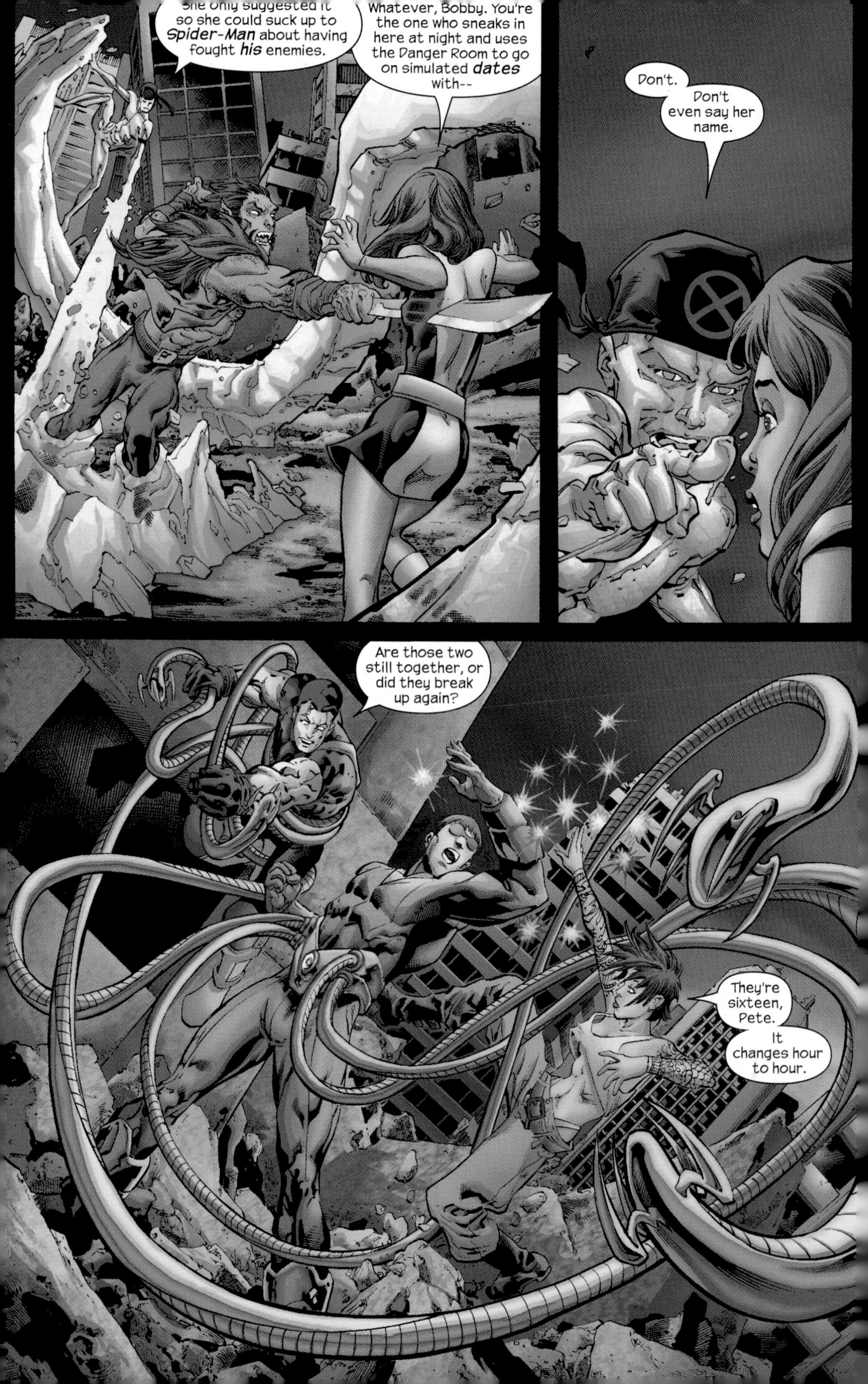
She only suggested it so she could suck up to *Spider-Man* about having fought *his* enemies.
Whatever, Bobby. You're the one who sneaks in here at night and uses the Danger Room to go on simulated *dates* with--
Don't.
Don't even say her name.
Are those two still together, or did they break up again?
They're sixteen, Pete.
It changes hour to hour.

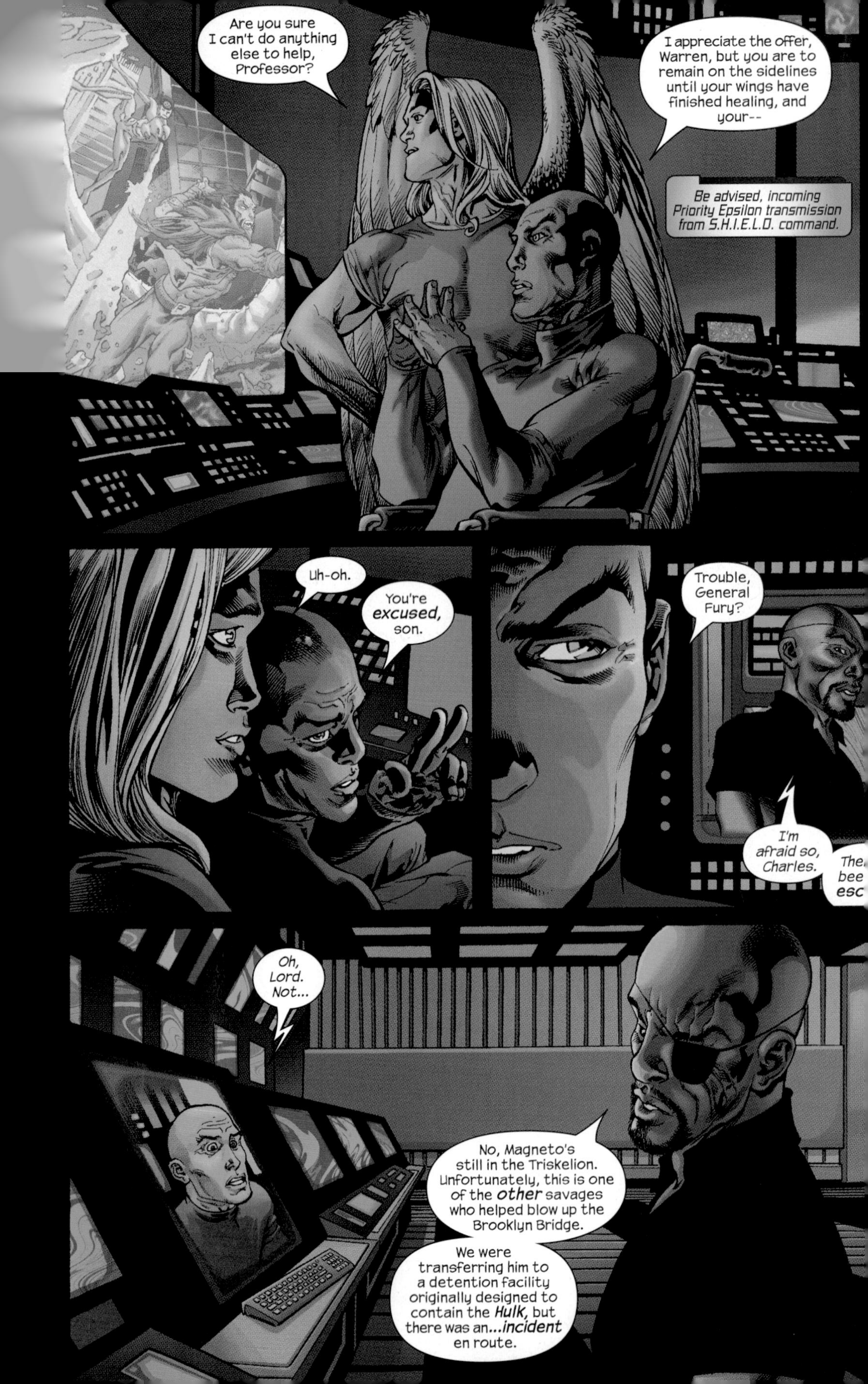
Are you sure I can't do anything else to help, Professor?
I appreciate the offer, Warren, but you are to remain on the sidelines until your wings have finished healing, and your--
Be advised, incoming Priority Epsilon transmission from S.H.I.E.L.D. command.
Uh-oh.
You're *excused*, son.
Trouble, General Fury?
I'm afraid so, Charles.
Oh, Lord. Not...
No, Magneto's still in the Triskelion. Unfortunately, this is one of the *other* savages who helped blow up the Brooklyn Bridge.
We were transferring him to a detention facility originally designed to contain the *Hulk*, but there was an...*incident* en route.

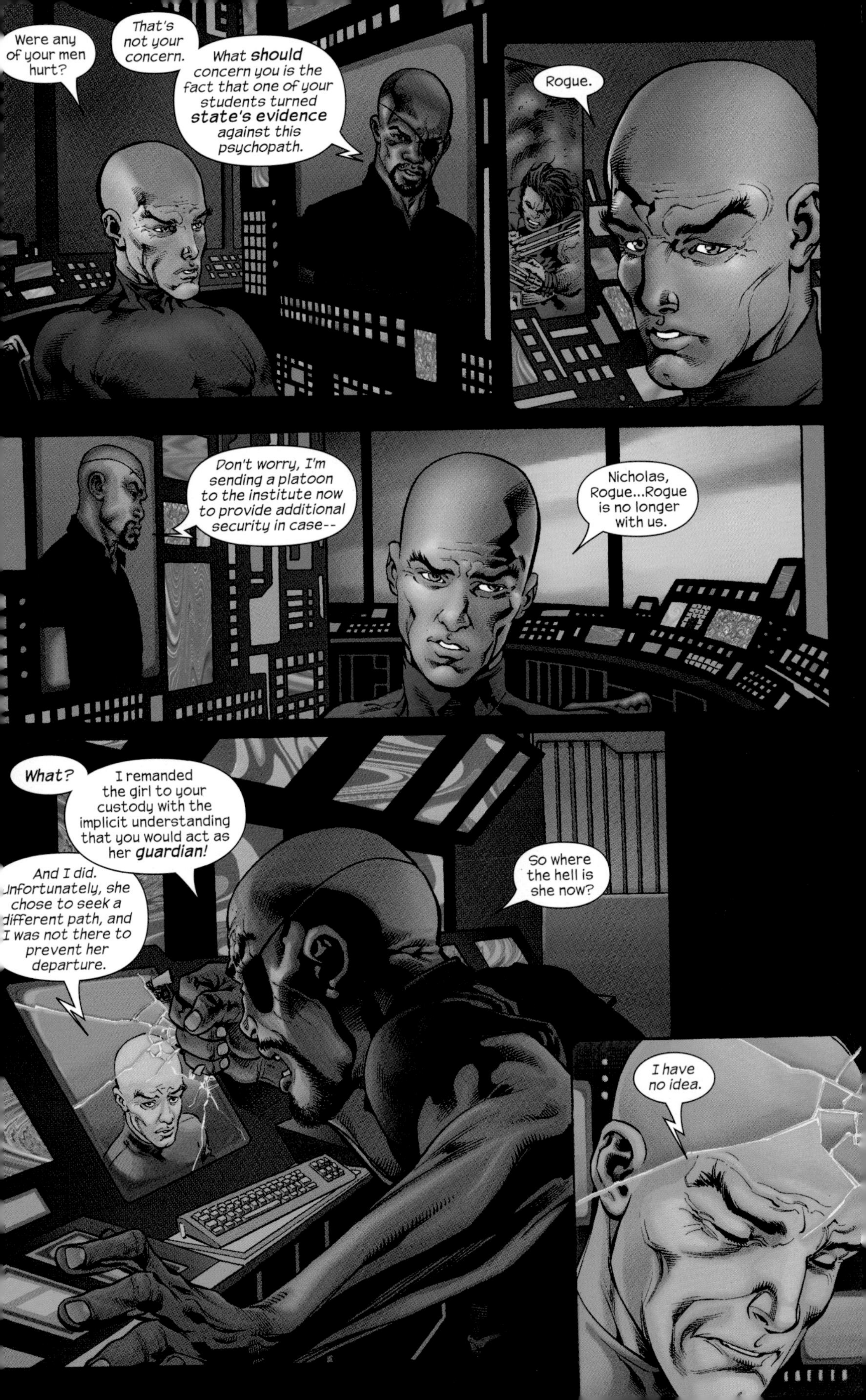
Were any of your men hurt?
That's not your concern.
What should concern you is the fact that one of your students turned state's evidence against this psychopath.
Rogue.
Don't worry, I'm sending a platoon to the institute now to provide additional security in case--
Nicholas, Rogue...Rogue is no longer with us.
What?
I remanded the girl to your custody with the implicit understanding that you would act as her guardian!
And I did. Unfortunately, she chose to seek a different path, and I was not there to prevent her departure.
So where the hell is she now?
I have no idea.

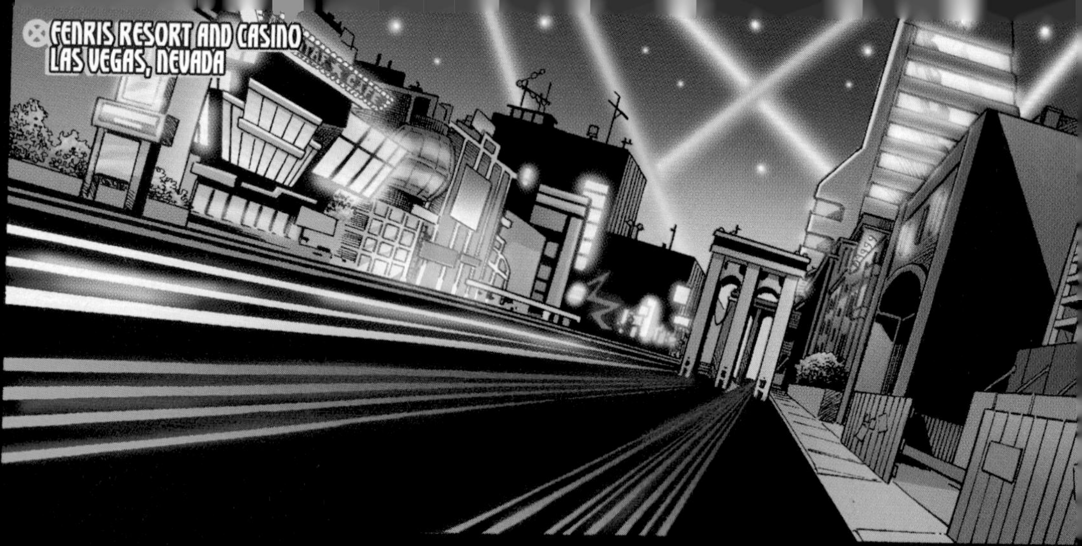
FENRIS RESORT AND CASINO
LAS VEGAS, NEVADA

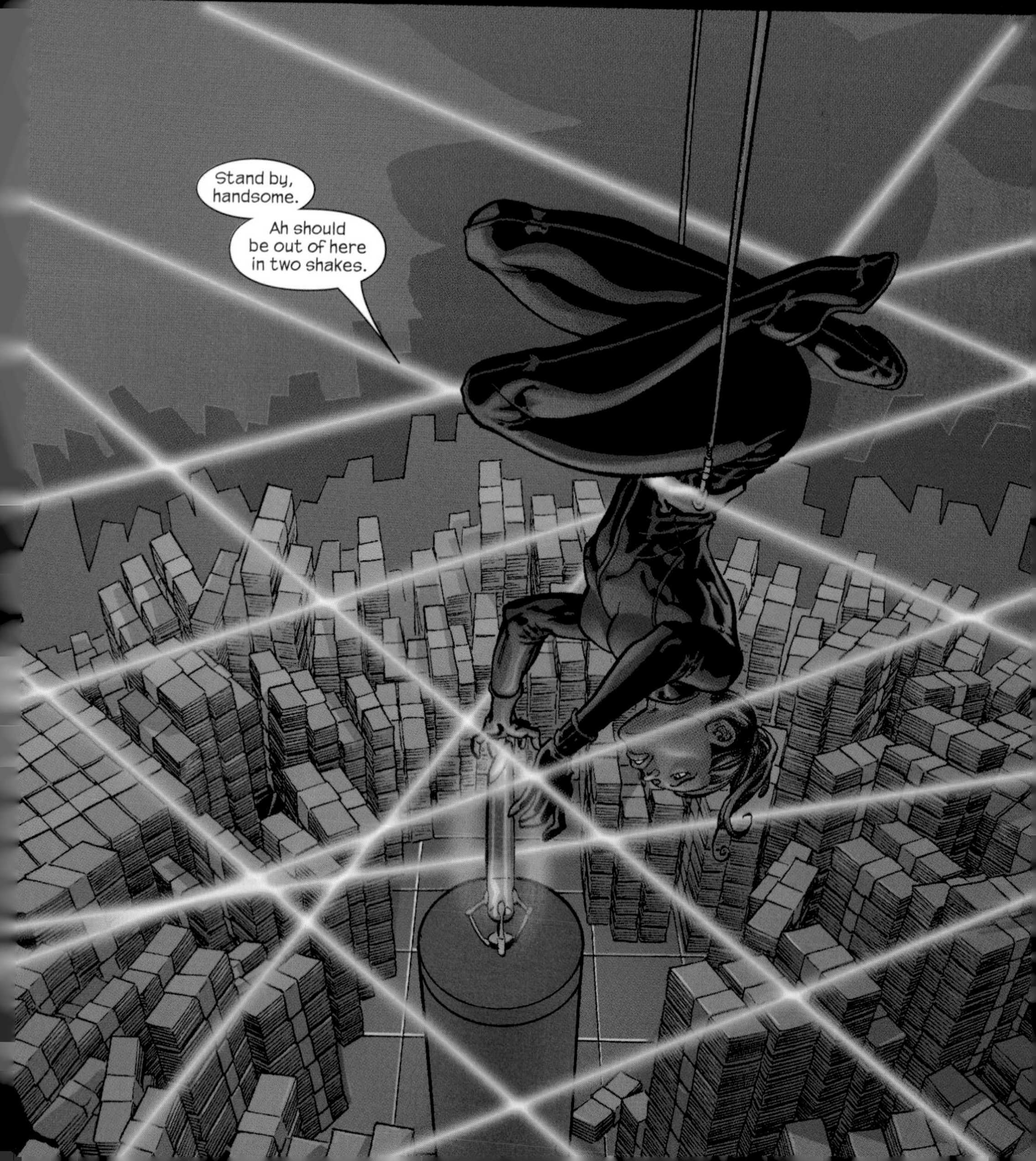
Stand by, handsome.
Ah should be out of here in two shakes.

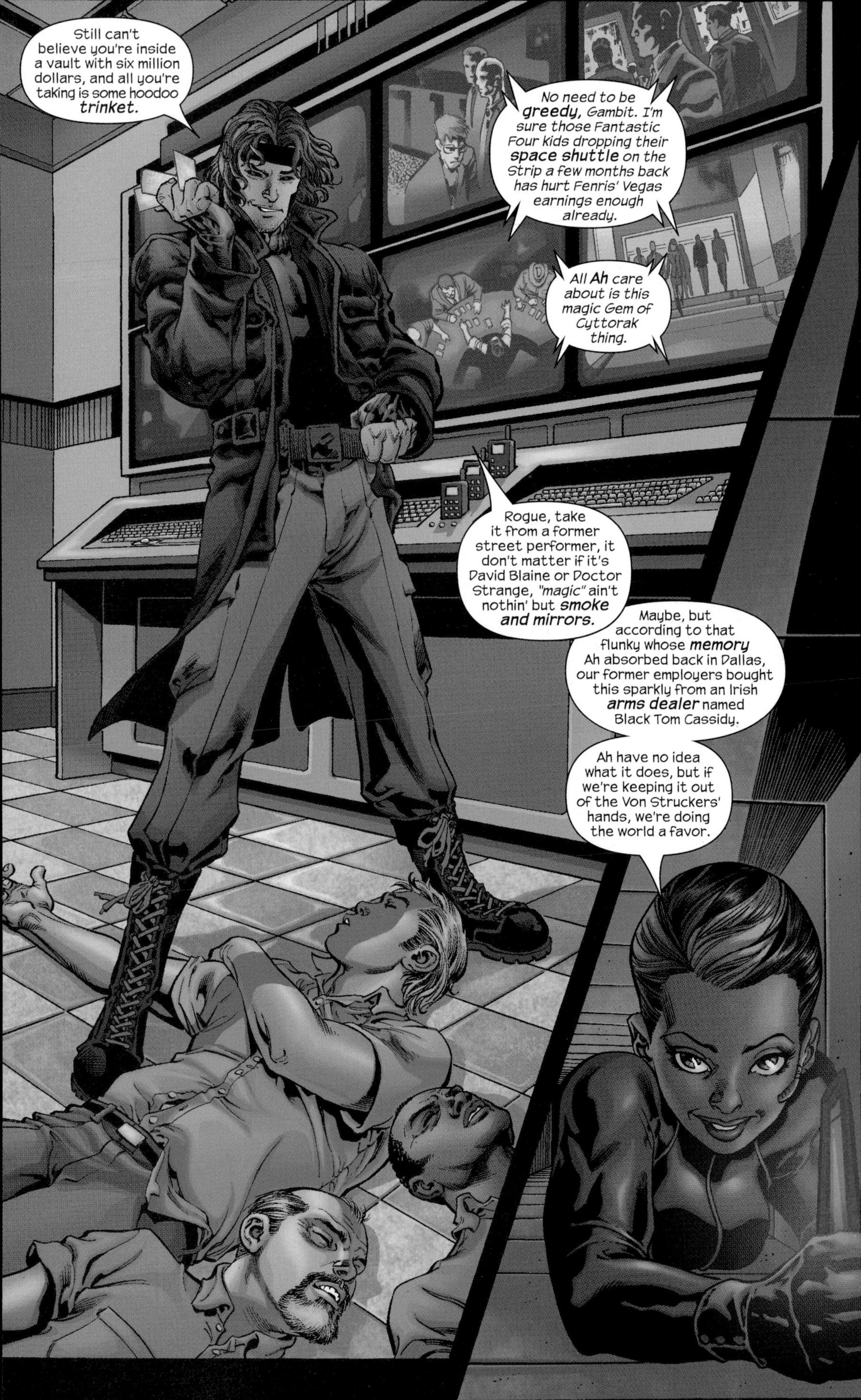
Still can't believe you're inside a vault with six million dollars, and all you're taking is some hoodoo trinket.
No need to be greedy, Gambit. I'm sure those Fantastic Four kids dropping their space shuttle on the Strip a few months back has hurt Fenris' Vegas earnings enough already.
All Ah care about is this magic Gem of Cyttorak thing.
Rogue, take it from a former street performer, it don't matter if it's David Blaine or Doctor Strange, "magic" ain't nothin' but smoke and mirrors.
Maybe, but according to that flunky whose memory Ah absorbed back in Dallas, our former employers bought this sparkly from an Irish arms dealer named Black Tom Cassidy.
Ah have no idea what it does, but if we're keeping it out of the Von Struckers' hands, we're doing the world a favor.

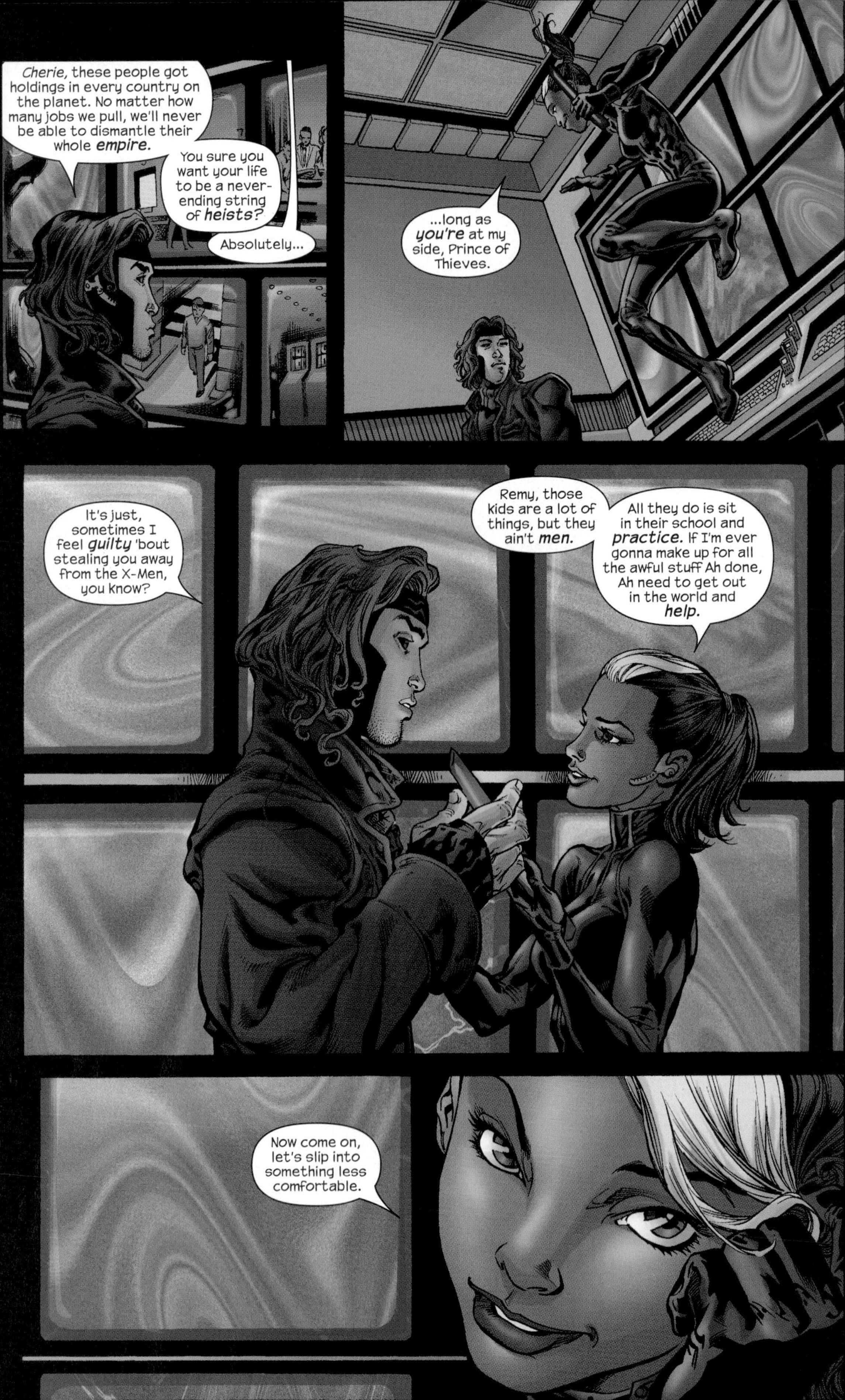
Cherie, these people got holdings in every country on the planet. No matter how many jobs we pull, we'll never be able to dismantle their whole empire.
You sure you want your life to be a never-ending string of heists?
Absolutely...
...long as you're at my side, Prince of Thieves.
It's just, sometimes I feel guilty 'bout stealing you away from the X-Men, you know?
Remy, those kids are a lot of things, but they ain't men.
All they do is sit in their school and practice. If I'm ever gonna make up for all the awful stuff Ah done, Ah need to get out in the world and help.
Now come on, let's slip into something less comfortable.

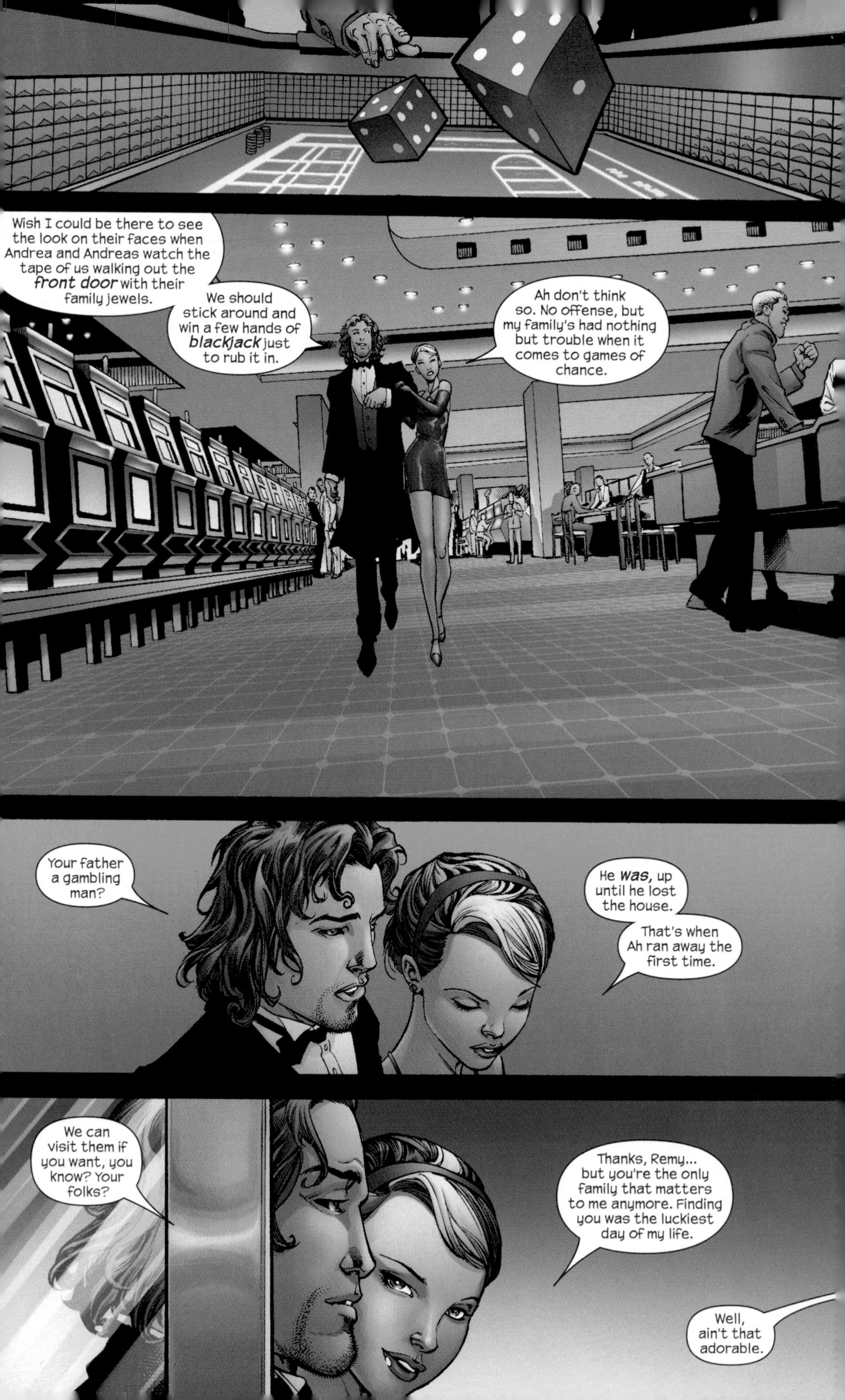

Wish I could be there to see the look on their faces when Andrea and Andreas watch the tape of us walking out the *front door* with their family jewels.
We should stick around and win a few hands of *blackjack* just to rub it in.
Ah don't think so. No offense, but my family's had nothing but trouble when it comes to games of chance.
Your father a gambling man?
He *was,* up until he lost the house.
That's when Ah ran away the first time.
We can visit them if you want, you know? Your folks?
Thanks, Remy... but you're the only family that matters to me anymore. Finding you was the luckiest day of my life.
Well, ain't that adorable.

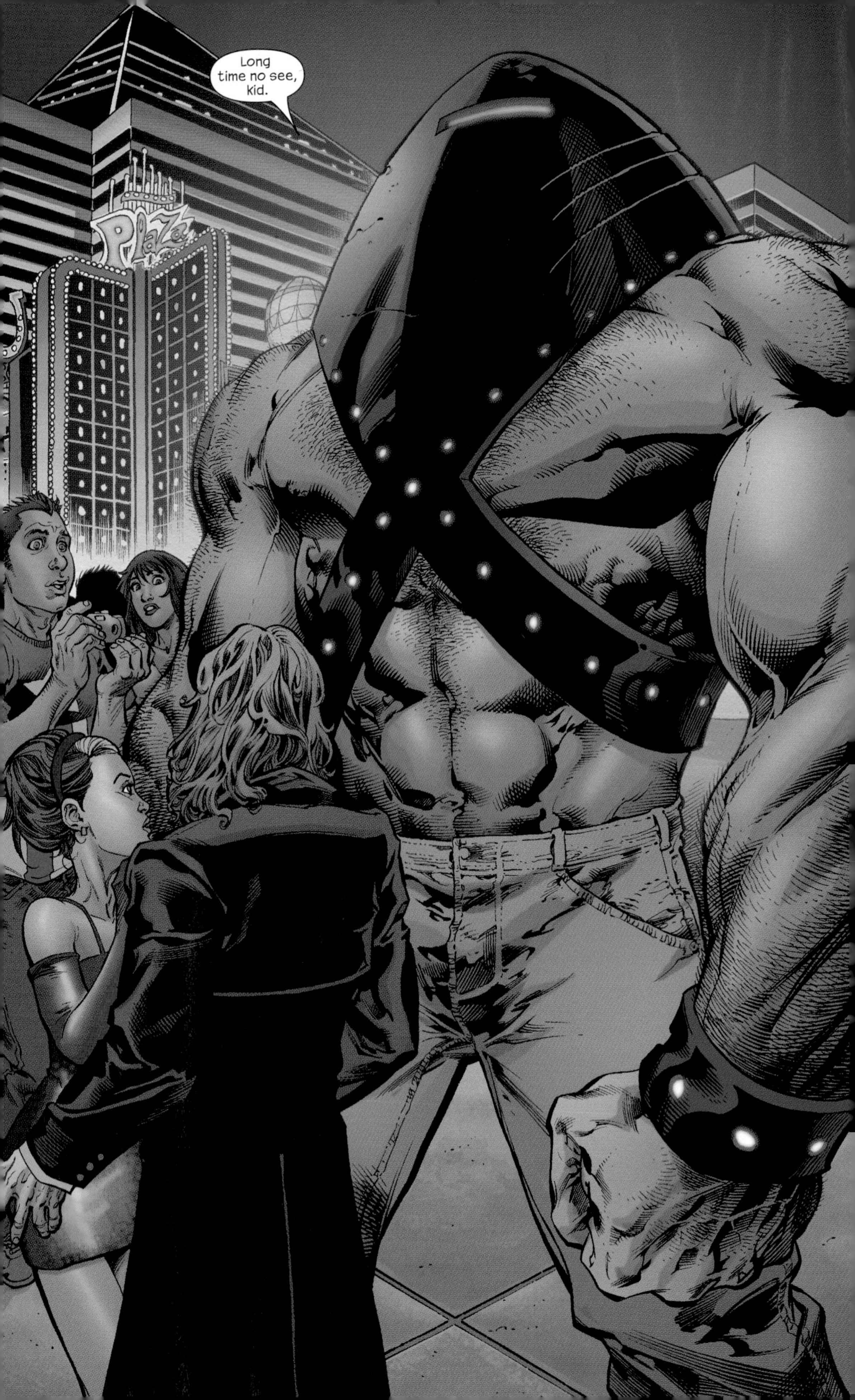
Long time no see, kid.

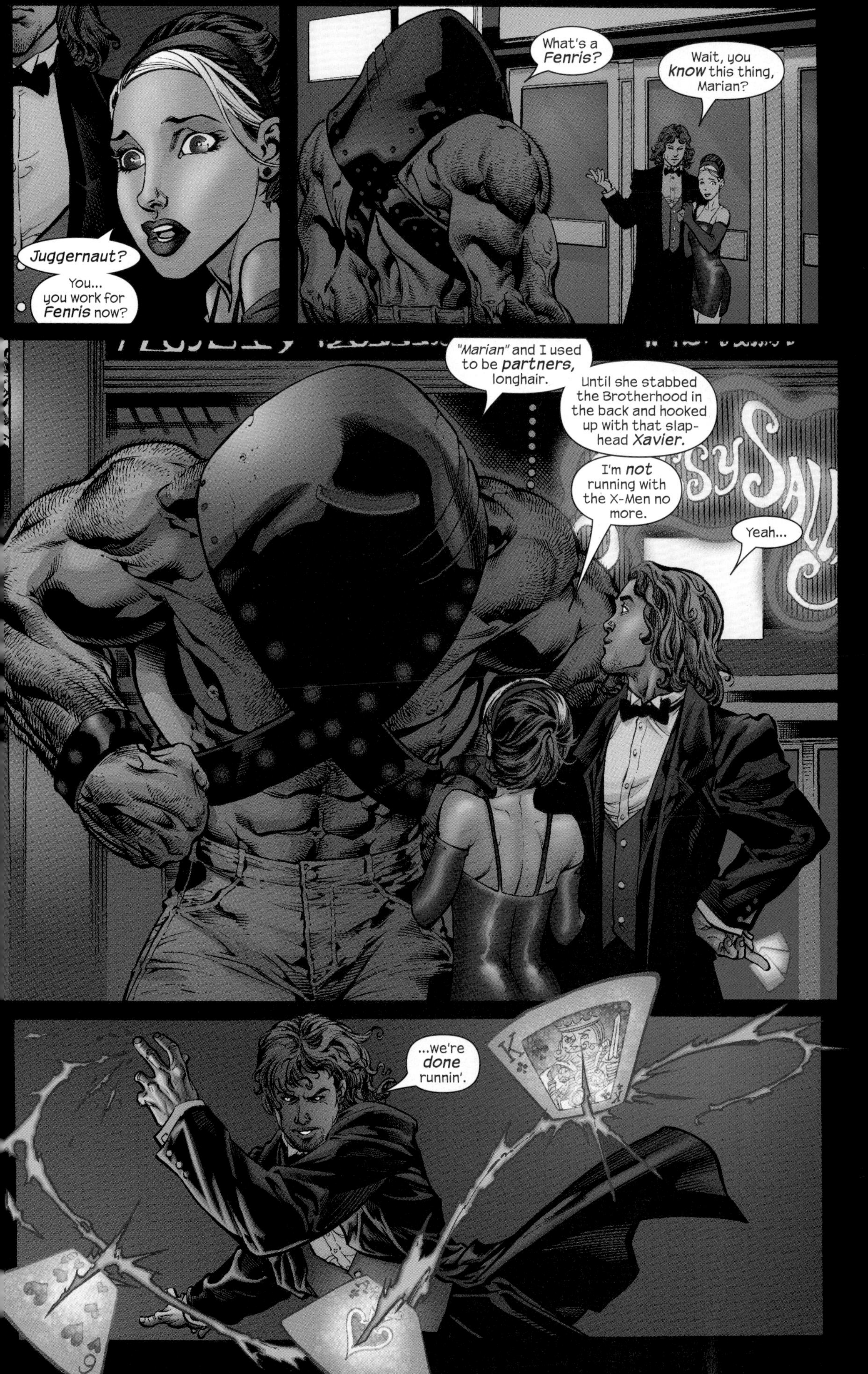
Juggernaut?
You... you work for Fenris now?
What's a Fenris?
Wait, you know this thing, Marian?
"Marian" and I used to be partners, longhair.
Until she stabbed the Brotherhood in the back and hooked up with that slap-head Xavier.
I'm not running with the X-Men no more.
Yeah...
...we're done runnin'.

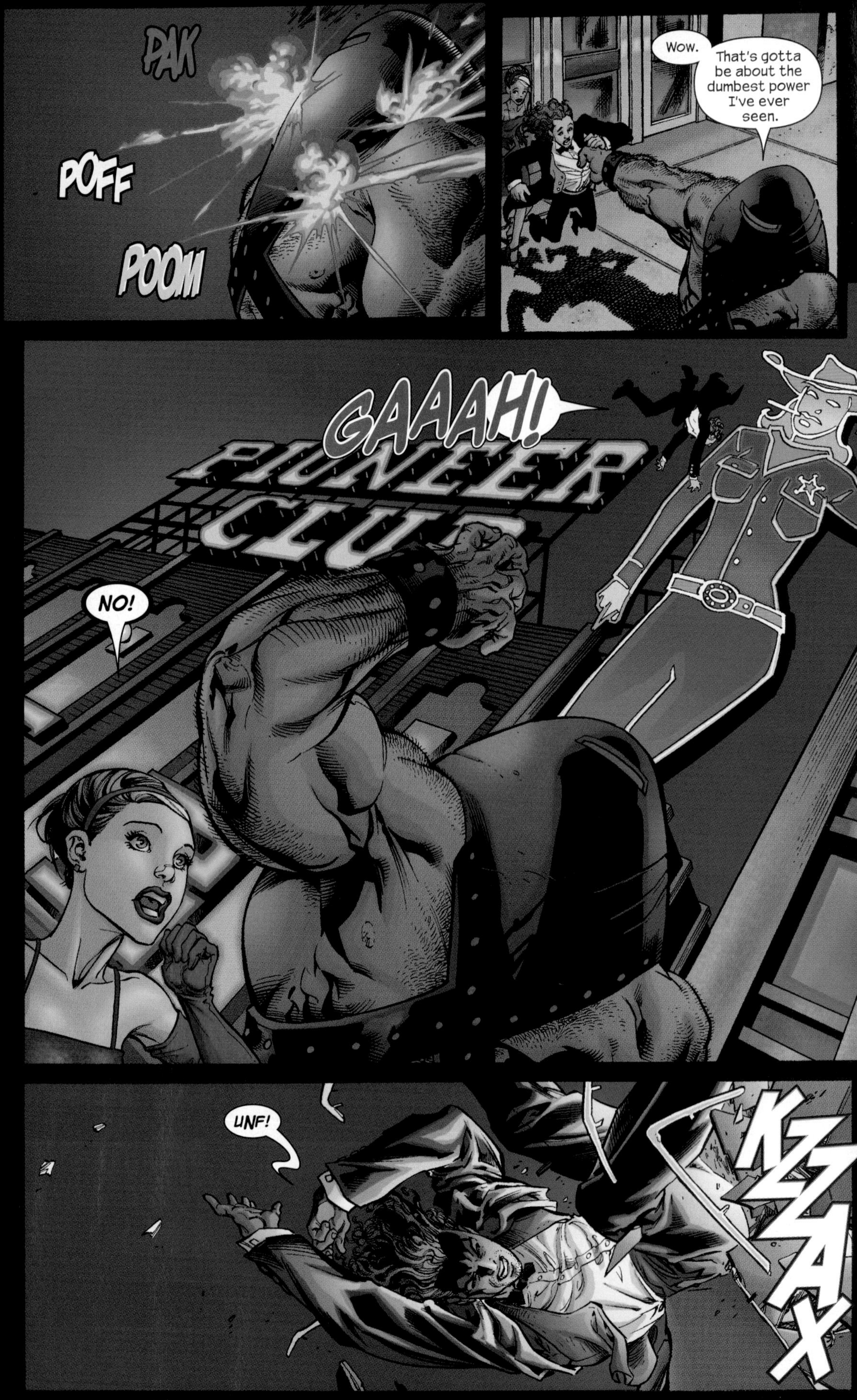
PAK
POFF
POOM
Wow.
That's gotta be about the dumbest power I've ever seen.
GAAAH!
PIONEER CLUB
NO!
UNF!
KZZZAX

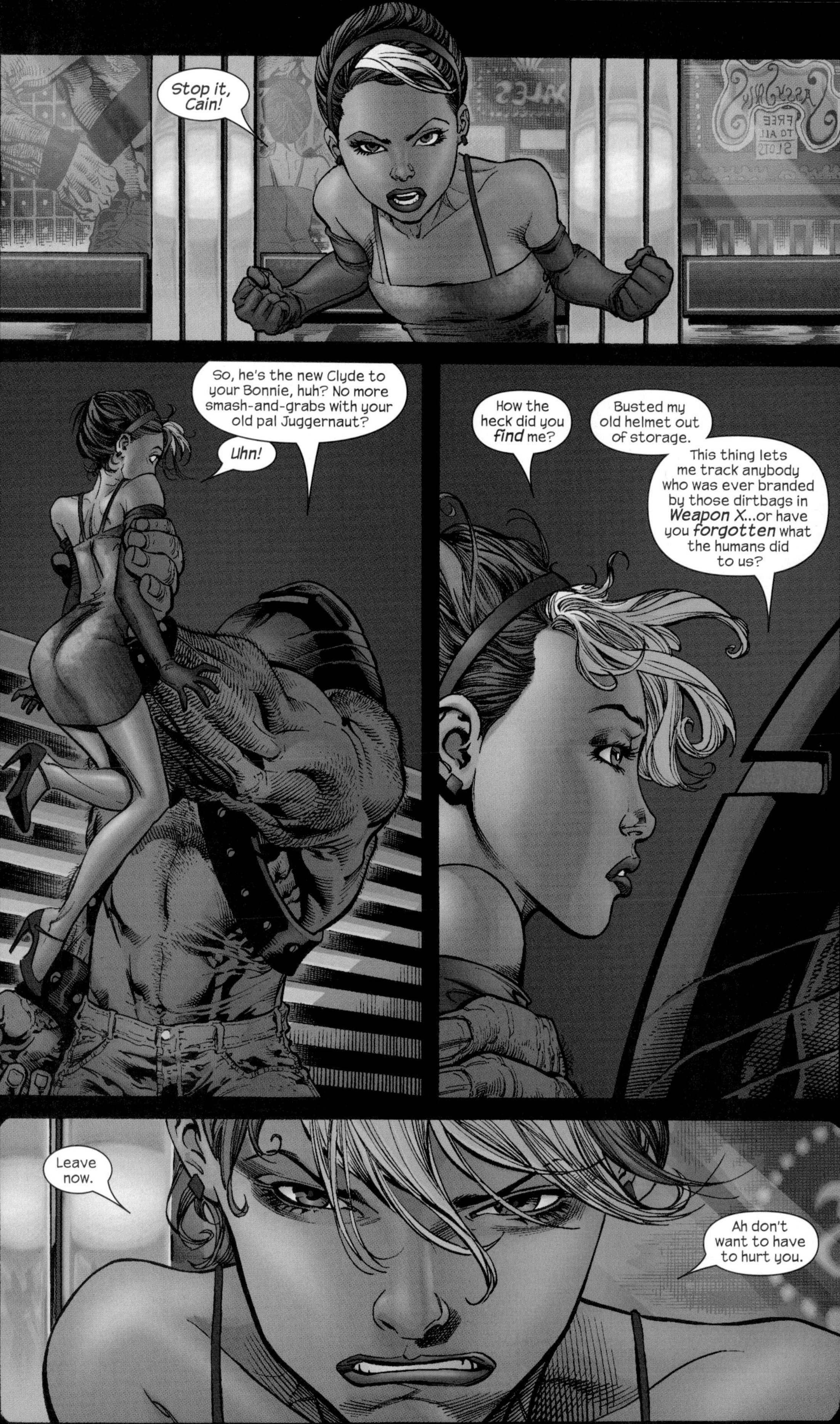
Stop it, Cain!
So, he's the new Clyde to your Bonnie, huh? No more smash-and-grabs with your old pal Juggernaut?
Uhn!
How the heck did you find me?
Busted my old helmet out of storage.
This thing lets me track anybody who was ever branded by those dirtbags in Weapon X...or have you forgotten what the humans did to us?
Leave now.
Ah don't want to have to hurt you.

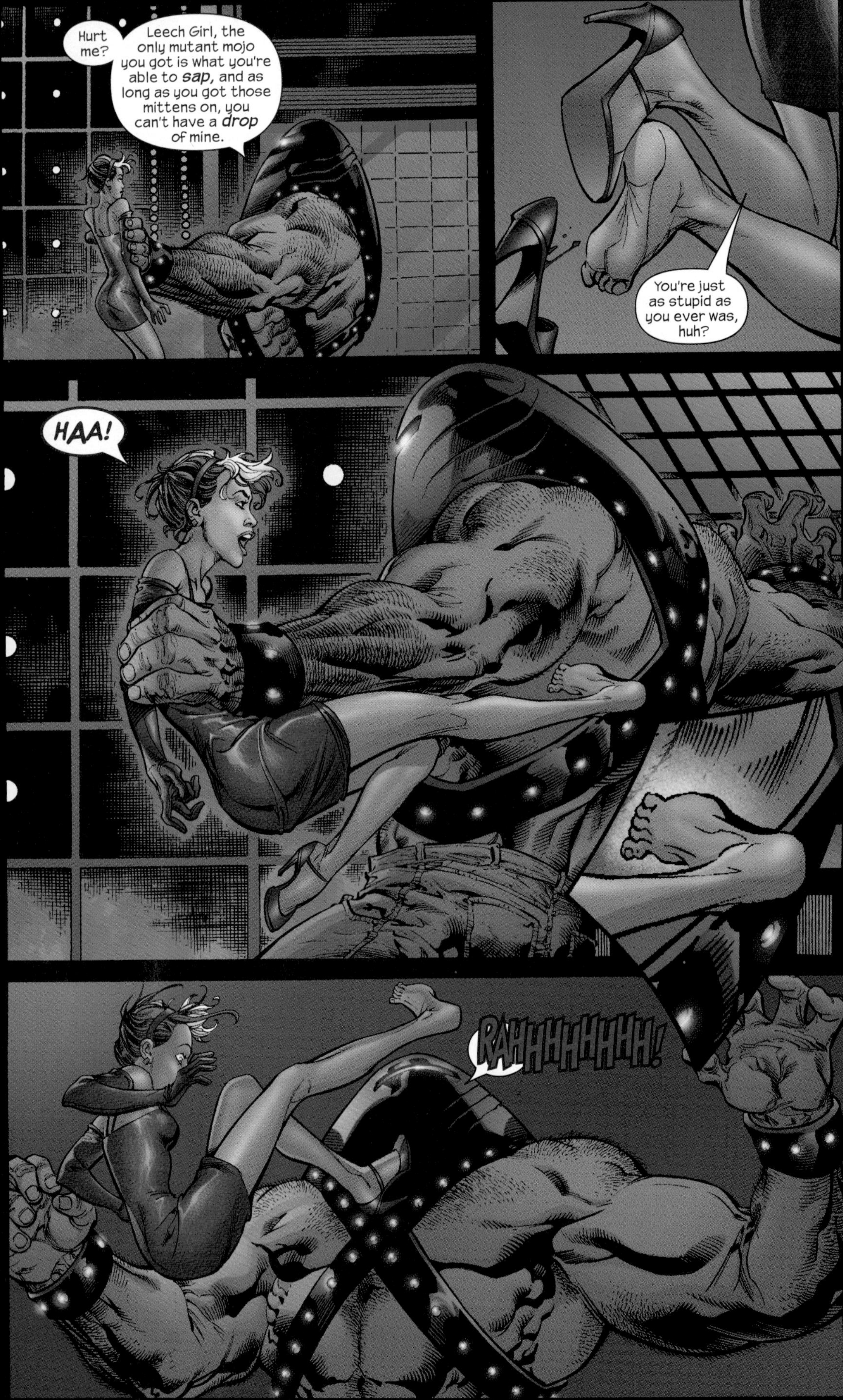

Hurt me?
Leech Girl, the only mutant mojo you got is what you're able to *sap,* and as long as you got those mittens on, you can't have a *drop* of mine.
You're just as stupid as you ever was, huh?
HAA!
RAHHHHHHHH!

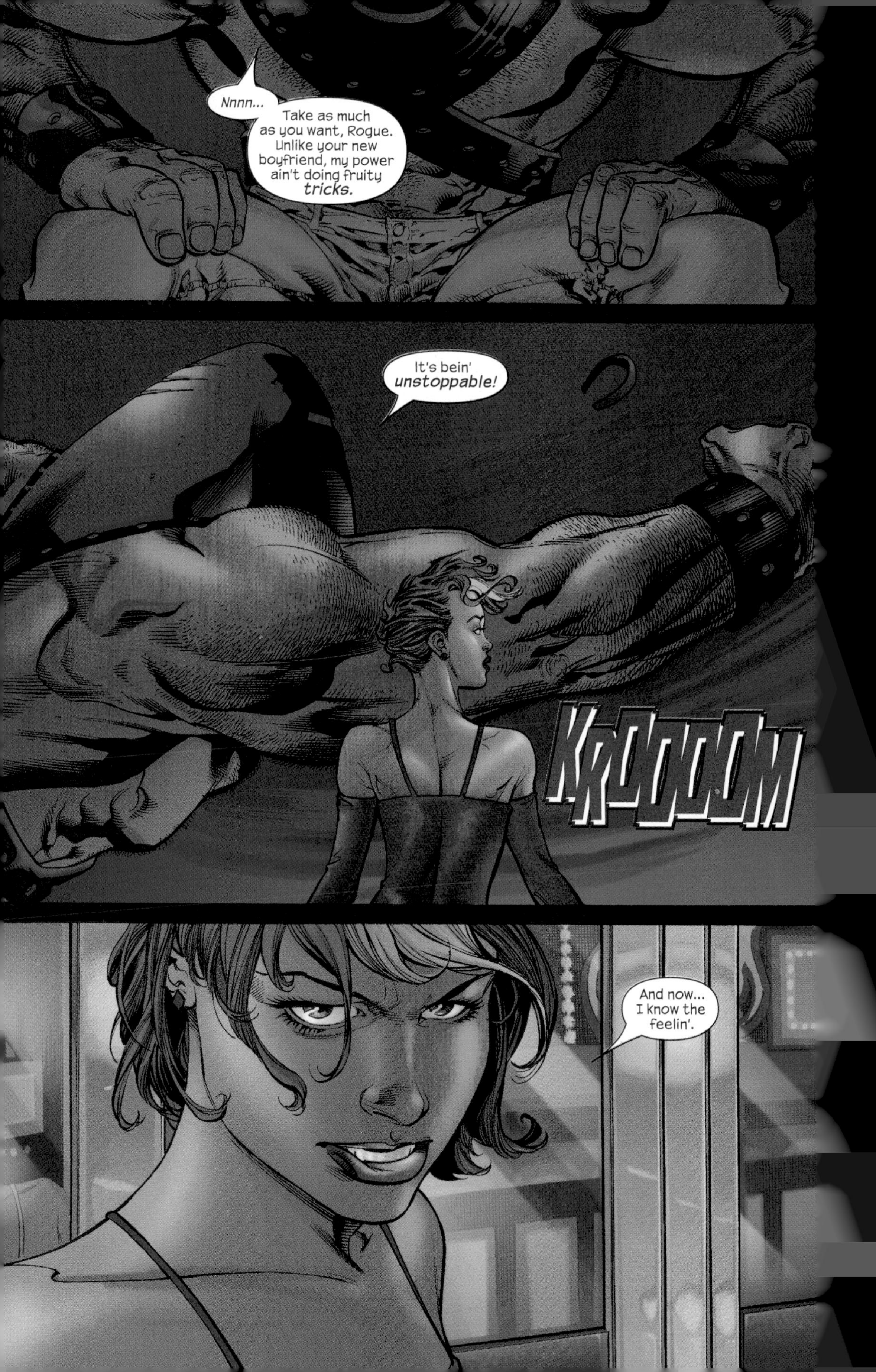
Nnnn...
Take as much as you want, Rogue. Unlike your new boyfriend, my power ain't doing fruity *tricks.*
It's bein' *unstoppable!*
KRDDDOM
And now... I know the feelin'.

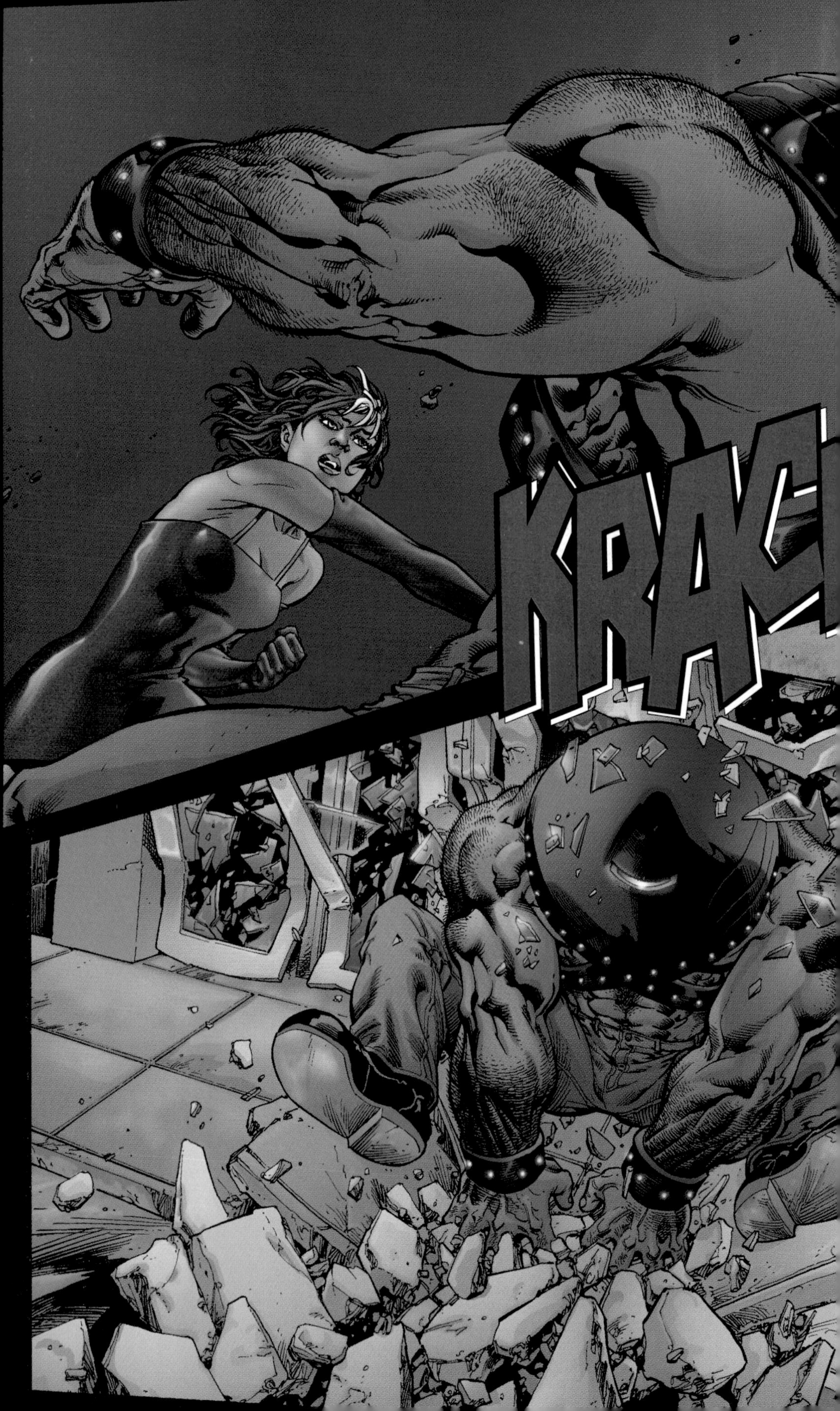
KRAC

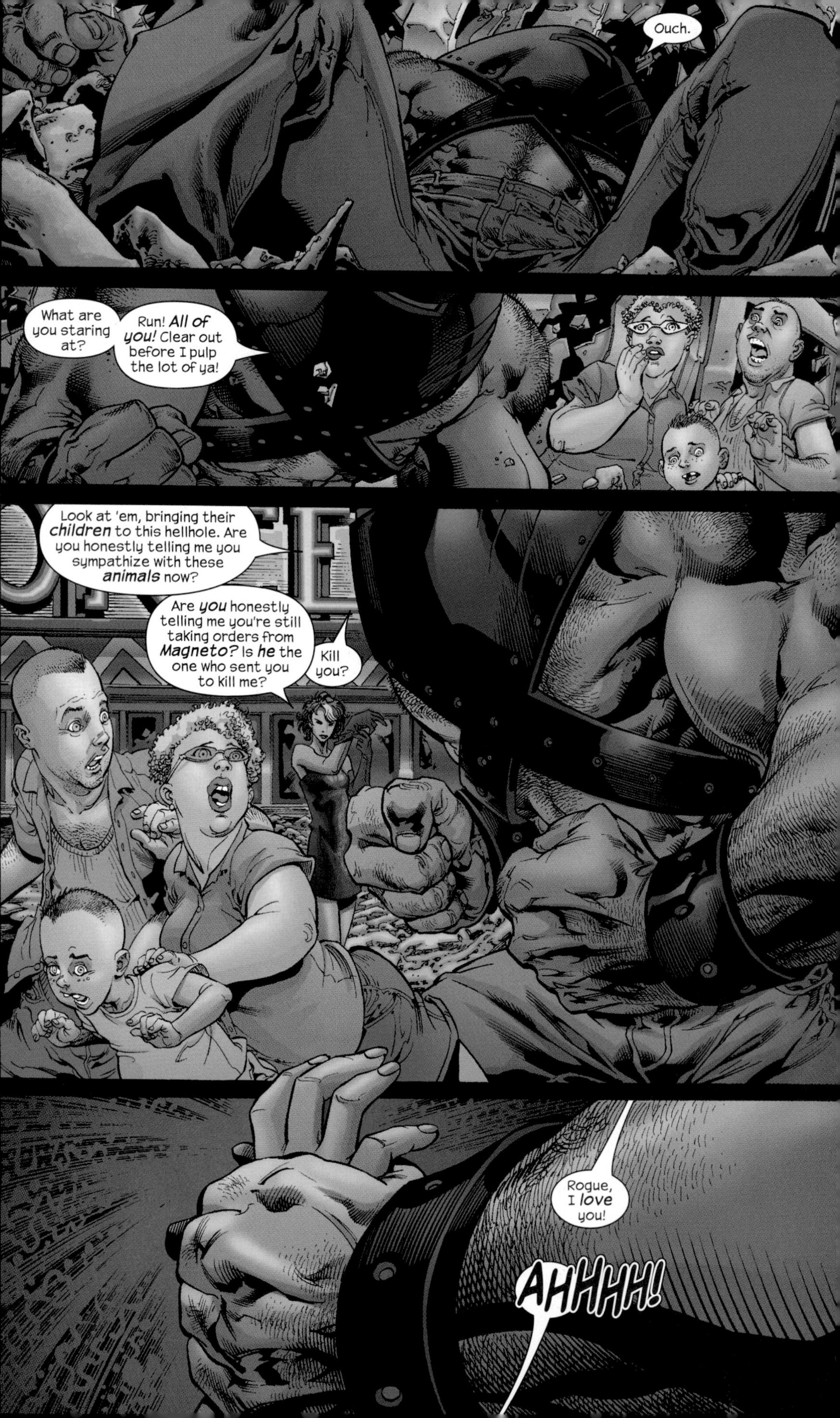
Ouch.
What are you staring at?
Run! All of you! Clear out before I pulp the lot of ya!
Look at 'em, bringing their children to this hellhole. Are you honestly telling me you sympathize with these animals now?
Are you honestly telling me you're still taking orders from Magneto? Is he the one who sent you to kill me?
Kill you?
Rogue, I love you!
AHHHH!

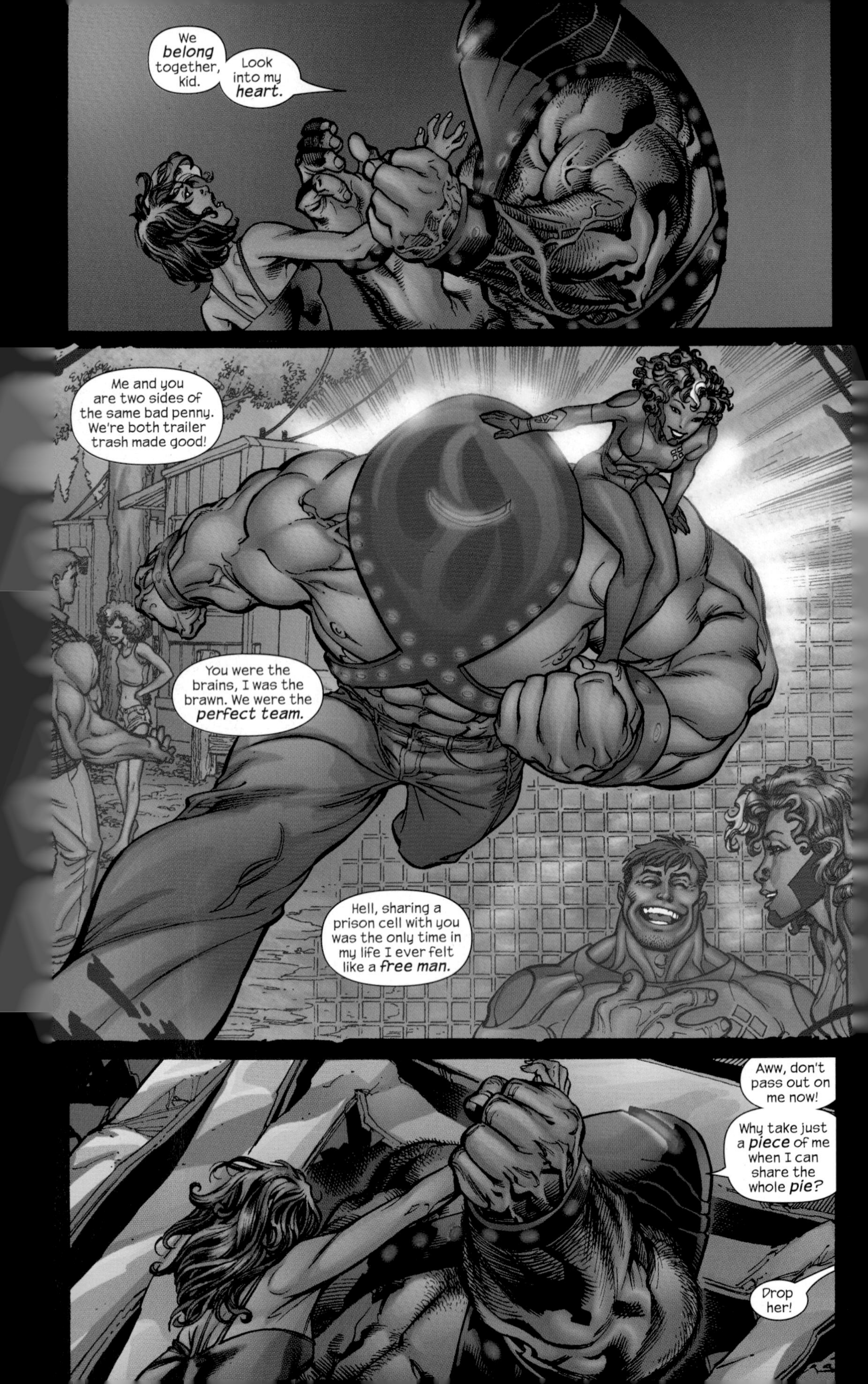
We belong together, kid.
Look into my heart.
Me and you are two sides of the same bad penny. We're both trailer trash made good!
You were the brains, I was the brawn. We were the perfect team.
Hell, sharing a prison cell with you was the only time in my life I ever felt like a free man.
Aww, don't pass out on me now!
Why take just a piece of me when I can share the whole pie?
Drop her!

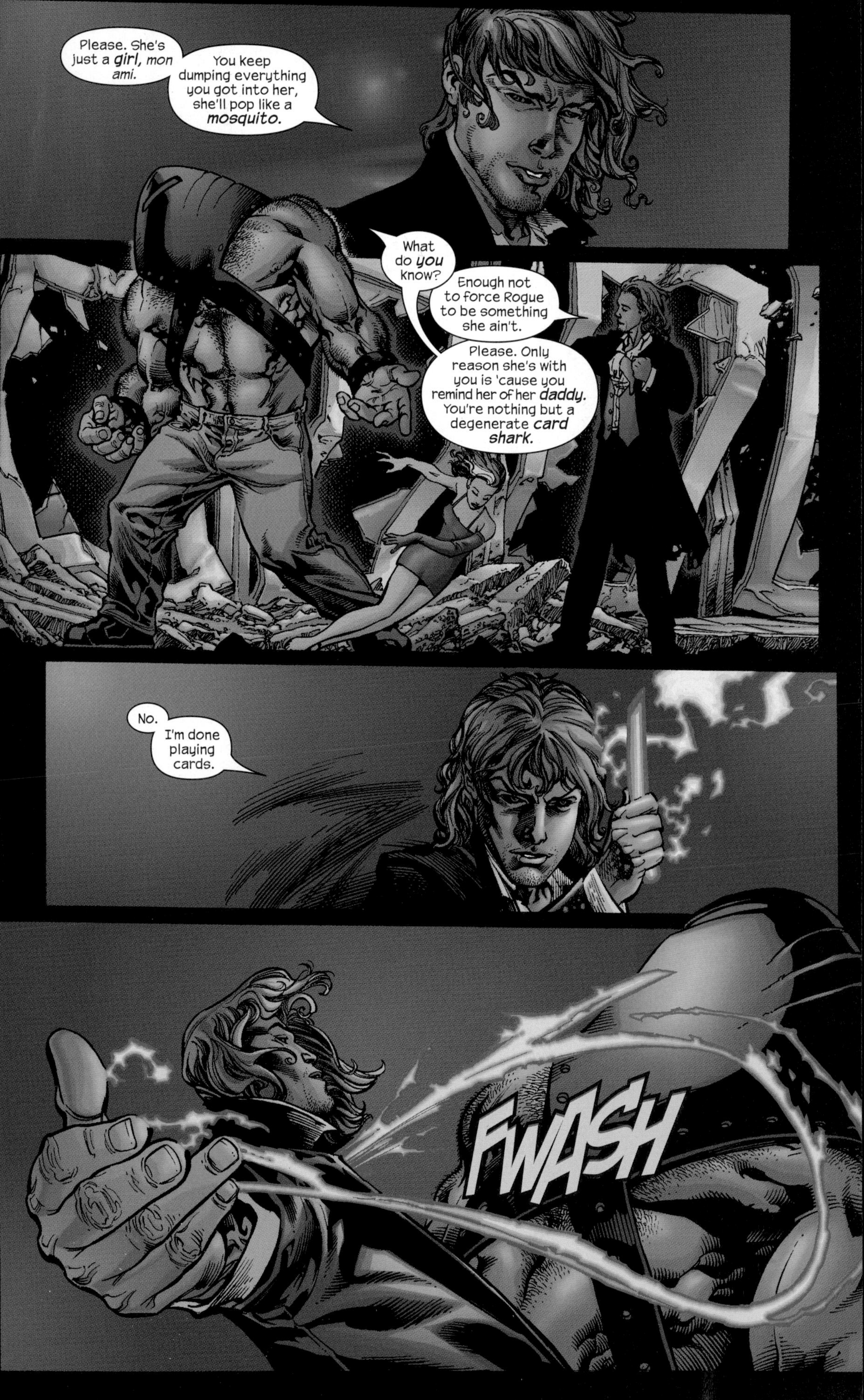
Please. She's just a **girl,** *mon ami.*
You keep dumping everything you got into her, she'll pop like a ***mosquito.***
What do ***you*** know?
Enough not to force Rogue to be something she ain't.
Please. Only reason she's with you is 'cause you remind her of her ***daddy.*** You're nothing but a degenerate ***card shark.***
No.
I'm done playing cards.
FWASH

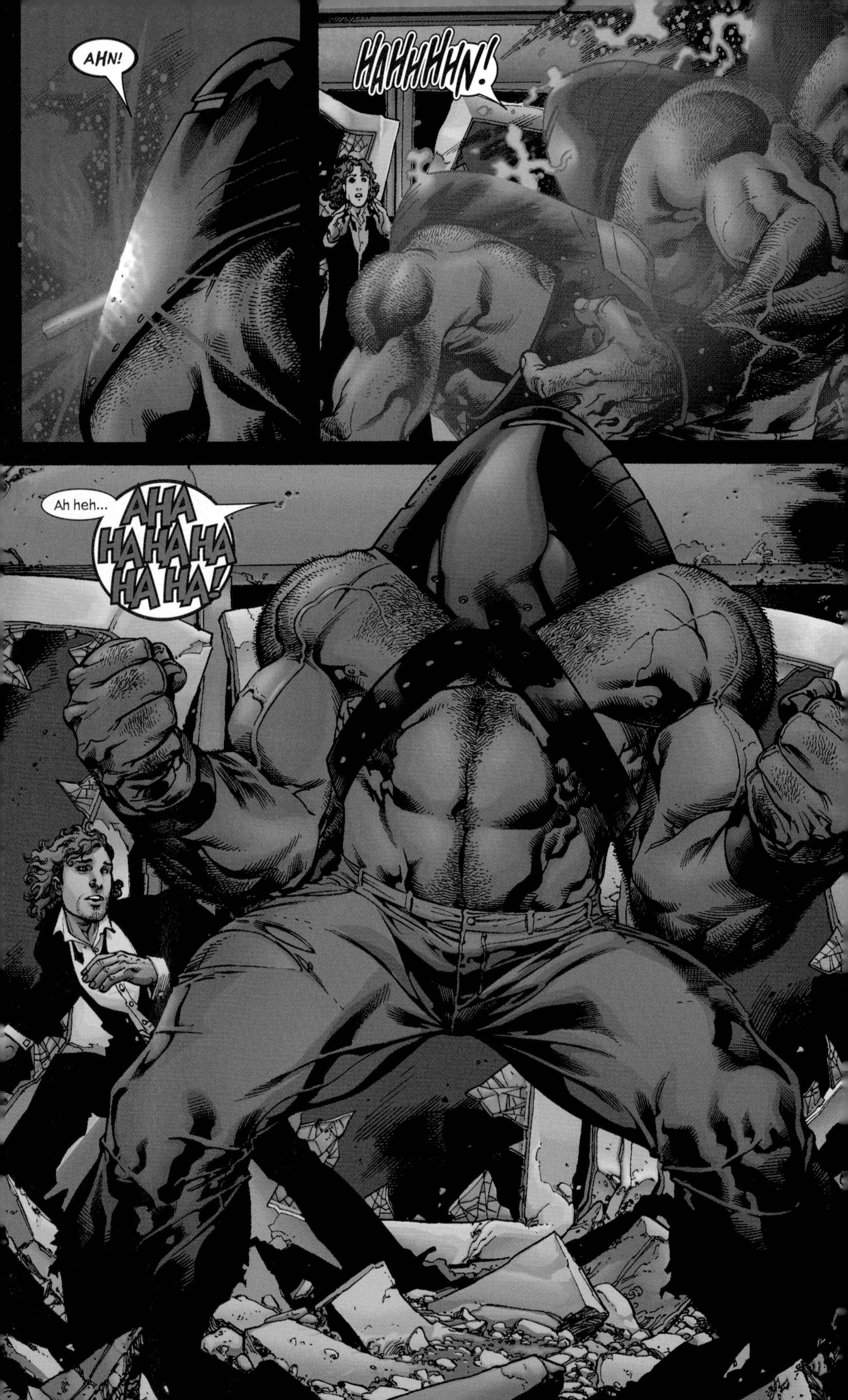
AHN!
HAHHHHN!
Ah heh... AHA HAHAHA HA HA!

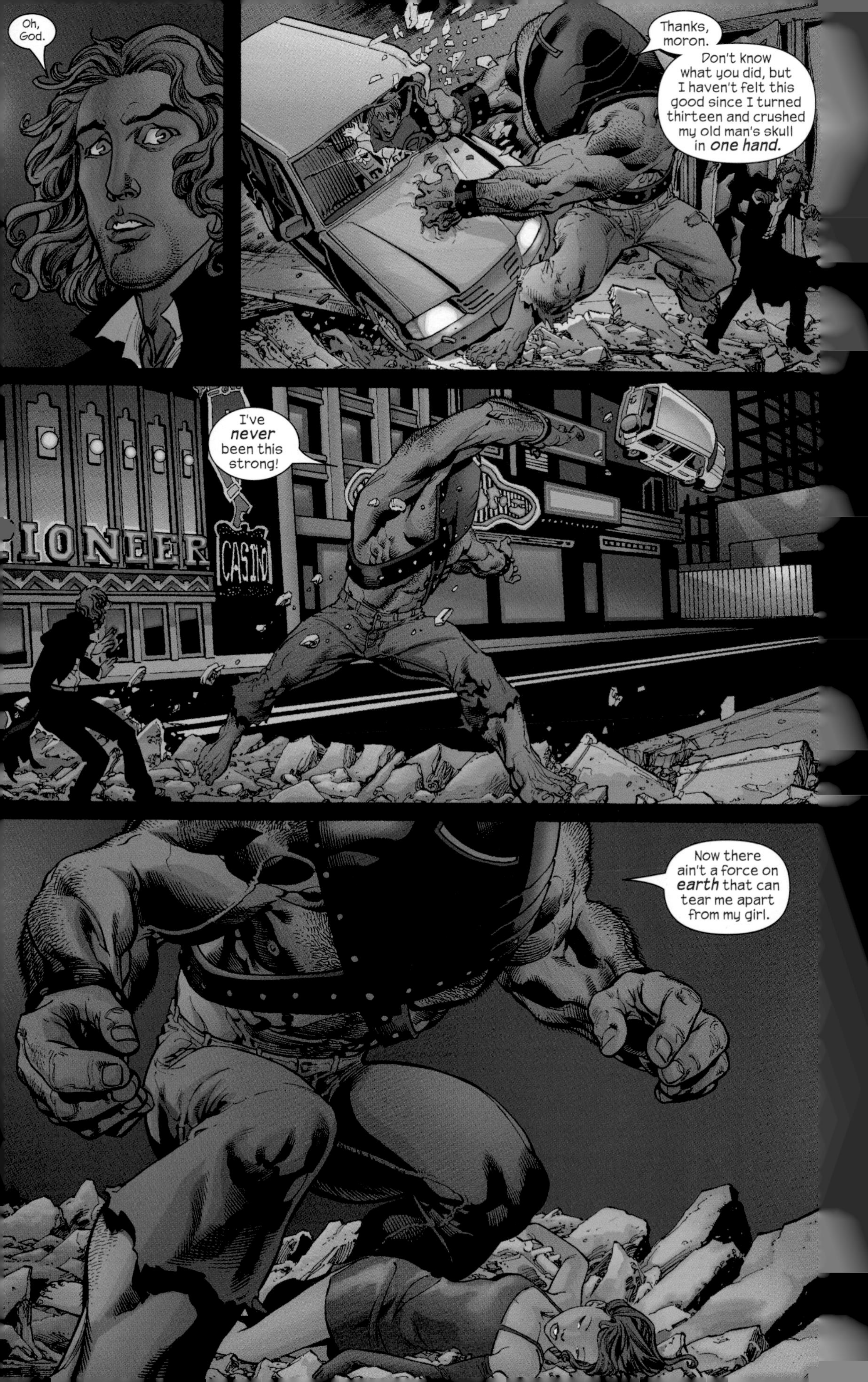
Oh, God.
Thanks, moron.
Don't know what you did, but I haven't felt this good since I turned thirteen and crushed my old man's skull in *one hand.*
IONEER
CASINO
I've *never* been this strong!
Now there ain't a force on *earth* that can tear me apart from my girl.

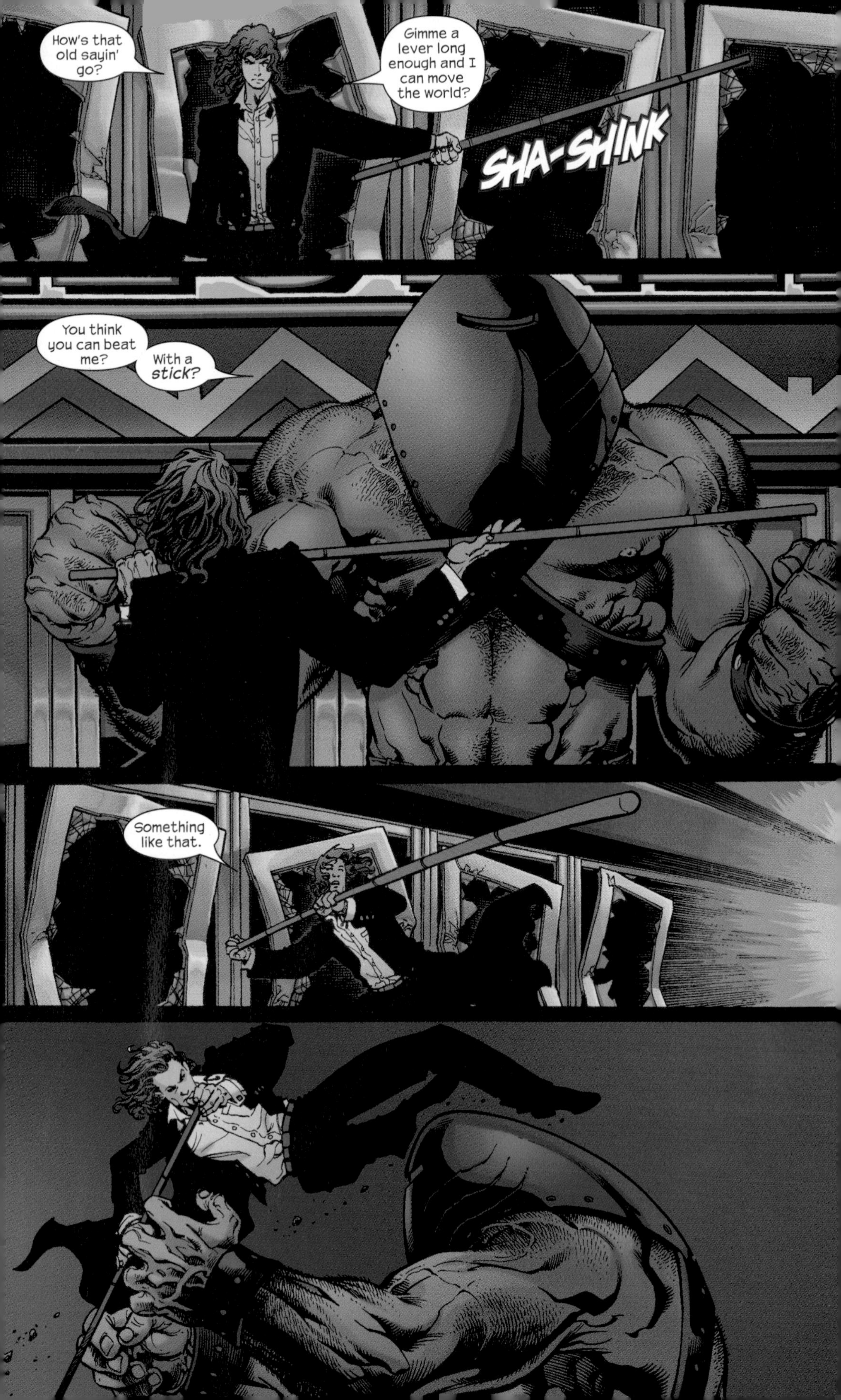

How's that old sayin' go?
Gimme a lever long enough and I can move the world?
SHA-SHINK
You think you can beat me?
With a *stick?*
Something like that.

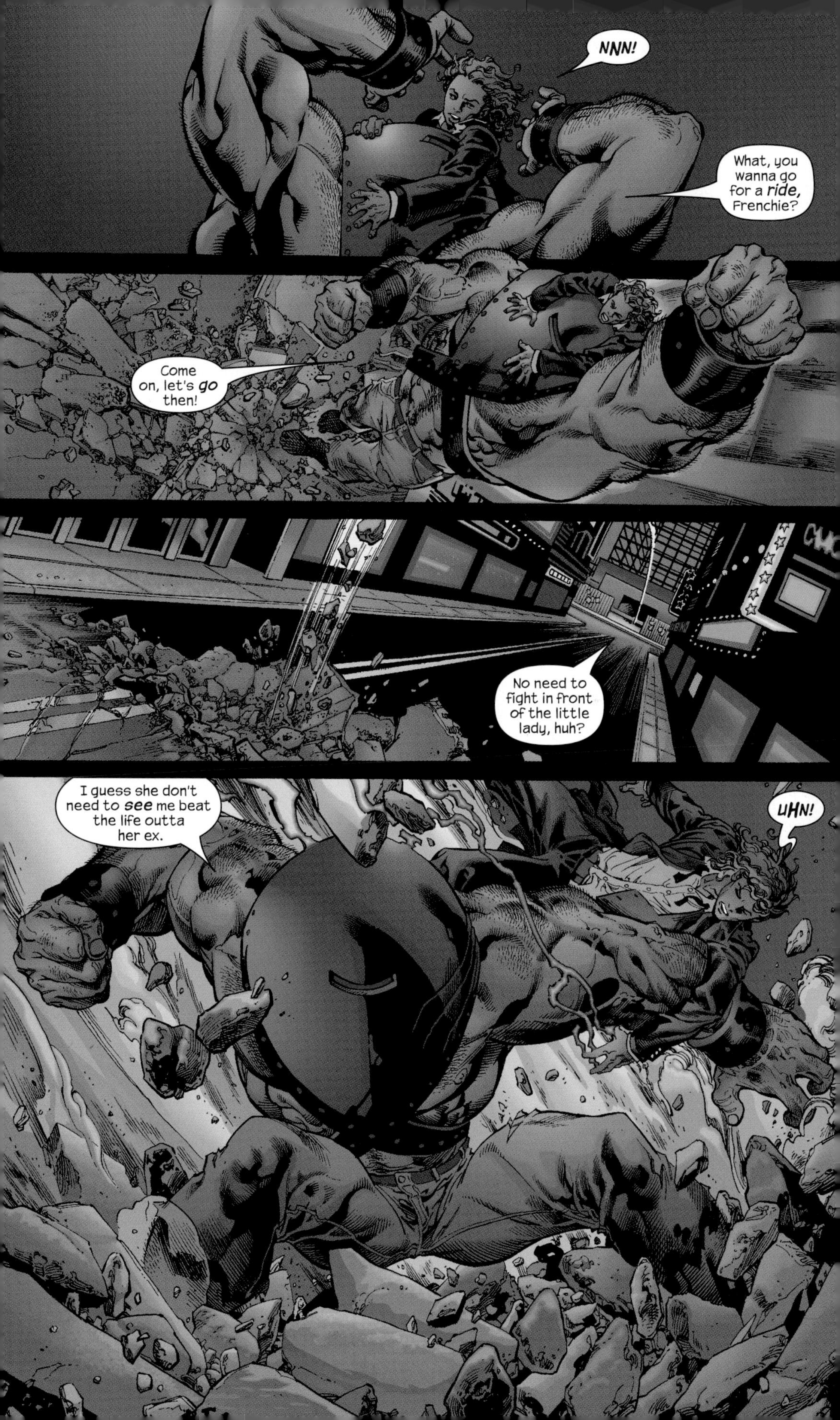
NNN!
What, you wanna go for a *ride,* Frenchie?
Come on, let's *go* then!
No need to fight in front of the little lady, huh?
I guess she don't need to *see* me beat the life outta her ex.
UHN!

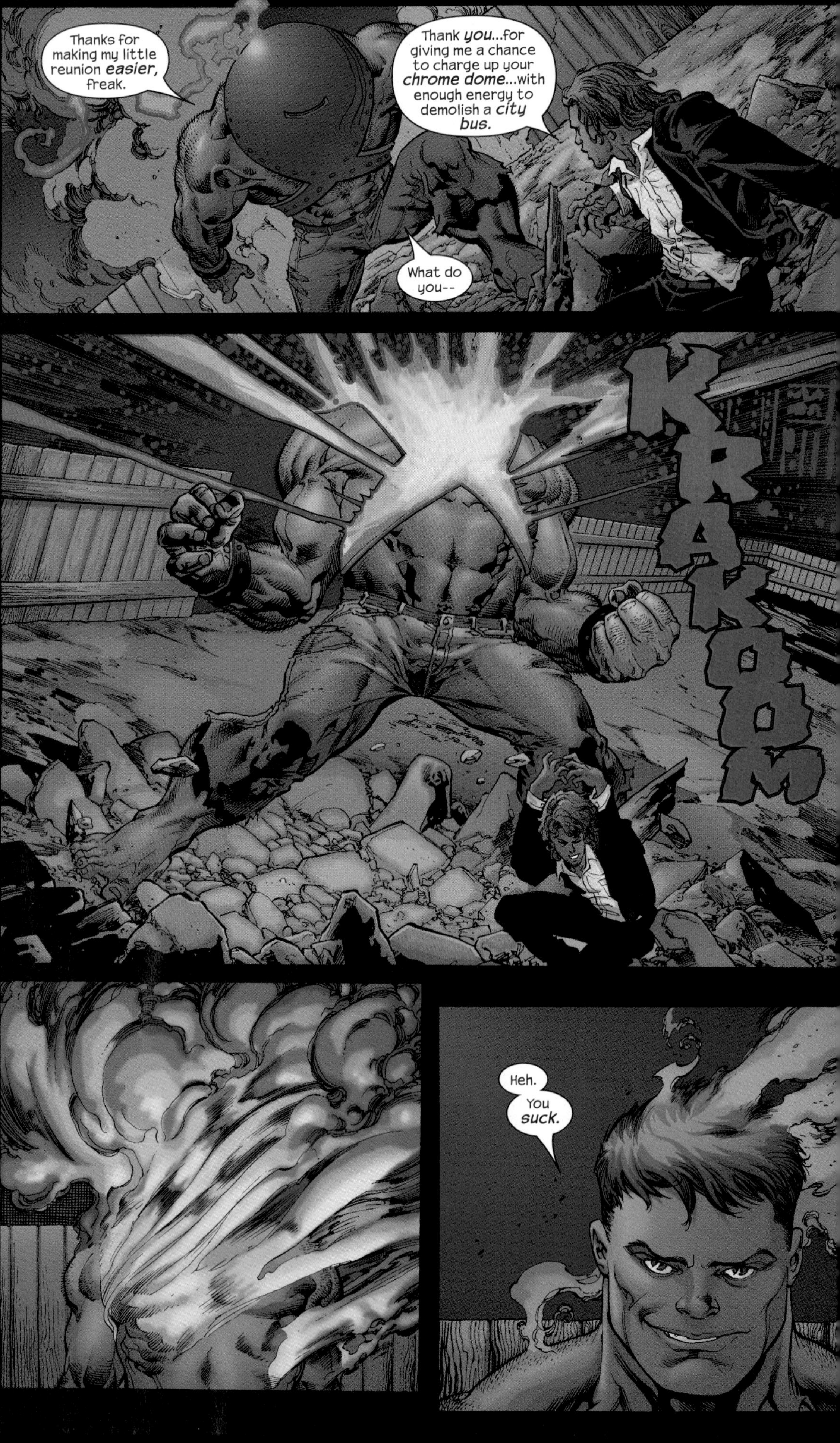
Thanks for making my little reunion *easier,* freak.
Thank *you*...for giving me a chance to charge up your *chrome dome*...with enough energy to demolish a *city bus.*
What do you--
KRAKOOM
Heh.
You *suck.*

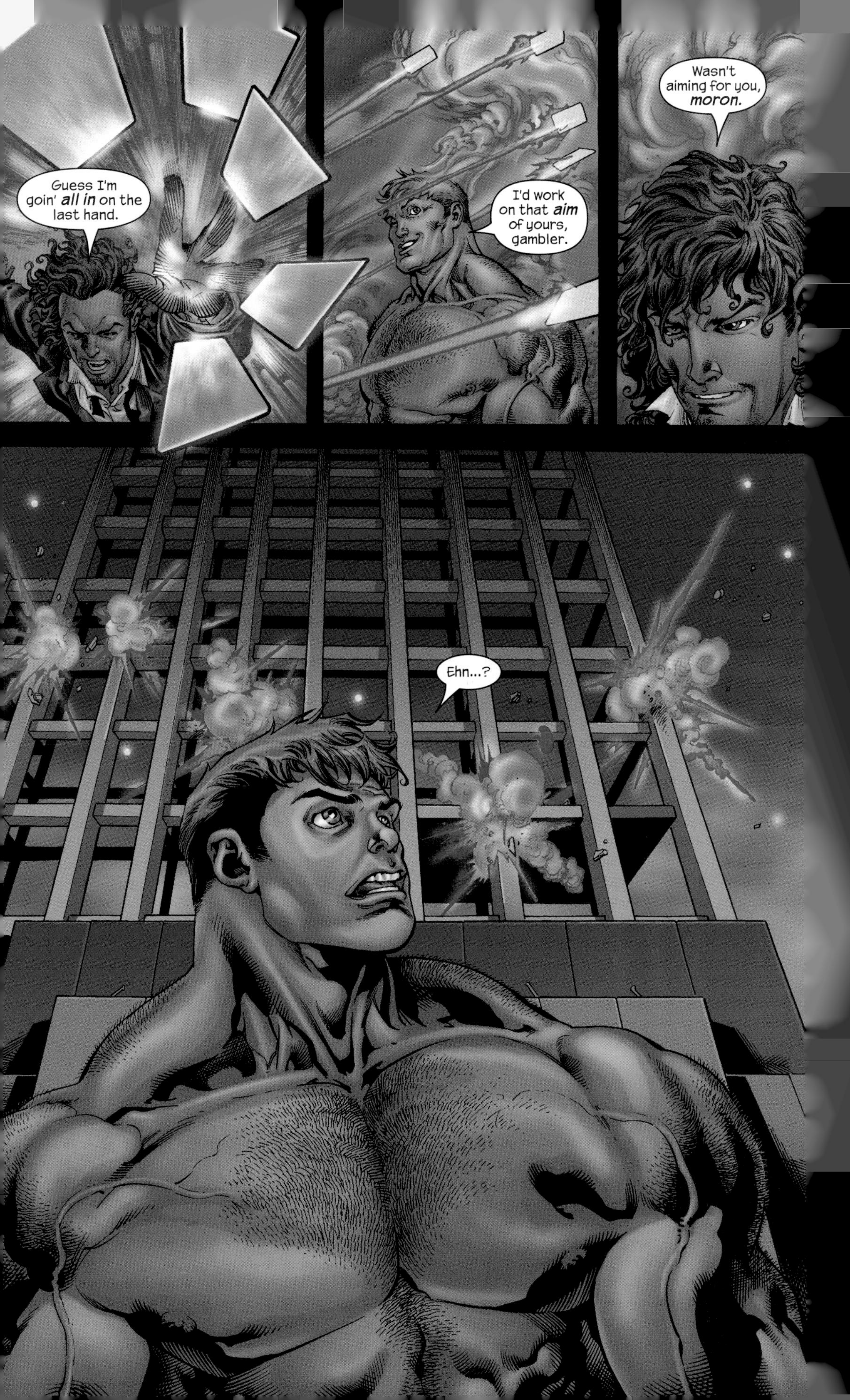
Guess I'm goin' **all in** on the last hand.
I'd work on that **aim** of yours, gambler.
Wasn't aiming for you, **moron.**
Ehn...?

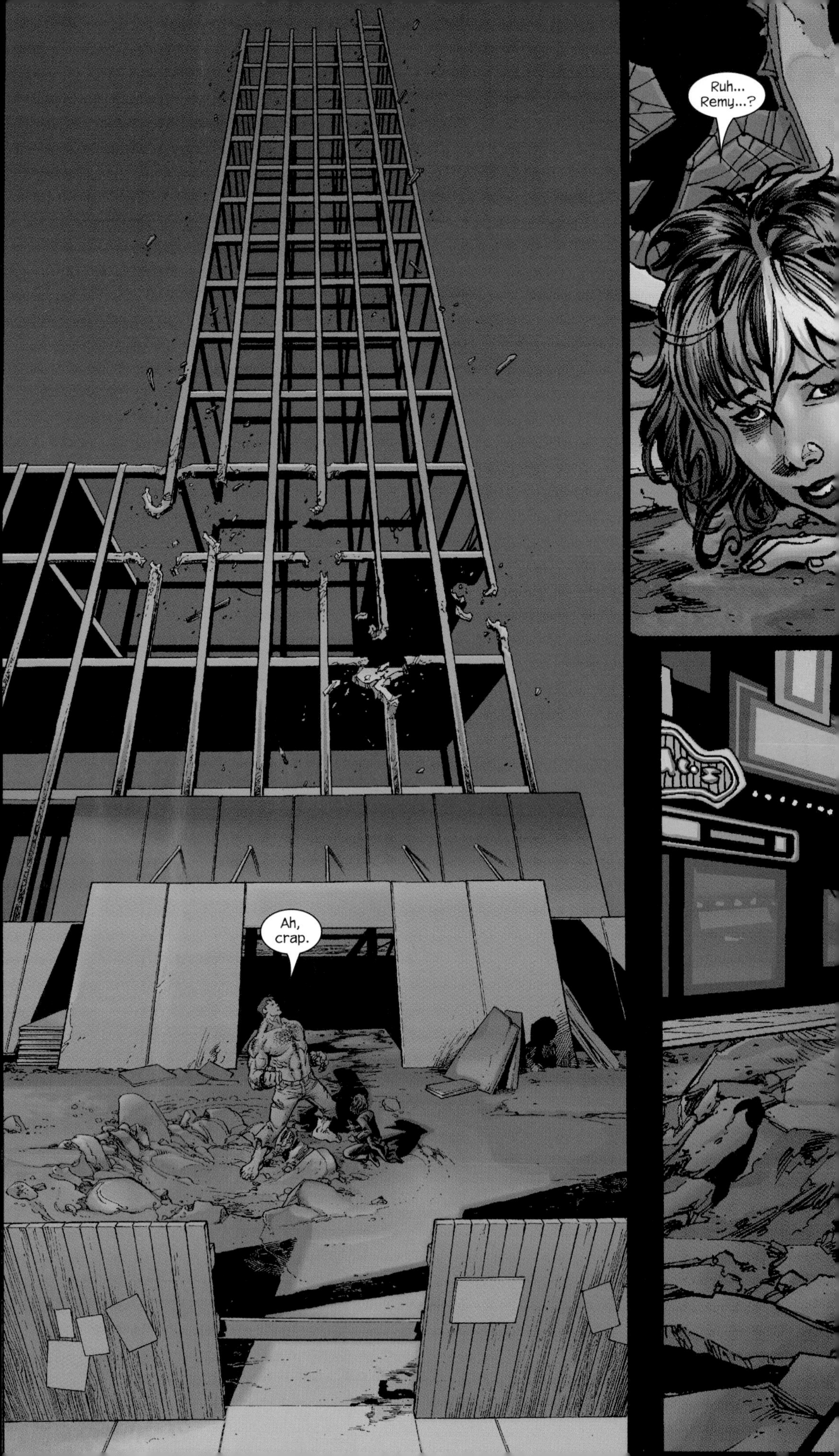
Ah, crap.
Ruh... Remy...?

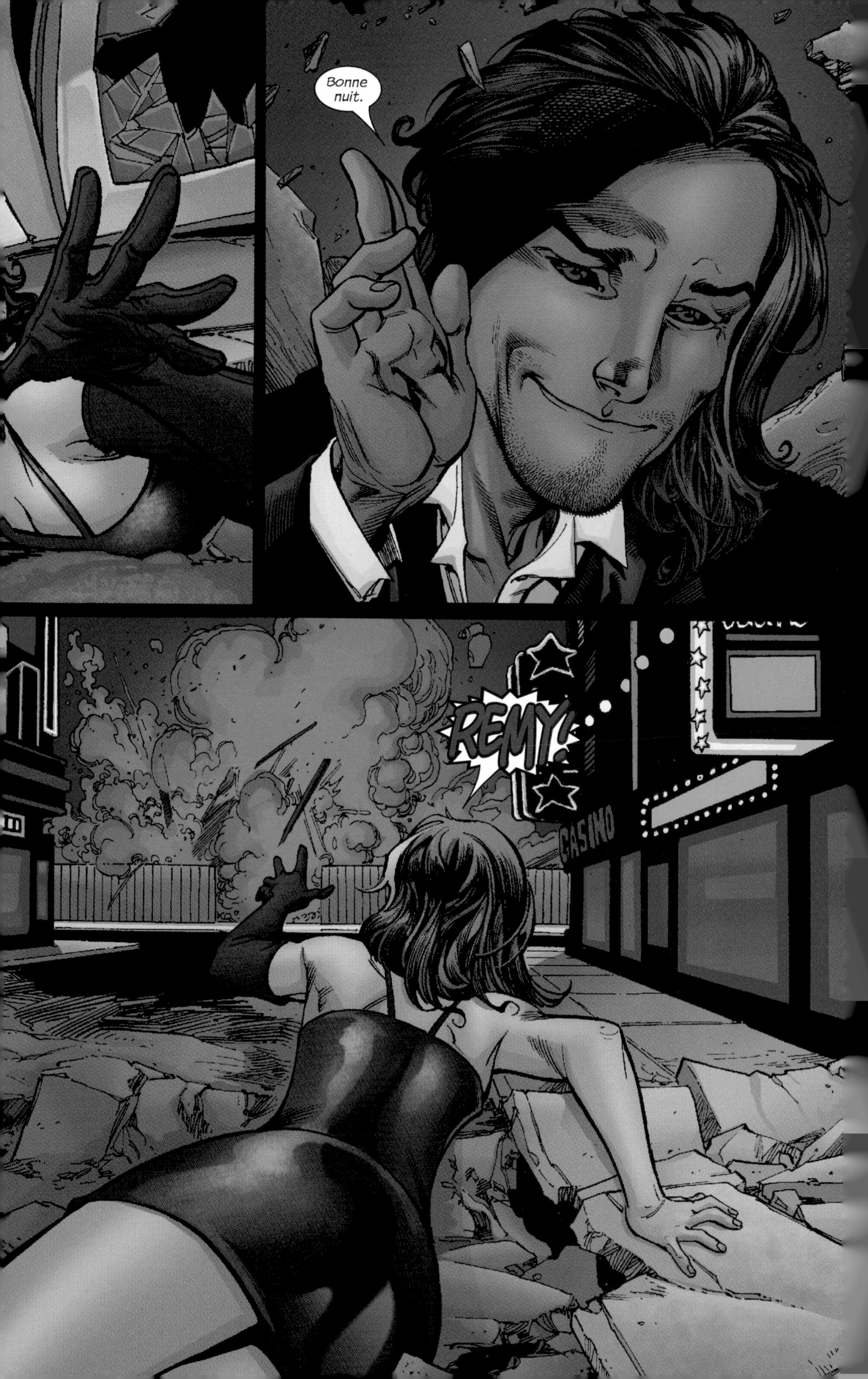
Bonne nuit.
REMY!
CASINO

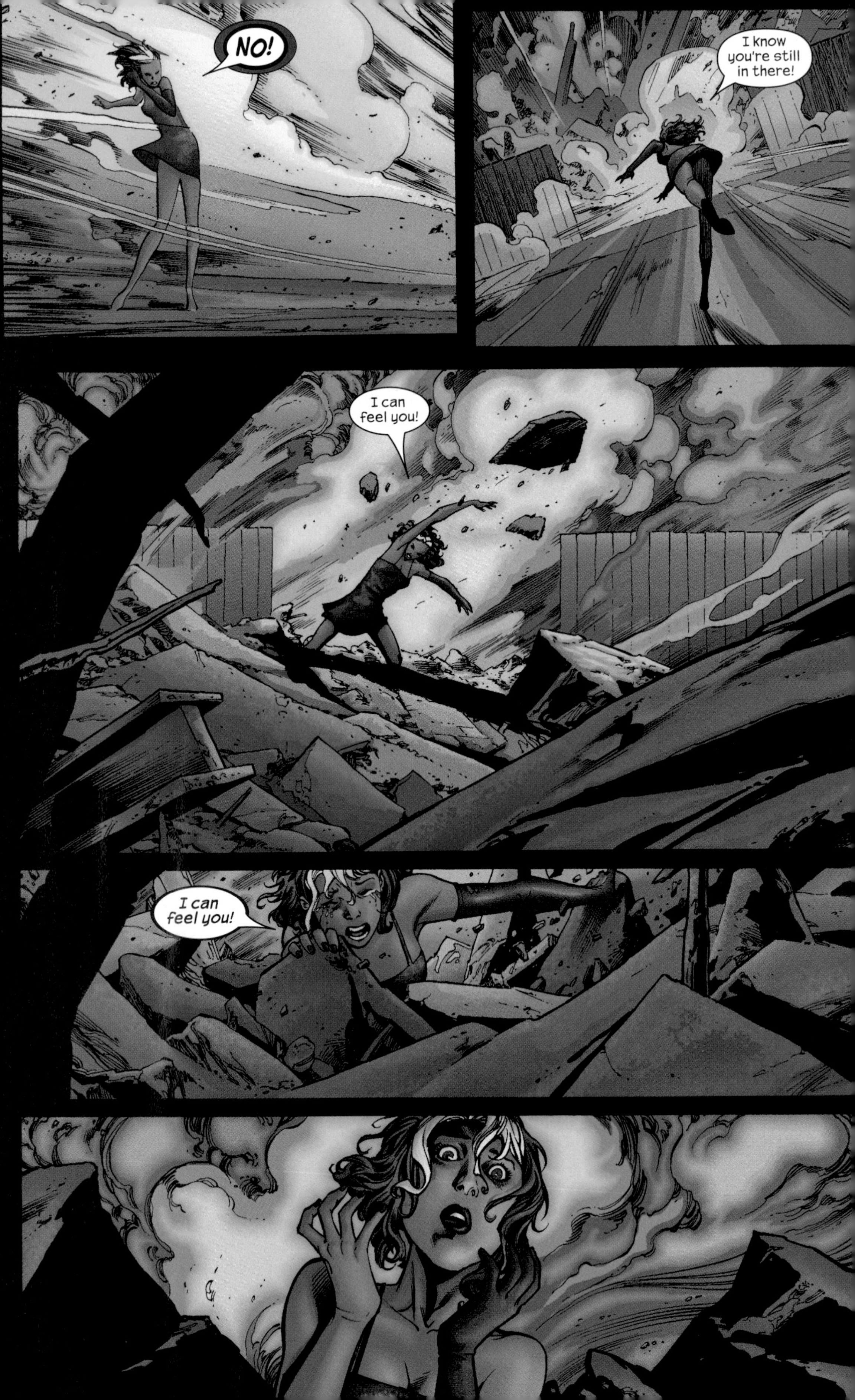
NO!
I know you're still in there!
I can feel you!
I can feel you!

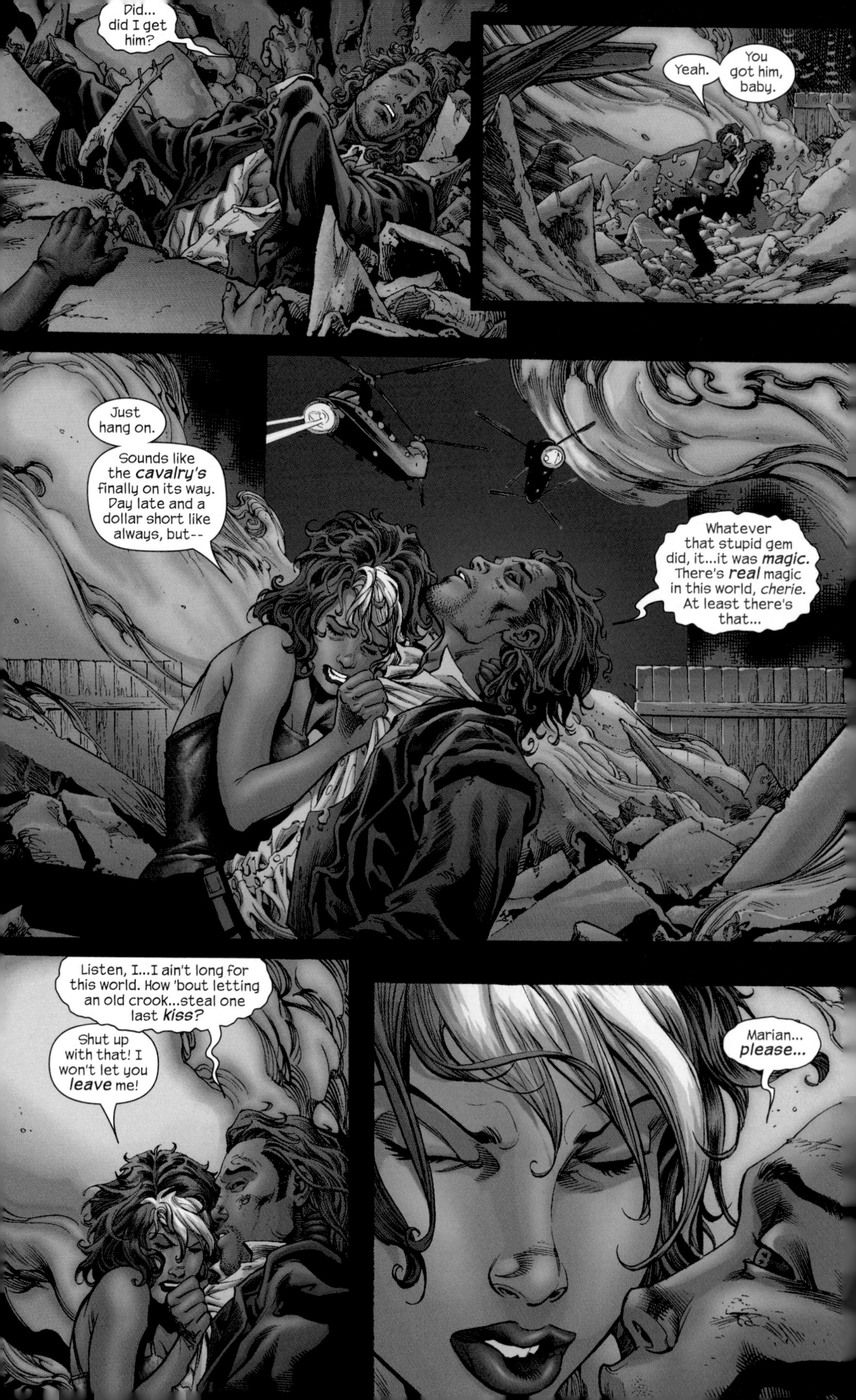
Did... did I get him?
Yeah.
You got him, baby.
Just hang on.
Sounds like the cavalry's finally on its way. Day late and a dollar short like always, but--
Whatever that stupid gem did, it...it was magic. There's real magic in this world, cherie. At least there's that...
Listen, I...I ain't long for this world. How 'bout letting an old crook...steal one last kiss?
Shut up with that! I won't let you leave me!
Marian... please...

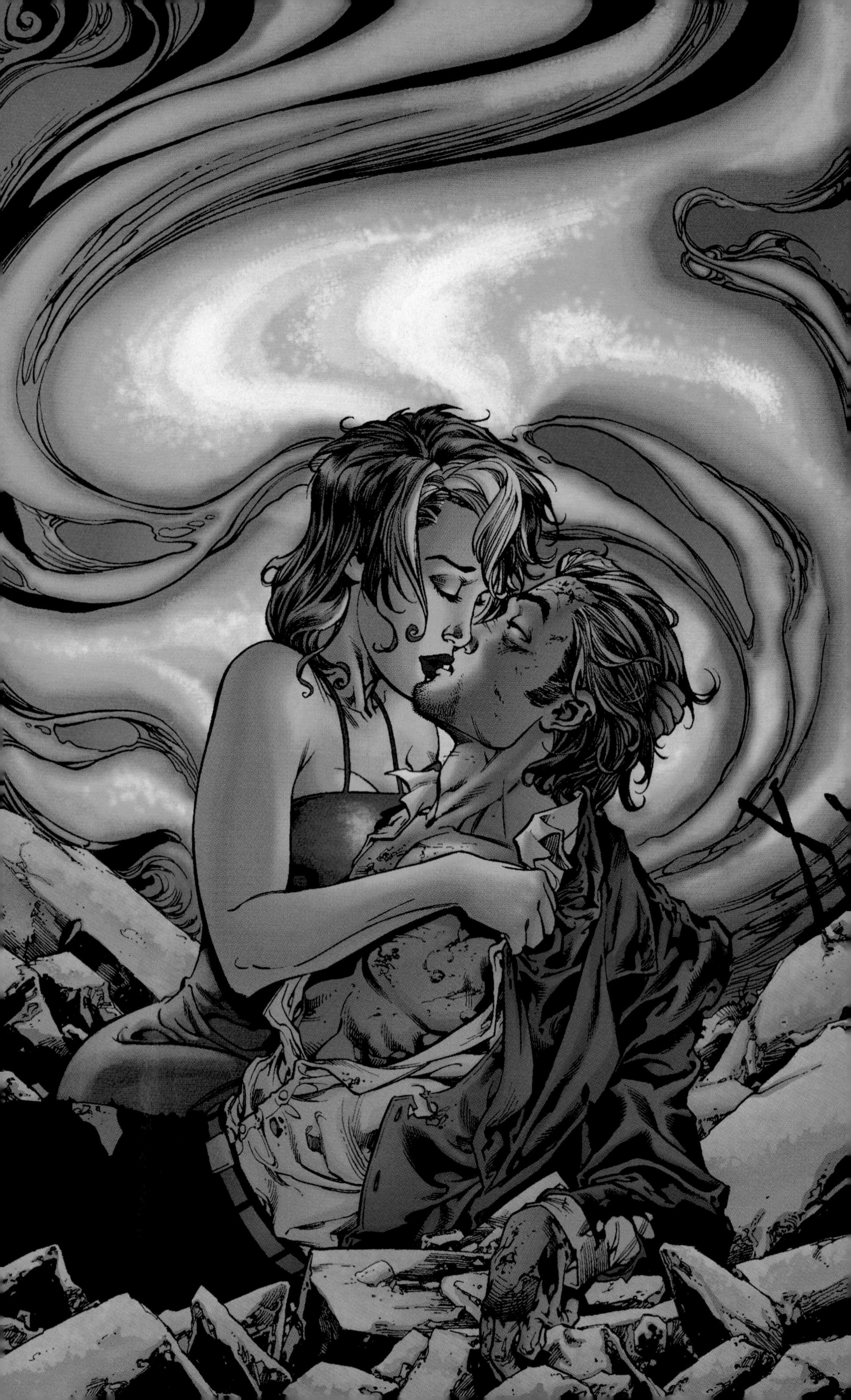

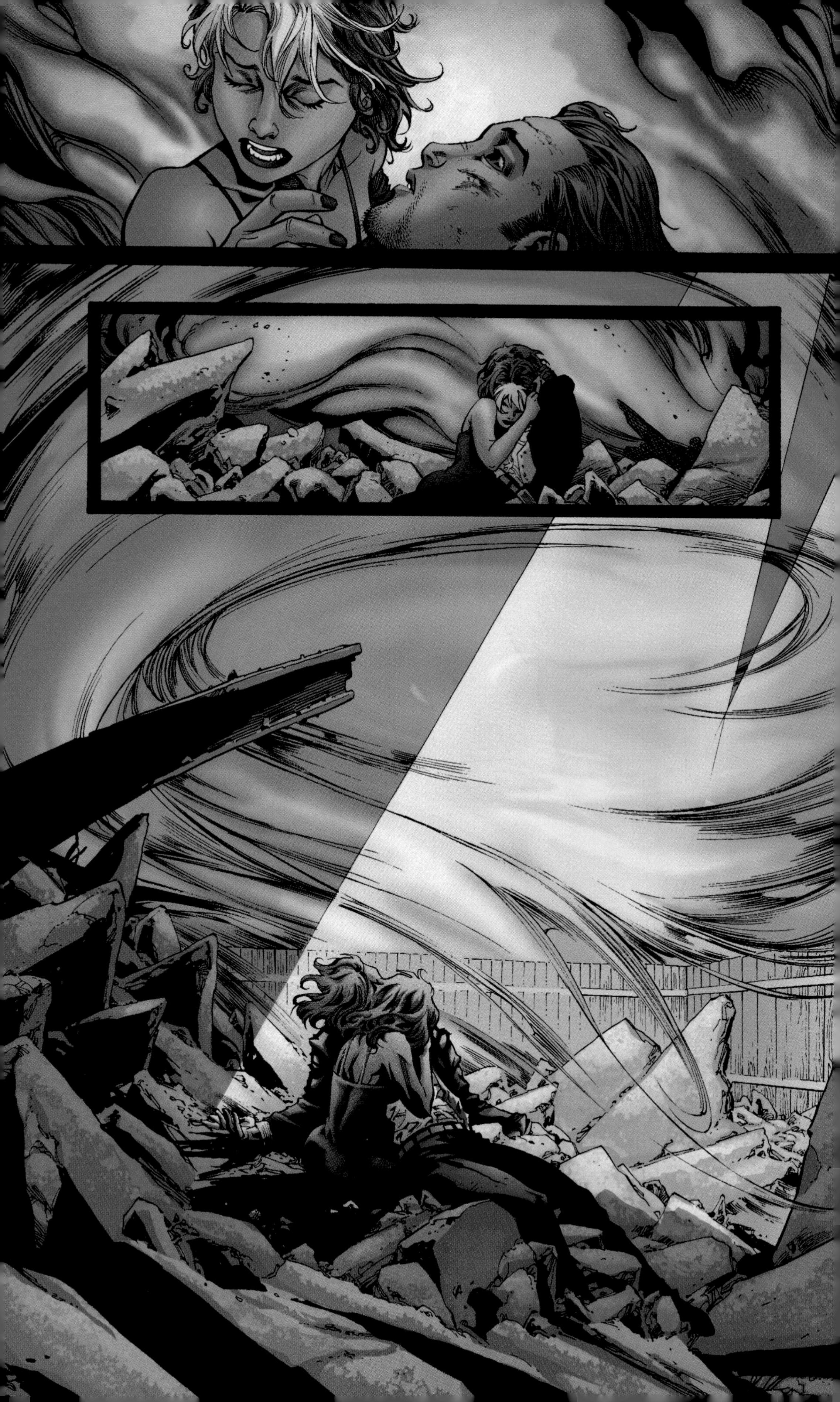

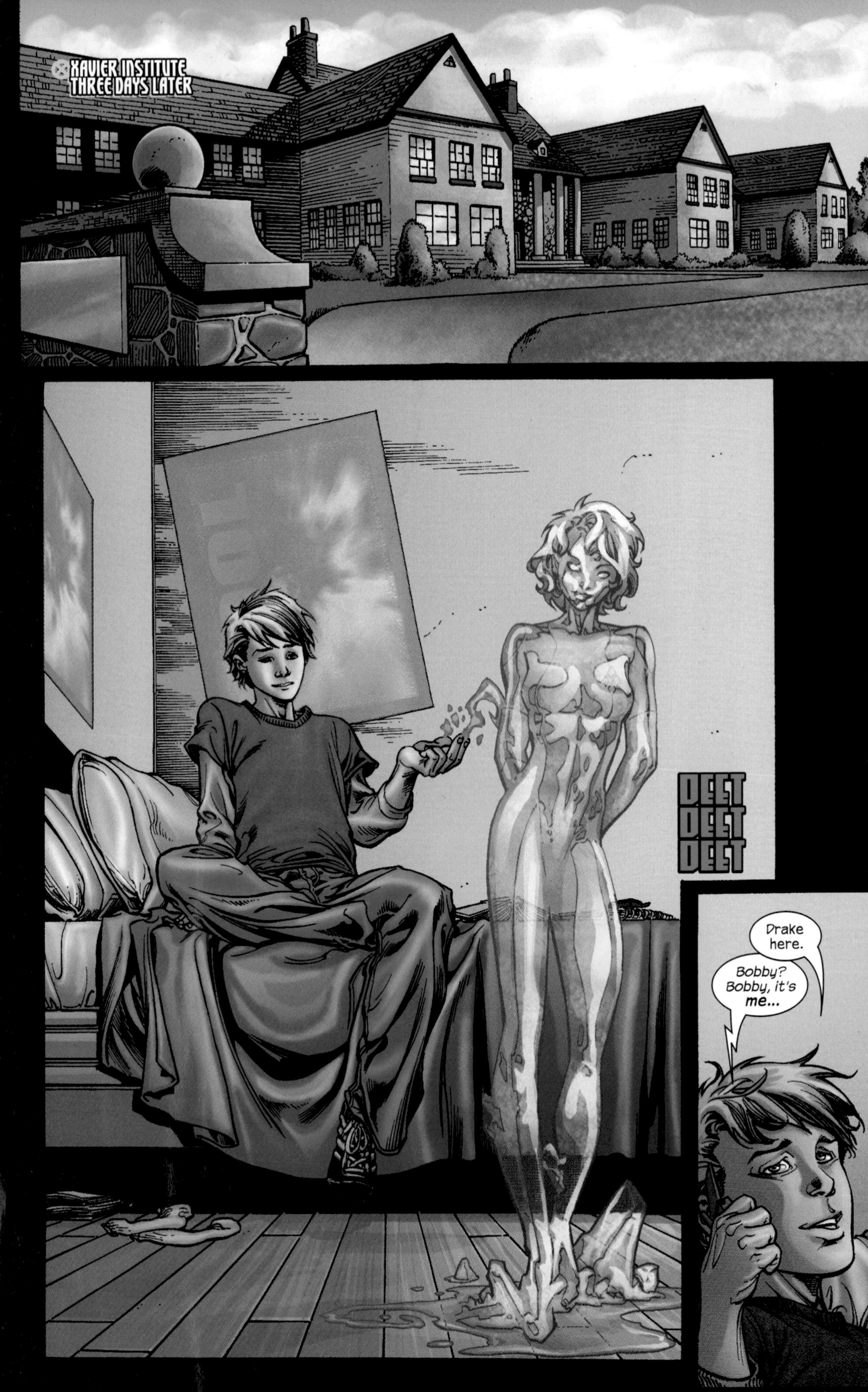
XAVIER INSTITUTE
THREE DAYS LATER
DEET
DEET
DEET
Drake here.
Bobby? Bobby, it's me...

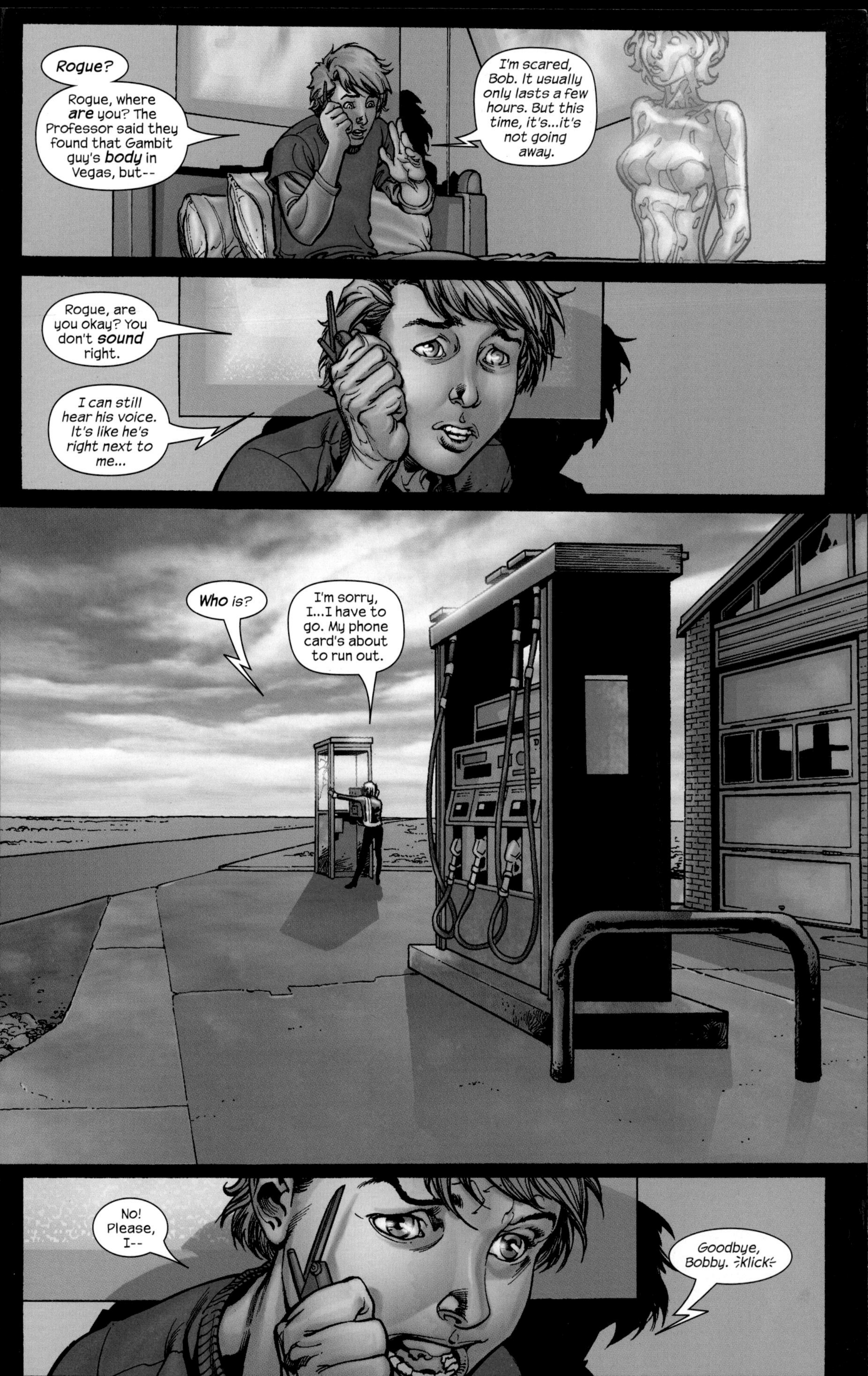
Rogue?
Rogue, where **are** you? The Professor said they found that Gambit guy's **body** in Vegas, but--
I'm scared, Bob. It usually only lasts a few hours. But this time, it's...it's not going away.
Rogue, are you okay? You don't **sound** right.
I can still hear his voice. It's like he's right next to me...
Who is?
I'm sorry, I...I have to go. My phone card's about to run out.
No! Please, I--
Goodbye, Bobby. ≑klick≑

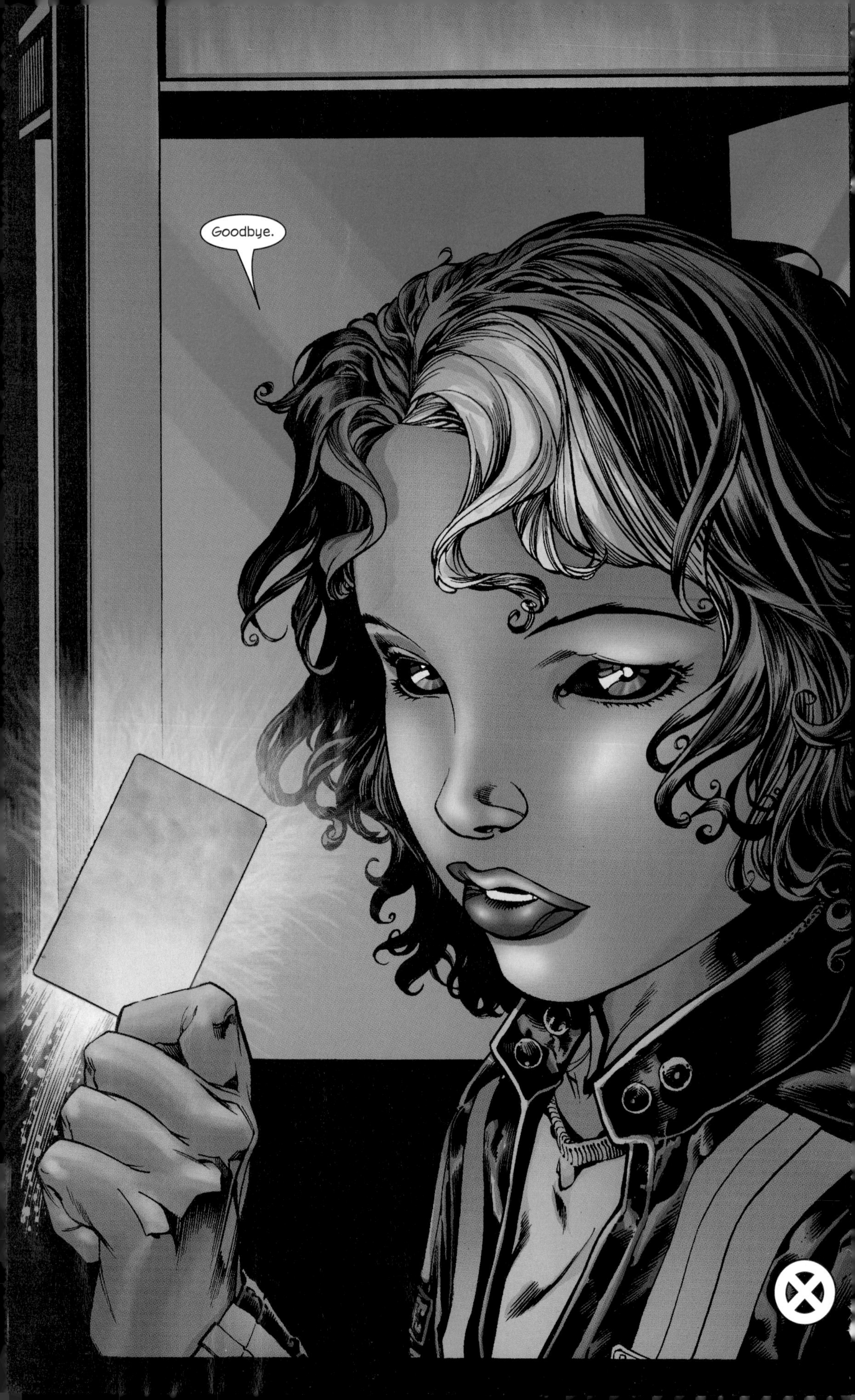
Goodbye.